MW01004364

Praise for *The World According to China*

"[an] excellent treatise"
The Atlantic

"In this marvelous (and sobering) book, Elizabeth Economy dissects China's grand strategy: a Sino-centric world order across all domains, with military and power projection to match. Western bromides will not counter China's determination."
Charlene Barshefsky, Chair, Parkside Global Advisors and Former US Trade Representative

"*The World According to China* is the best book I've read on the country's push for a new Sino-centric world order. In one accessible work the reader gets a thorough and balanced understanding across multiple regions and domains."
Bookish Asia

"Having long revered Elizabeth Economy's China expertise, I had lofty expectations. After reading this book, my admiration for her only amplified. Thoroughly researched, Economy's analysis of Xi's – and thus China's – view of the world both engages and educates. A must-read!"
Chris Fenton, author of *Feeding the Dragon*

"Economy's book is superb. It is well-written, well-researched, and notably balanced in its presentation of China's policies and the effects of these policies' implementation."
Joshua Huminski, *The Diplomatic Courier*

"Employing her trademark thoroughness, clarity, and insight, Elizabeth Economy probes deeply into China's ambitions and actions to reorder the world order. Business leaders must read this book as inducing and coercing multinationals to go along is an indispensable part of China achieving success."
James McGregor, Chairman of Greater China for APCO Worldwide

"If you want to understand the most important competition of this century, read *The World According to China*. Elizabeth Economy illuminates the Chinese Communist Party's grand ambition and forces us to confront the reality that if it succeeds, our world will be less free, less prosperous, and less safe."
H.R. McMaster, author of *Dereliction of Duty* and *Battlegrounds: The Fight to Defend the Free World*

The World According to China

The Council on Foreign Relations (CFR) is an independent, nonpartisan membership organization, think tank, and publisher dedicated to being a resource for its members, government officials, business executives, journalists, educators and students, civic and religious leaders, and other interested citizens in order to help them better understand the world and the foreign policy choices facing the United States and other countries. Founded in 1921, CFR carries out its mission by maintaining a diverse membership, with special programs to promote interest and develop expertise in the next generation of foreign policy leaders; convening meetings at its headquarters in New York and in Washington, DC, and other cities where senior government officials, members of Congress, global leaders, and prominent thinkers come together with CFR members to discuss and debate major international issues; supporting a Studies Program that fosters independent research, enabling CFR scholars to produce articles, reports, and books and hold roundtables that analyze foreign policy issues and make concrete policy recommendations; publishing *Foreign Affairs*, the preeminent journal on international affairs and US foreign policy; sponsoring Independent Task Forces that produce reports with both findings and policy prescriptions on the most important foreign policy topics; and providing up-to-date information and analysis about world events and American foreign policy on its website, www.cfr.org.

The Council on Foreign Relations takes no institutional positions on policy issues and has no affiliation with the US government. All views expressed in its publications and on its website are the sole responsibility of the author or authors.

THE WORLD ACCORDING TO CHINA

Elizabeth C. Economy

A Council on Foreign Relations Book

polity

First published in 2022 by Polity Press
This edition published in 2023 by Polity Press

Polity Press
65 Bridge Street
Cambridge CB2 1UR, UK

Polity Press
111 River Street
Hoboken, NJ 07030, USA

ISBN-13: 978-1-5095-3749-5
ISBN-13: 978-1-5095-3750-1 (pb)

A catalogue record for this book is available from the British Library.

Library of Congress Cataloging-in-Publication Data

Names: Economy, Elizabeth, 1962- author.
Title: The world according to China / Elizabeth C. Economy.
Description: Medford: Polity Press, 2022. | Includes bibliographical references and index. | Summary: "A penetrating analysis of China's global ambitions from one of the world's leading China experts"-- Provided by publisher.
Identifiers: LCCN 2021013890 (print) | LCCN 2021013891 (ebook) | ISBN 9781509537495 (hardback) | ISBN 9781509537518 (epub)
Subjects: LCSH: China--Foreign relations--21st century | China--Politics and government--2002- | China--Foreign economic relations--21st century. | China--Relations. | Geopolitics--China. | Xi, Jinping.
Classification: LCC DS779.47 .E27 2022 (print) | LCC DS779.47 (ebook) | DDC 327.51--dc23
LC record available at https://lccn.loc.gov/2021013890
LC ebook record available at https://lccn.loc.gov/2021013891

Typeset in 11.5 on 14 pt Adobe Garamond
by Cheshire Typesetting Ltd, Cuddington, Cheshire

For further information on Polity, visit our website:
politybooks.com

Contents

Figures, Maps, and Tables

Abbreviations

ADB	Asian Development Bank
AI	artificial intelligence
AIIB	Asian Infrastructure Investment Bank
ASEAN	Association of Southeast Asian Nations
BARF	Belt and Road Forum
BIS	Security Information Service (Czech Republic)
BRI	Belt and Road Initiative
CBA	Chinese Basketball Association
CCP	Chinese Communist Party
CCTV	China Central Television
CDB	China Development Bank
CGTN	China Global Television Network
CIs	Confucius Institutes
CICIR	China Institutes of Contemporary International Relations
CMC	Central Military Commission
COSCO	China Ocean Shipping Company
CPEC	China–Pakistan Economic Corridor
CPTPP	Comprehensive and Progressive Agreement for Trans-Pacific Partnership
DPP	Democratic Progressive Party
DRAM	dynamic random-access memory
DSR	Digital Silk Road
EDA	electronic design automation
FAO	Food and Agriculture Organization
FDI	foreign direct investment
FOIP	Free and Open Indo-Pacific
GSM	Global System for Mobile Telecommunications
HKHRDA	Hong Kong Human Rights and Democracy Act
HKSAR	Hong Kong Special Administration Region
HSMC	Wuhan Hongxin Semiconductor Manufacturing

HSR	Health Silk Road
ICAO	International Civil Aviation Organization
ICCPR	International Covenant on Civil and Political Rights
ICT	information and communications technology
IDA	Institute for Defense Analysis
IEC	International Electrotechnical Commission
IFC	International Finance Corporation
IMF	International Monetary Fund
IP	intellectual property
IPO	initial public offering
ISO	International Standards Organization
ITU	International Telecommunication Union
KMT	Kuomintang
MIC	Made in China
NBA	National Basketball Association
NDRC	National Development and Reform Commission
NED	National Endowment for Democracy
NÚKIB	National Cyber and Information Security Agency (Czech Republic)
PKU	Peking University
PLA	People's Liberation Army
PPE	personal protective equipment
PRC	People's Republic of China
R&D	research and development
RCEP	Regional Comprehensive Economic Partnership
SCO	Shanghai Cooperation Organization
SDGs	Sustainable Development Goals
SIA	Semiconductor Industry Association
SSF	Strategic Support Force
SOEs	state-owned enterprises
TCM	traditional Chinese medicine
THAAD	Terminal High Altitude and Area Defense
TRA	Taiwan Relations Act
UFWD	United Front Work Department
UMC	United Microelectronics Corporation
UN DESA	United Nations Department of Social and Economic Affairs

UNCLOS United Nations Convention on the Law of the Sea
UNHRC United Nations Human Rights Council
UNIDO United Nations Industrial Development Organization
WHA World Health Assembly
WHO World Health Organization

Acknowledgments

This book has benefited greatly from the support of both the Hoover Institution and the Council on Foreign Relations (CFR), my two homes away from home. The dedication of these institutions to rigorous and informed policy debate created a vibrant intellectual environment that encouraged me to research and write this book. Even more importantly, the Hoover Institution and CFR are filled with wonderful scholars and colleagues who make going to work a privilege and a joy. In addition, I have been fortunate that the presidents of these institutions, Condoleezza Rice and Richard Haass, have provided me with guidance and inspired me through their scholarship and leadership in the policy world.

I am also grateful for the insightful advice and help I have received in reviewing the manuscript. Richard Haass and James Lindsay, CFR's Director of Studies, read the entire manuscript and offered valuable advice, as did two anonymous reviewers. My good friends and colleagues Adam Segal and Karl Eikenberry each read parts of the book and made it better. I owe special thanks to Endy Zemenides, who opened the doors of Greece's foreign policy community to me and provided me with a range of perspectives into how China is exercising its diplomatic and economic power outside its borders. Other friends, colleagues, and officials in China, Central Europe, Latin America, and the United States also generously shared their knowledge and insights.

I owe special thanks to my research associates, Lucy Best and Michael Collins. They provided outstanding research assistance throughout the writing process, brought their editing skills to bear as the manuscript neared completion, and, most importantly, brought a positive attitude and good humor to their work every day.

I also would like to thank my editor, Louise Knight, and editorial assistant, Inès Boxman, at Polity Press for their help and patience throughout the writing process. It was a joy to work with them. Justin Dyer also provided invaluable copyediting assistance.

Throughout the years, the Ford Foundation, the Luce Foundation, and the Starr Foundation have consistently encouraged and assisted me in my work. For this project, I am once again deeply grateful for their support.

All views and mistakes are my own and in no way should be attributed to anyone I have thanked above.

I wrote much of the book over the course of the COVID-19 pandemic, which reminded the world of the fragility of life and the importance of spending time with those we care about most. The unexpected time that I was able to spend with my husband, David – who is a constant source of energy and optimism – and our three (mostly) grown children, Alexander, Nicholas, and Eleni, was an unexpected bright spot in a very dark year. Our time together, along with the weekly Zoom calls I had with my parents, James and Anastasia, and my siblings, Peter, Katherine, and Melissa, served as a constant reminder to me of what matters most in this world.

1

Politics and the Plague

Chinese Communist Party (CCP) General Secretary and President of China Xi Jinping made the most of the moment. Speaking via video-conference at the opening ceremony of the United Nations World Health Assembly (WHA) on May 18, 2020 (Figure 1.1), he offered $2 billion over two years to help with the global response to the COVID-19 pandemic. The virus had first come to international attention in China and was now sweeping through the rest of the world. China itself had largely contained the spread. Everyday life was rapidly returning to normal, and Xi was prepared to assist other countries more in need. He pledged that when China was ready with a vaccine, the country would make it "a global public good." And in a nod to the mounting calls from over 120 countries for an international investigation into the origins of the virus – a demand China had until then resisted – Xi declared his support for a "comprehensive review of the global response to COVID-19."[1] It was a deft move designed to ensure that China would not be singled out in an international investigation and that any report would include Beijing's impressive success in containing the virus. It was also a personal diplomatic coup for the embattled Xi: the speech brought back memories of his January 2017 triumphs in Davos, where he touted Chinese leadership on globalization and free trade, and Geneva, where he pledged to defend the Paris Agreement on climate change. And his rhetorical magnanimity positioned China once again in stark contrast to the United States, whose president at the time, Donald Trump, had questioned the viability of the World Trade Organization, withdrawn from the Paris Agreement, and announced, just one month before Xi's WHA speech, that the United States would withhold all its funding from the World Health Organization (WHO).

If Xi Jinping's pledge before the WHA had represented the sum total of China's foreign policy over the course of the pandemic, the rest of the world could have walked away from the speech confident that it

Figure 1.1   Xi Jinping speaks at the 73rd World Health Assembly on
May 18, 2020
Source: Xinhua/Alamy

had found the global leader it needed for the 21st century. But China's pandemic diplomacy is not only a story about a newly emerged global power shouldering responsibility for responding to a humanitarian crisis. It is also the canary in the coal mine – a warning of the potential challenge that China's ambition and growing global influence portend for the current international system and the institutions, values, and norms that have underpinned it for more than 75 years.

Xi's ambition, as his words and deeds over the past decade suggest, is to reorder the world order. His call for "the great rejuvenation of the Chinese nation" envisions a China that has regained centrality on the global stage: it has reclaimed contested territory, assumed a position of preeminence in the Asia Pacific, ensured that other countries have aligned their political, economic, and security interests with its own, provided the world's technological infrastructure for the 21st century, and embedded its norms, values, and standards in international laws and institutions. The path to achieving this vision is a difficult one. It requires challenging both the position of the United States as the world's dominant power and the international understandings and institutions that have been in place since the end of World War II.

To achieve his ambition, Xi has transformed how China does business on the global stage. He has developed a strategy that reflects his domestic governance model: a highly centralized Party-state system that takes as its central priority preservation of its own power at home and realization of its sovereignty ambitions abroad. It is a system that grants Xi a unique capability to mobilize and deploy political, economic, and military resources – both public and private – across multiple domains: reinforcing his strategic priorities within China, in other countries, and in global governance institutions. He also seeks to control the content and flow of information – both within China and among international actors – to align them with Beijing's values and priorities. In addition, the CCP penetrates societies and economies abroad to shape international actors' political and economic choices in much the same way as it does with domestic actors. Moreover, Xi leverages the economic opportunities offered by China's vast market both to induce and to coerce others to adopt his policy preferences. Finally, Xi's model is underpinned by the hard power capability of an increasingly formidable Chinese military.

Will China succeed? Xi and many other top Chinese officials express confidence that the answer is yes. They argue that their efforts are already bearing fruit, aided by the inexorable trends of globalization and technological change, as well as the decline of the United States. As former senior Chinese official He Yafei has suggested, "Pax Americana is no more."[2] The dominant narrative in China is that the shift in the balance of power is already well underway, and the outcome is inevitable.

Yet there are signals that such confidence may be misplaced. Even as Xi's strategy achieves gains in the near term, it simultaneously creates conditions that constrain its success over the longer term. The greater the degree of CCP control or economic coercion that Xi exerts, the less credibility and attraction many of his initiatives hold for others and the more challenging additional gains become. Actors in the international community possesses agency that is not available to Chinese citizens. As the discussion of China and the pandemic later on in this chapter reveals, for example, the same elements of state mobilization, penetration, and coercion that achieved success within China played out very differently on the global

3

stage. Xi's determination to use China's provision of personal protective equipment (PPE) to the rest of the world to control the narrative around the pandemic, coerce thanks, and bolster CCP legitimacy, for example, caused Beijing's international standing to plummet and countries to begin considering how to move their supply chains out of China. What began as a diplomatic triumph transformed into a diplomatic debacle.

A Pandemic High

At China's annual gathering of its nearly 5,000 representatives to the National People's Congress and Chinese People's Political Consultative Conference in Beijing in March 2021, Xi Jinping stated that the country had been the first to tame the coronavirus, first to resume work, and first to attain positive growth. It was the result, he argued, of "self-confidence in our path, self-confidence in our theories, self-confidence in our system, self confidence in our culture. Our national system can concentrate force to do big things." And he further shared his pride that "Now, when our young people go abroad, they can stand tall and feel proud – unlike us when we were young."[3] Former Party Secretary of the Xinjiang Uyghur Autonomous Region Zhang Chunxian shared Xi's confidence, asserting that "the phenomenon of China advancing and the US retreating has also been conspicuous" and reiterating an earlier Xi claim that "the East is rising and the West is declining."[4]

China's robust response to the pandemic marked a defining moment in Xi's almost decade-long drive to reclaim Chinese centrality on the global stage. At his very first press conference as CCP General Secretary in November 2012, he had called for the "great rejuvenation of the Chinese nation" – a China that would "stand more firmly and powerfully among all nations around the world and make a greater contribution to mankind." This was not a new notion. Chinese leaders since Sun Yat-sen, the first provisional president of the Republic of China in 1911, have all invoked the theme of rejuvenation to remind the Chinese people of the country's past glories and future destiny. As Tsinghua University scholar Yan Xuetong wrote in 2001,

> The rise of China is granted by nature. . . . Even as recently as 1820, just
> twenty years before the Opium War, China accounted for 30 percent of the

world's GDP. This history of superpower status makes the Chinese people very proud of their country on the one hand, and on the other hand very sad about China's current international status. They believe China's decline to be a historical mistake, which they should correct.[5]

China had experienced a similar burst of national pride during the 2008 global financial crisis. Its economy had emerged relatively unscathed, while the United States experienced its worst economic disaster since the Great Depression. At the time, Vice Premier Wang Qishan told US Treasury Secretary Hank Paulson: "You were my teacher. But now I am in my teacher's domain, and look at your system, Hank. We aren't sure we should be learning from you anymore." The official Chinese news service Xinhua captured the zeitgeist: "The changing posture is related to the new reality. The depreciating US dollar, sub-prime crisis, and financial market instability have weakened the American position when dealing with China. In the meantime, China's high-speed economic growth has massively increased the country's confidence."[6]

Yet the country did not truly capitalize on its economic success until Xi Jinping took the reins of power. Xi is the first Chinese leader to align the country's capabilities with a vision and strategy to realize the long-held dream of rejuvenation. He and the rest of the Chinese leadership are not satisfied with their country's position within the international system, the values and policy preferences that the system embodies, how power is distributed, and how decisions are made. They want to reorder the world order.

To begin with, China's leaders want to reclaim their country's centrality on the global stage. A frequent refrain among Chinese officials today is that the last two centuries in which China was not the dominant global economy were an historical aberration. The current period, however, in which China's economy will soon surpass that of the United States, will mark a return to its rightful place and cement a shift in the two countries' relative influence on the global stage.

As a new geostrategic landscape emerges, China will be at the center, but with an altered geography that includes Chinese control over contested territories. There is no rejuvenation of the great Chinese nation without reunification. Chinese leaders are particularly focused on maintaining control within their own border regions, including the Xinjiang

Uyghur Autonomous Region, the Tibet Autonomous Region, and the Hong Kong Special Adminstrative Region, and asserting control over areas they consider core interests, such as Taiwan and a vast swath of the South China Sea. China also has outstanding territorial disputes that it wants resolved in its favor with other countries, including India, Japan, Nepal, Bhutan, and South Korea. In 2018, speaking before the National People's Congress, Xi stated, "It is the shared aspiration of all Chinese people and in the fundamental interests of the Chinese nation to safeguard China's sovereignty and territorial integrity and realize China's complete reunification . . . [A]ny actions and tricks to split China are doomed to fail."[7] Xi is particularly insistent that Taiwan, which thus far remains out of his grasp, is already part of China: "People on both sides of the Straits are one family, with shared blood" and, as such, "no one can ever cut the veins that connect us."[8] Although Chinese leaders often discuss the country's rejuvenation as part of a peaceful and inevitable trend in international relations, Xi also makes clear that peace and stability will never come at the cost of China's sovereignty: "While pursuing peaceful development, we will never sacrifice our legitimate rights and interests or China's core interests. No foreign country should expect China to trade off its core interests or swallow bitter fruit that undermines China's sovereignty, security or development interests."[9]

From there, Chinese influence and power extend through the Asia Pacific, which Chinese leaders portray as seamlessly integrated through Chinese-powered trade, technology, infrastructure, and shared cultural and civilizational ties. Xi likens the nations of the Asia Pacific to a "big family," in which "the region cannot prosper without China" and "China cannot develop in isolation from the region."[10] While much of Xi's emphasis is on the value of integration through trade, security also plays a central role. In 2014, Xi proposed the establishment of a new regional security cooperation architecture for Asia, arguing: "In the final analysis let the people of Asia run the affairs of Asia, solve the problems of Asia and uphold the security of Asia."[11] According to Xi, cooperation could include a code of conduct for regional security, an Asian Security partnership program, and coordination on law enforcement. He reiterated the idea in 2015, when he proposed a uniquely "Asian community with a shared future."[12] Implicit in Xi's "Asia for Asians" construct is a much-diminished role for the United States, which is the current dominant power and guarantor of regional security. In the new world order, the United States has largely retreated back across the Pacific, returning to its historic role as an Atlantic power. Wang Jisi of Peking University (PKU) explains the Chinese leader's views as natural and designed to "solidify China's role as a regional power."[13]

Chinese influence further radiates through the rest of the world via infrastructure, ranging from ports, railways, and highways to fiber optic cables, e-commerce, and satellite systems. In the same way that US, European, and Japanese companies led the development of much of the world's 20th-century infrastructure development, Chinese companies are competing to lead in the 21st century. The spoils of the competition will be long-lasting, entrenching the winner's technology, standards, and know-how throughout the world for decades to come.

Xi Jinping's ambition to embed Chinese influence globally also extends beyond physical constructs. One of his most dramatic foreign policy innovations has been the promotion of China's political model and the export of some of its authoritarian elements, such as state control over the internet. Although scholars and officials had engaged in initial discussions of a China model after the global financial crisis – web entries on the topic jumped from approximately 750 in 2008 to 3,000 in 2009[14] – the Chinese leadership at the time rejected the notion of an exportable Chinese model. Then premier Wen Jiabao stated definitively that "China never sees its development as a model. . . . All countries have their own development paths that suit their national conditions."[15] Xi, however, has introduced a different, more confident and more competitive approach.

In a January 2013 speech before the CCP's top 200-odd officials, only two months after becoming CCP General Secretary, Xi posited an existential competition between China's model and that of the West. He described the post-Cold War period as one in which many developing countries were forced to adopt the Western model, leading to "party feuds, social unrest, and people left homeless and wandering." He continued on to argue: "We firmly believe that as socialism with Chinese characteristics develops further, our system will inevitably mature; it is likewise inevitable that the superiority of our socialist system will be increasingly apparent."[16] Four years later at the 2017 19th Party Congress, Xi became the first Chinese leader since Mao Zedong to suggest that China had a political model worth emulating: "The China model for a better social governance system offers a new option for other countries and nations who want to speed up their development while preserving their independence. And it offers Chinese wisdom and a Chinese approach to solving the problems facing mankind."[17] While Chinese scholars acknowledge the existence of competition among models, many remain wary of promoting a Chinese model. Yan Xuetong, for example, sounds a cautionary note: "Setting the China model as an example and hoping other countries to follow China can easily lead to an ideological confrontation. . . . [T]here is no need to compare China with Western countries or to promote the superiority of the China model. This won't help improve China's international image."[18]

Finally, Xi has expressed his desire to "lead in the reform of the global governance system"[19] – transforming the institutions, norms, and values that govern relations among international actors, as well as China's place within that system. For Xi, this is a long-term ideological battle. In 2014, he asserted, "We should be keenly aware of the protracted nature of the contest over the international order."[20]

While Chinese leaders have long insisted that they support the international system and do not want to undermine it, they also believe that their inability to participate in the development of the post-World War II Bretton Woods System left them at a disadvantage. The rules-based order did not reflect the values, norms, or policy preferences of the newly established People's Republic of China (PRC). Huang Jing, dean of the Beijing Language and Cultural University, acknowledges that every Chinese leader from Deng Xiaoping to Xi Jinping has pledged to maintain the international system, but that China's political system is "incompatible with the mainstream of the existing international order." As a result, he suggests, when faced with the two choices – China changing to accommodate the system or China changing the system to be accommodated – Beijing has selected the latter.[21] And with China's greater standing on the global stage, Xi now claims a new mandate to reform the international system. Changes in global governance, he noted in September 2016, originate in changes in the balance of power.[22]

Chinese officials often mask their global governance ambitions in vague and benign-sounding concepts, such as "a new relationship among major powers" and a "community of shared future (or common destiny) for mankind." These concepts, nonetheless, hold within them the promise of radical change in the values currently expressed in international institutions on issues such as human rights, internet governance, and trade and investment. A main focus of Chinese efforts, for example, is to rebalance the international system's support away from individual to state-determined rights. These concepts also call for the dissolution of the US-led alliance system. Chinese foreign policy officials often frame US alliances as exclusive and contributing to the insecurity of others;[23] as Fu Ying, a former high-ranking Chinese diplomat, articulated in a 2016 speech: "China has long been alienated politically by the western world. The US-led military alliance puts their interests above others and pays little attention to China's security concerns."[24] Xi has called frequently for a new form of security partnership that is based on "non-confrontation and non-alliance."[25]

Although Chinese officials leave open the question of whether they expect their country to replace the United States as the world's hegemon, many Chinese scholars believe that China will soon surpass the United States. Wang Jisi acknowledges that within China, there is a popular perception that US power is declining and that sooner or later China will succeed the United States as "number one" in the world.[26] Fudan University professor Shen Dingli believes China already occupies the "moral high ground" in the international community and is now "poised to act as the leading country in the new era."[27] These scholars refrain from answering, however, whether China is ready to play a dominant role in not only defining the rules that govern the international system but also marshaling the international community to respond to global challenges and to serve as the world's policeman.

China's desire to reorder the world order is a tall one. US leadership on the global stage, its democratic alliance system, and the post-World War II liberal international order are deeply entrenched. Moreover, while Beijing's initial successful management of the pandemic at home reinforced the Chinese people's confidence in their system, its sustained lockdowns during 2021 and 2022, as well as its strategy on the global stage, ultimately harmed the CCP's legitimacy at home and reputation abroad. Chinese actions presented a complex and, ultimately for many foreign observers, concerning picture of what future Chinese global leadership might entail.

The COVID-19 Test

In late December 2019, hospitals in Hubei, a relatively well-off province in central China, reported a string of cases of a "pneumonia of unknown etiology." Dr. Ai Fen, the director of the Emergency Room of Wuhan Central Hospital, was the first to make a connection between the cases coming into the hospitals and reports of people at the Huanan Seafood Wholesale Market falling ill with high fevers. After alerting her hospital, she posted a warning to a number of colleagues. Her message caught the attention of other doctors, including Dr. Li Wenliang, a 34-year-old ophthalmologist, who worked at the same hospital. He sent a message to a group chat with his former medical school classmates: "A new coronavirus infection has been confirmed and its type is being identified. Inform all family and relatives to be on guard."[28] Wuhan's public security officials moved quickly to silence Li, calling him in for questioning on January 1, 2020. They issued Li a formal reprimand for "making untrue comments" and "severely disturbing social order." They also detained seven other Chinese citizens for "spreading rumors."[29] Li nonetheless continued to warn people. A few weeks later, he himself contracted the virus. For her part, Ai received a serious reprimand from the hospital's disciplinary inspection committee, criticizing her for spreading false rumors and warning her not to tell anyone – not even her husband.[30]

As China's leaders moved to control the spread of the virus, the strengths and weaknesses of the country's political model were on full display. The high degree of political centralization and control over information prevented medical officials from alerting the Chinese people and the rest of the world about the virus and contributed to millions of Chinese leaving Wuhan, the virus' epicenter, to travel during the Lunar New Year celebration, many unknowingly carrying the virus with them. Yet this same centralization of authority also enabled the government to lock down Wuhan on January 23, effectively preventing 11 million people from leaving the city and anyone else from entering. Public transport and highways were closed, and restrictions were placed on a number of other nearby cities and towns. All told, 50 million people in Hubei province were placed under strict quarantine by the end of January. The world watched in awe as Beijing mobilized 7,500 workers to construct two makeshift hospitals in under two weeks and commandeered enterprises across the country to manufacture much-needed PPE, including masks, gowns, and gloves. The CCP's surveillance technology – more than 200 million cameras tracking people everywhere – and symbiotic relationship with the country's leading technology companies, such as Tencent and Alibaba, allowed the government to track and ultimately contain the spread of the virus with a relatively high degree of efficiency.

Despite the government's success, for the first time since Xi Jinping had come to power in 2012, Chinese citizens took to the internet in large numbers to challenge the official narrative. The death of Dr. Li prompted more than one million Chinese citizens to post their thoughts online: the British Broadcasting Corporation (BBC) reported that the top two hashtags were "Wuhan government owes Dr. Li Wenliang an apology" and "We want freedom of speech." The internet activism was short-lived, however. Many citizen journalists who reported on the pandemic were later detained and sentenced to jail for "picking quarrels,"[31] while others went missing.[32]

By the end of 2020, the Chinese government had erased from the public record any signs of early missteps or public dissent. The Chinese people had largely returned to their pre-pandemic lives, and China emerged as the world's only large economy to post a positive growth rate. Within China, the story of China and the COVID-19 pandemic became a triumphal one: the Chinese government contained the virus and its critics in record time. Its state-centered model, which enabled the mobilization of resources, the CCP's penetration of society and the economy, and control over information, not only succeeded but also stood in stark contrast to the disastrously chaotic response of the United States, the world's leading democracy. Rather than spark a crisis in the CCP's authority, the pandemic reinforced its legitimacy. On the international front, however, China's pandemic diplomacy resulted in a far different outcome.

The Pandemic Goes Global

On December 31, 2019, the day after Drs. Ai and Li shared their fears, two separate WHO offices, as well as officials from Taiwan, sounded their own alarm bells. The WHO requested further information the following day from Chinese authorities, who acknowledged the existence of a cluster of cases but provided very little additional insight. That same day, however, local Wuhan officials closed the Huanan Seafood Wholesale Market, which had been identified as a suspected center for the outbreak. Meanwhile, Chinese researchers successfully mapped the coronavirus' complete genetic information on January 2 – a feat that would help researchers all over the world understand where and how the virus spread – although they didn't make it publicly available to the rest of the world until more than a week later on January 11. That day, China also reported its first death, that of a 61-year-old man.

As cases mounted and Chinese officials moved to lock down Wuhan, Beijing mobilized its resources on the global stage, much as it had at home. The CCP's United Front Work Department (UFWD), which is responsible for maintaining ties with overseas Chinese, reached out to local Chinese civic groups abroad and encouraged them to assist China in the country's moment of need. The response was immediate and overwhelming. Bloomberg News reported that Chinese volunteers in Nagoya, Japan bought 520,000 masks in three days.[33] Churches, philanthropic organizations, multinationals, and governments across the world also mobilized to send PPE to China. One of those who answered the call was Li Lu. A former student leader of the 1989 democracy protests in Tiananmen Square, Li had fled China for the United States in the wake of the government crackdown. In short order, he graduated with a BA, JD, and MBA from Columbia University, became an American citizen, and started his own investment fund, Himalaya Capital Management. Li and I were at a conference in San Diego in late January when I overheard him on the phone during a break desperately attempting to secure PPE to send to China. As he later explained to me, he had lived through the 1976 Tangshan earthquake and remembered the chaos of the Chinese government's efforts at the time. He saw some of the same confusion during the early months of the pandemic as Chinese leaders tried to manage the PPE supply through only two government-designated organizations: the International Red Cross and the All-China Federation of Philanthropy. Both were ill equipped to manage the situation. Li found his own way to get more than $1,500,000 in PPE and financial assistance where it needed to go by using "layers of friends" and networks both in and outside China. In addition, the day after the death of Dr. Li, Li established a foundation to help take care of the families of nurses and doctors who had died or were permanently incapacitated. Overall, organizations in the United States provided 18 tons of masks, gowns, respirators, gauze, and other needed materials.[34] By the end of February, the international community had provided China with items worth $1.2 billion.[35]

Beijing also directed its ambassadors to fan out to try to control the narrative. At the conclusion of the San Diego conference, I sat in a half-empty auditorium listening to China's ambassador to the United States Cui Tiankai deliver a keynote address. His message was straightforward: China was behaving in a transparent manner and sharing information with the international community. Moreover, China's sacrifice was not only for the Chinese people but also for the rest of the world. Cui, like his fellow ambassadors, avoided any hint of culpability for the virus' initial spread. And behind the scenes, Chinese officials requested that other countries not publicize their assistance to China or stoke fear by banning travel or closing their borders to Chinese nationals.[36] These requests betrayed the fragility of the CCP's legitimacy at home; in a system of performative rather than electoral accountability, a perceived failure in pandemic management could result in a governance crisis.

By mid-March, the Chinese government had largely arrested the spread of the virus. Chinese officials and the media pivoted quickly to sell a new message: China was the world leader in pandemic response.[37] The country had amassed the world's largest cache of PPE. (China itself was already the world's largest manufacturer of PPE, producing 60 percent of protective garments,[38] and a critical source of the precursor materials necessary to develop COVID-19 vaccines and drug therapies.) And with PPE to spare and a demonstrable record of success in beating back the virus, the government brought the same actors back on duty, but with a different mission.

Chinese ambassadors now promoted Beijing's "Knowledge Center for China's Experiences in response to COVID-19" on their embassy websites, featuring QR codes that provided access to scientific papers, short policy briefs, and videos with Chinese doctors that touted Xi Jinping's leadership and the country's impressive COVID-19 response.[39] The government also encouraged Chinese companies such as Alibaba and Huawei to become informal brand ambassadors for Beijing by providing PPE and other assistance to countries struggling with shortages.

Overseas Chinese followed suit. Li Lu organized a webinar featuring three Chinese doctors from Wuhan and Shanghai who had been at the forefront of fighting the pandemic. Hundreds of US scientists, doctors, and other health professionals attended. In addition, he used his personal funds to buy millions of dollars of PPE to supply to US hospitals. And in a stroke of good luck, the head of one of China's premier electric car makers, BYD (also one of Himalaya Capital's portfolio companies), happened to be in the United States, and Li persuaded him to start producing face masks. With 3,000 engineers behind the effort, BYD became the largest face mask producer in the world – and one of only two Chinese companies that received official US National Institute for Occupational Safety and Health certification and Emergency Use Authorization from the Food and Drug Administration for medical equipment. "Viruses don't recognize borders or ideology," Li reminded me when we talked again in fall 2020. "They affect people equally. Things that can protect Chinese can help Americans, and drugs will work both ways."

A Period of Strategic Opportunity

For Chinese leaders, the second stage of the pandemic represented what they like to refer to as a "period of strategic opportunity." Xi managed to use the pandemic to make progress on several health-related priorities, most notably bolstering his still nascent Health Silk Road (HSR), an off-shoot of his 2013 grand-scale global infrastructure plan "One Belt, One Road" (later translated as the Belt and Road Initiative or BRI).[40] Thirty countries, as well as the WHO and UN Programme on HIV/AIDS, had previously signed memoranda of understanding as HSR partners;[41] now China was sending them doctors, medical devices, and technology, such as contact-tracing capabilities and e-medicine.[42] In a March phone call with then Italian prime minister Giuseppe Conte, Xi Jinping stated, "Italy and China are the cornerstones of the new Silk Road of Health,"[43] and he sent 300 doctors to Italy to cement the partnership. Foreign Minister Luigi Di Maio criticized Europe for providing less assistance than China,[44] although not all Italians agreed with his assessment. As one Italian observer noted, China's aid was provided primarily as part of a commercial deal, whereas European assistance was "more substantial" and arrived in the form of donations.[45]

In addition, Xi seized the opportunity presented by the pandemic to promote traditional Chinese medicine (TCM). Xi had long supported TCM, describing it as "the treasure of ancient Chinese science and the key to the archive of Chinese civilization."[46] TCM is both lucrative – with a global market value of more than $400 billion – and an important source of potential Chinese cultural or soft power influence. Early in his tenure, Xi set targets for the production and use of TCM within China, established TCM centers, programs, and workshops in several African and other countries,[47] and worked with Margaret Chan, a former Hong Kong health official and WHO head, to develop and release a 10-year strategy to integrate TCM into the world's healthcare systems. (The plan called for countries to educate their citizens on TCM's benefits and ensure that insurance companies provided reimbursement for TCM.)[48] In 2019 – over the objection of much of the international scientific community – the WHO agreed to include TCM in its International Classification of Diseases (a document that validates certain treatments and medicines for doctors to diagnose patients) without subjecting TCM practices to the same rigorous testing demanded of Western treatments.[49] This provided TCM with an invaluable official seal of approval.

Despite limited medical evidence as to the benefits of TCM for treating COVID-19, Xi instructed Chinese hospitals to prescribe it as part of their COVID-19 treatment protocol.[50] He also pushed the distribution of TCM and TCM medical specialists through the HSR and advertised its usefulness in pandemic treatment on Chinese embassy websites. At the same time, Chinese-based international professional associations lobbied the United Nations to formally recognize the value of TCM in responding to COVID-19.[51]

Wolves at the Door

While the world lauded China's leadership in providing PPE, much of the goodwill Beijing earned evaporated as Chinese officials began to adopt a more coercive and combative form of diplomacy colloquially referred to as "wolf warrior diplomacy." The latter term reflected the tag line from the second of two Chinese blockbuster *Wolf Warrior* movies in which elite Chinese forces triumph over foreign mercenaries and others: "Even though a thousand miles away, anyone who affronts China will pay."[52]

The same diplomats who had earlier requested that other countries not advertise their assistance to China now trumpeted their provision of PPE to these same countries and insisted on public displays of gratitude. While Italian prime minister Guiseppe Conte complied, others, such as German chancellor Angela Merkel, stressed the two-way nature of pandemic assistance: "The European Union sent medical equipment to China [when] China asked for help at that time. What we are seeing here is reciprocity."[53] The wolf warrior diplomats also weaponized the country's control over PPE and access to China's vast market to try to coerce countries into aligning their interests with those of China. China reportedly told France that ample PPE would be forthcoming if the latter bought Huawei 5G equipment. And when Australian prime minister Scott Morrison called for an investigation into the origins of the virus in April, China's ambassador to the country suggested it would pay a steep economic price: "[M]aybe the ordinary [Chinese] people will think why they should drink Australian wine or eat Australian beef."[54] Shortly afterward, China banned Australian beef imports and placed tariffs on Australian barley, following this up in fall 2020 with bans on Australian coal and wine, as well as recommendations to Chinese tourists not to travel to Australia.[55]

Chinese foreign affairs officials and the media also tried to deflect attention from China's role in the pandemic by spreading disinformation about other countries' management of it. Ministry of Foreign Affairs spokesman Zhao Lijian tweeted: "It might be the US army who brought the epidemic to Wuhan. Be transparent! Make public your data! US owe [*sic*] us an explanation!"[56] The Chinese embassy in Paris published an article on its website claiming that French healthcare workers had abandoned their jobs in nursing homes and left the residents to "die of starvation and illness." And at one point, a number of Chinese media organizations and government officials tweeted out a video that purported to show Italians chanting "Grazie, China," with China's national anthem playing in the background. It later emerged that the Italians were cheering for their own healthcare workers.[57]

Chinese foreign minister Wang Yi explicitly encouraged such diplomatic hardball, claiming: "We never pick a fight or bully others. But we have principles and guts. We will push back against any deliberate insult, resolutely defend our national honor and dignity, and we will refute all groundless slander with facts."[58] While such nationalistic rhetoric had its supporters within China, it came at a steep reputational cost outside the country. International media coverage portrayed Beijing's mask diplomacy as bullying, and foreign governments lost faith in China as a reliable source of PPE. Concern over Chinese-manufactured PPE was also compounded by widespread reports of substandard products. Health officials in Spain, the UK, Turkey, the Philippines, the Netherlands, and Finland, among other countries, complained that the Chinese masks lacked adequate filters, testing kits were inaccurate, and disinfectants were fake.[59] The Netherlands alone recalled 600,000 faulty Chinese-made masks. In the wake of both the quality issues and the coercive nature of Beijing's mask diplomacy, countries began to discuss the need to reorient their supply chains away from China.

A Friend in Need Is a Friend Indeed

Over the course of the pandemic, the WHO emerged as a critical ally for Beijing. The head of the WHO, Tedros Adhanom Ghebreyesus, whose candidacy Beijing had championed, consistently downplayed the potential threat of the virus and any Chinese responsibility for its spread. Even after the WHO formally declared the COVID-19 outbreak a Public Health Emergency of International Concern, Tedros stated that the designation "was not issued because of what is happening in China, but what is happening in other countries." Moreover, in a January 30 news conference, he reiterated his opposition to limiting either trade or travel to China, despite the fact that there were 17,238 confirmed cases and 361 deaths in China as well as 151 confirmed cases and one death in 23 other countries.[60] During a brief trip to China the week before, Tedros had even lauded Beijing's actions: "We appreciate the seriousness with which China is taking this outbreak, especially the commitment from top leadership, and the transparency they have demonstrated, including sharing data and [the] genetic sequence of the virus."[61]

The WHO had earlier deferred to China's wishes on naming the disease.[62] The organization acknowledged privately that China did not like the name – SARS-CoV-2 – selected by the official study group of the International Committee on Taxonomy of Viruses (likely because it reminded the world of China's role in the 2003 SARS outbreak).[63]

More significantly, the WHO also respected Beijing's wishes by refusing to allow Taiwan to participate in WHA briefings unless it adopted Beijing's preferred name for it: Chinese Taipei.

China's influence in the WHO, perhaps surprisingly, is not the result of a substantial financial contribution to the organization; the country contributes less than 1 percent of the organization's budget. It is, however, deeply integrated into the WHO politically: a Chinese official holds a seat on the governing board and a second is in charge of overseeing the organization's work on communicable and noncommunicable diseases. China is also viewed as a very important partner in developing public health programs for the Global South.[64] And Tedros has been an outspoken supporter of Chinese initiatives. Speaking at the August 2017 "High-Level Meeting for Health Cooperation: Towards a Health Silk Road" in Beijing, he applauded the HSR as the "groundwork for essential health services needed to ensure universal health care."[65]

The WHO's unreserved support for Beijing throughout the pandemic raised alarm bells in other countries over undue Chinese influence. According to one public health expert, Tedros avoided criticizing China for fear of losing access to critical information. Other WHO staffers, however, were less reticent. Australian professor John Mackenzie asserted that China had tried to hide cases during the first weeks of the outbreak.[66] He leaked recordings of internal WHO staff meetings that revealed consensus among many staffers that China was not sharing information in a timely manner. In particular, Beijing only released the gene sequence after a lab in Shanghai had already published it on a virologist website. (It later emerged that one Chinese lab had sequenced most of the genome as early as December 27, a full two weeks before it was released to the public.) In addition, the WHO's chief of emergencies, who had praised China publicly, claimed in an internal meeting that China was not cooperating the way other countries – such as the Democratic Republic of the Congo – did during the Ebola outbreak.[67]

The Siren Call of Sovereignty

China's unwillingness to put its sovereignty conflict with Taiwan aside in 2020 was indicative of a much larger strategic push by Beijing to reinforce its sovereignty claims while other countries were preoccupied with the pandemic. Most notably, it implemented a politically repressive National Security Law in Hong Kong; continued its detention of more than one million Uyghur Muslims in labor and reeducation camps in the country's westernmost region, Xinjiang; and deployed its naval and other military forces across the South and East China Seas, threatening Taiwan, Japan, Indonesia, Malaysia, and the Philippines. As we will see in chapter 3, it also sunk a Vietnamese fishing boat and named more than 80 features in the South China Sea, 55 of which were underwater. China and India also engaged in their first deadly border conflict in more than four decades.

Criticism of China's coercive political and aggressive military behavior mounted, particularly in Europe, North America, and parts of Asia. India banned a wide array of popular Chinese apps; Europe, the UK, the US, and Canada levied sanctions against Chinese officials and entities for their actions in Xinjiang; and many countries revised their decision to allow Huawei components or software in their 5G networks. Global public opinion polls indicated that distrust in Xi Jinping's motivations and ambitions was rising precipitously (see Figure 1.2).[68] Yet Chinese officials did not relent. In fact, in the face of the Xinjiang sanctions, they retaliated against a number of European entities, jeopardizing an investment deal with Europe that had been seven years in the making. It was an important signal both of the relative weight of sovereignty as opposed to trade and investment among China's strategic priorities, and of Beijing's willingness to tolerate significant disequilibrium in the international system in pursuit of a new steady state: a reunified and politically insulated China.

The Recovery

During fall 2020, China mounted a renewed effort to assume a leadership position in responding to the pandemic. It joined COVAX, the international initiative to ensure a degree of equity in the distribution of COVID-19 vaccines, after initially rejecting participation. Several senior Chinese foreign policy analysts had argued publicly that joining would be in China's best interest. They noted that it would send an important signal to the international community that China was not simply "sweeping its own snow

Figure 1.2 Comparison of global levels of faith in Xi Jinping from 2019 to 2020

Source: https://www.pewresearch.org/global/2020/10/06/unfavorable-views-of-china-reach-historic-highs-in-many-countries/

in front of the door" but instead was interested in helping others. They also offered an array of less altruistic motivations, including improving Beijing's image, assisting in the global economic recovery (which they suggested would serve the country's economic interests), and establishing China's vaccine as an internationally recognized brand.[69]

By the time it joined COVAX, China had already vaccinated one million people domestically and in the United Arab Emirates, Bahrain, Peru, and Argentina. But there was growing concern in the international scientific community over Beijing's lack of transparency in its vaccine trials. China had not provided information concerning the vaccine trial results, leaving the international community questioning the efficacy and safety of the vaccines.[70] It was not until April 2021 that the head of China's Center for Disease Control and Prevention, Gao Fu, acknowledged that the efficacy of the country's vaccines was relatively low and measures should be taken to improve their protection rates. (He later asserted that his comments had been misinterpreted.)[71]

In addition, China's zero-COVID policy and frequent, strict lockdowns throughout 2021 and 2022 contributed to serious food shortages, lack of sufficient medical care, and localized protests. As a result, the CCP's triumphal COVID narrative lost credibility both at home and abroad.[72]

Mapping China's Ambition, Influence, and Impact

The conduct of Chinese foreign policy over the course of the first year of the pandemic and beyond offers some initial insights into how Xi has adapted his domestic governance model to the pursuit of his strategic ambitions. For example, he mobilized and deployed domestic resources across multiple domains – within China, through the BRI, and in the WHO – to promote the adoption of TCM internationally. He also used the penetration of the CCP in other countries' societies to collect and distribute PPE via state-directed overseas Chinese organizations and to enable Chinese officials to spread disinformation on Western social media platforms such as Twitter. Moreover, he leveraged the Chinese market to try to coerce countries into thanking

China publicly for PPE and into dropping their calls for an investigation into the origins of the virus.

The chapters outlined below explore in detail how Xi has utilized this model and the consequences – both intended and unintended – for his ability to realize his broader strategic objectives. Chapter 2 outlines how China utilizes soft, sharp, and hard power to shape the perceptions and policy preferences of other actors and evaluates the relative strengths and weaknesses of these tools. It argues that context matters. Countries that are geographically distant from China, for example, are typically less concerned about the country's deployment of hard power than those in its backyard. And while multinationals often succumb to Chinese coercive economic leverage, countries generally do not. Perhaps most surprisingly, the level of Chinese trade and investment does not correlate closely with countries' support for Beijing on other issues, such as its policies in Xinjiang or its actions in the South China Sea. Other factors matter more.

Chapter 3 delves into the heart of Xi's rejuvenation ambition: the creation of a unified China. It investigates how China realized its sovereignty claims in Hong Kong, and the steps it is taking to make progress in the South China Sea and Taiwan. It reveals that China's willingness to use soft power, as opposed to more coercive or even military actions, diminishes rather than expands as opposition among other actors to its sovereignty efforts grows. China is also willing to ignore international law, such as the UN Convention on the Law of the Sea (UNCLOS), and to endure significant disequilibrium in the international system in pursuit of its sovereignty objectives. One consequence of China's use of economic coercion and military power has been to bolster the Quadrilateral Security Dialogue (Japan, India, the United States, and Australia) and to invite deeper military engagement from actors outside the region, such as Germany, France, and the UK. This expanding coalition challenges Xi's ability to make further progress on his sovereignty ambitions for the South China Sea and Taiwan.

The heart of chapter 4 is an exploration of whether and in what ways China is selling its model and imprinting its political, economic, and security preferences on other countries through its flagship foreign policy initiative, Belt and Road. The BRI captures the essence of Xi's strategic ambition. It places China at the center of a vast network of global physical and technological infrastructure, as well as political and security influence. The chapter delineates the sprawling and opportunistic nature of the BRI, illuminates the debates within and outside China over its sustainability, and reveals the differential impacts of Belt and Road across a range of countries. It concludes that while the BRI, more than any other initiative, has helped China realize its ambitions for a reordered world, its continued success may be derailed by discontent within host countries over Beijing's weak governance practices and low environmental and labor standards. In addition, the spread of Chinese political, economic, and military influence via the BRI has heightened the global influence competition with other advanced economies.

Chapter 5 examines China's effort to lead the world's technological transformation over the 21st century. It finds that its strategic playbook has experienced mixed success. Its governance model has yielded significant gains in Chinese domestic technological capabilities and has enabled Beijing to take a commanding lead in developing the technological infrastructure for a significant number of developing economies through the Digital Silk Road and to reinforce its technological priorities in international standard setting bodies. Beijing's relationship with advanced market democracies in Europe, North America, and Asia, however, has encountered increasing difficulty. The growing CCP control over the private sector has contributed to Chinese technology companies' exclusion from some of these countries' markets. Moreover, the linkages between Chinese technology companies and the Chinese military or surveillance activities, particularly in Xinjiang, have resulted in US sanctions to deprive these companies of necessary technology. In addition, CCP financial and other support for international scientific talent through its Thousand Talents Plan has triggered concerns over spying and intellectual property (IP) theft, contributing to a significant political backlash in the United States and elsewhere.

Chapter 6 investigates China's efforts to reform global governance norms, values, and institutions in four policy arenas: the Arctic, human rights, the internet, and development finance. It reveals how Beijing has successfully enforced its own policy preferences through assuming leadership positions in international institutions; a long-term strategy of setting targets and timetables to benchmark accomplishments; mobilizing Chinese government, business, and civil society actors; leveraging its economic power; and reinforcing its priorities in multiple domains. As with the BRI and China's global technology push, however, the more overtly China's policies impinge on or undermine established norms and values, the more likely the international community will resist.

The final chapter offers thoughts on how the United States and the rest of the world should respond to China's strategic ambitions. It argues that neither the traditional US policy of "constructive engagement" nor the more recent Trump administration approach of "compete, counter, and contain," is adequate to meet the challenge. The US strategy, along with that of its allies and partners, must account for Xi Jinping's unique policy playbook as well as to assert a positive and proactive vision of the world's future and their place within it. Given China's global reach and impact, moreover, the United States and traditional allies and partners must expand the tent to engage the rest of the world in this vision. While there is broad scope for cooperation between China and the United States on global challenges such as climate change, this is unlikely to alter the contest underway between two distinct sets of values and world visions.

Conclusion

The findings from these chapters reveal how Xi Jinping uses the various elements of his unique foreign policy playbook to realize his strategic ambitions. Taken together, they also suggest several broader conclusions.

First, Xi's overarching strategic priority is to maintain sovereignty and social stability in the near term, and to realize the unification of China over the longer term. Moreover, he is willing to tolerate significant disequilibrium in the international system to achieve a new, more desirable end steady state of a reunified China. Xi's repressive policies in Xinjiang and Hong Kong, for example, resulted in international censure, as well as coordinated economic sanctions by the European Union, UK, Canada, and the United States; his retaliatory sanctions then threatened a major trade deal with the EU. The border conflict with India led Prime Minister Modi to strengthen security and other ties with the Quad. In addition, China's wolf warrior diplomacy – designed to control the international political narrative to avoid a domestic legitimacy crisis – contributed to a steep drop in Xi's and China's global standing. Yet this backlash failed to persuade China to change course. Finally, Beijing's willingness to exclude Taiwan from the WHA briefings during the pandemic further demonstrated its determination to place its sovereignty interests over both the welfare of the Taiwanese people and the larger global good.

Second, while China is not exporting communism, it is exporting elements of its authoritarian political model. In the same way that it controls speech domestically, Beijing seeks to limit the ability of international actors to speak freely about China. Traditionally, Beijing has concentrated on ensuring that other countries acknowledge its sovereignty claims, using the leverage of its market or access to the country to coerce them to do so or to punish them if they do not. Chinese red lines are proliferating, however. China initiated a boycott against Australian exports in response to Canberra's call for a COVID-19 inquiry; it also expelled three *Wall Street Journal* reporters in response to an article that referred to China as the "sick man of Asia." Virtually any issue can now be labeled a threat to Chinese sovereignty or social stability. China also exports its model more directly via the BRI. It trains officials in some BRI countries on how to censor the internet, control civil society, and build a robust single-party state. It also transfers its development model through the BRI in the form of debt-induced infrastructure development with weak transparency, labor, environmental, and legal standards. Finally, Chinese officials use their leadership positions within the UN and other international institutions to shape the values and norms of those bodies in ways that align with China's political interests: for example, by preventing Uyghur Muslim dissidents from speaking before UN bodies and by advancing Chinese technology norms, such as a state-controlled internet in global standard setting bodies.

Third, Xi has made substantial progress in realizing his strategic vision, but continued success is far from inevitable. The very characteristics that have enabled China to achieve its foreign policy objectives in the near term now risk undermining its future progress. Within its own backyard, China has defeated a broad-based push for democracy and cemented CCP control in Hong Kong, prevented Taiwan from gaining voice within the United Nations, and enhanced its sovereignty claims in the South China Sea. Efforts to create a more Sinocentric Asia Pacific have also made progress. The Chinese leadership successfully led the negotiations for the Regional Comprehensive Economic Partnership (RCEP) in November 2020, which stands as the largest trading bloc in the world and serves as an important step forward in asserting China's leadership within the Asia

Pacific. The Chinese military has also significantly enhanced its capabilities in the region. In addition, China has managed impressive gains in shaping the world beyond its backyard. Through the BRI, and particularly the Digital Silk Road, China is increasingly the provider of choice as the world builds out its technological infrastructure for the 21st century. It has won contracts to deploy Huawei 5G technology throughout much of Africa and, increasingly, in Latin America and the Middle East. Its media companies project a more positive China narrative to tens of millions of citizens globally. And in international institutions, China has made headway in advancing its human rights, internet governance, and development norms.

Increasingly, however, China's state-centered model has limited the credibility and attraction of many of its initiatives. Private Chinese technology companies such as Huawei and ByteDance face growing constraints in accessing global markets. Countries are increasingly rejecting Chinese investments over concerns that they are part of a CCP-directed strategy to support its military expansion. Chinese cultural initiatives such as Confucius Institutes (CIs) have also diminished in popularity because they are perceived to be agents of Chinese propaganda. In addition, the predilection of some Chinese officials who serve in UN bodies to act in the interest of China as opposed to the broader mission of the UN has provoked efforts by other countries to push back against Chinese initiatives and support alternative candidates for senior UN positions. China's future ability to achieve its broader foreign policy objectives is thus increasingly compromised by its insistence that it control both state and non-state actors.

In many developing and middle-income countries, as well, the export of China's development model through the BRI is incurring significant political and economic costs. There are frequent popular protests around the lack of transparency, weak environmental and labor safeguards, and concerns around debt repayment plans. COVID-19 placed particular stress on BRI deals, with the Chinese government reporting that 60 percent had been adversely affected. Newly elected leaders often seek to reset BRI deal terms, describing them as grossly unfair and the product of their predecessors' corruption or weak negotiation skills. Several countries in Central and Eastern Europe have become disillusioned with the paucity of Chinese investment and have withdrawn from the 17+1 framework. The BRI also has not yielded significant political benefits for China more broadly. There is no correlation, for example, between states that receive the most BRI investment and those that support China on thorny political issues such as Xinjiang, Hong Kong, or the South China Sea.

Fourth, China's exercise of sharp and hard power in the Asia Pacific has served to bind more tightly rather than unravel US-led alliances and partnerships. Beijing's wolf warrior diplomacy, defiance of freedom of navigation norms in the South China Sea, aggressive military activity around sovereignty issues, including Taiwan, the South China Sea, the Sino-Indian border, and the Diaoyu/Senkaku islands, and crackdown on Hong Kong have all contributed to strengthen relations among the larger Asian powers, such as the United States, Japan, Australia, and India. In the face of Chinese assertiveness, major European countries, including the UK, France, and Germany, are also all becoming more deeply engaged in Asian regional security. Popular opinion polls throughout Asia indicate significant distrust of Xi Jinping and little interest in Chinese regional leadership, even among countries deeply dependent on China, such as Cambodia. And China's unwillingness to condemn Russia's invasion of Ukraine has contributed to additional international backlash against Beijing and heightened concern over potential Chinese military action against Taiwan. This backlash raises the costs for China of future efforts to assert sovereignty over Taiwan and the South China Sea and constrains its ability to achieve its objective of replacing the United States as the preeminent power in the Asia Pacific.

Fifth, China does not appear prepared to supplant the United States as the world's sole superpower. China's leaders desire to occupy a position in which their values and policy preferences determine the nature of institutions, but in which their contribution to those institutions and to global public goods is aligned closely with their own narrower domestic political and economic interests. They seek a voice in shaping the international system that is equivalent to, or greater than, that of the United States, but they do not want to shoulder the burdens associated with the latter's sole superpower status.

Finally, China's emergence as a global power is typically portrayed as a story of a rising power threatening the status quo power, in this case the United States. Xi himself gives credence to this framing with his frequent references to "the East is rising and the West is declining," and by asserting in March 2021 that the United States was the "biggest threat to our country's development and security."[73] Certainly, the United States has played an important role in identifying the challenges presented by Xi's ambition and strategy and in mobilizing others to resist Chinese efforts to transform the geostrategic landscape in ways that undermine norms and values such as freedom of navigation or the rule of law.

Framing the challenge in this bilateral, zero-sum way, however, is misleading and serves China's interest: any relative gain by China as the rising power is immediately perceived as a loss for the United States; Beijing can characterize any competitive or even confrontational US policy as simply trying to contain China; and it isolates the United States from its allies and partners by suggesting that it has a unique set of China-related interests and concerns.

Instead, the fundamental challenge presented by China is to the broader values, norms, and institutions that underpin the current rules-based order. As China's senior-most foreign official, Yang Jiechi, stated in March 2021, "What China and the international community follow or uphold is the United Nations-centered international system and the international order underpinned by international law, not what is advocated by a small number of countries of the so-called rules-based international order."[74] Notwithstanding the fact that the rules-based order established in the post-World War II period is enshrined in a wide array of UN laws and conventions, as the following chapters reveal, the challenge China is delivering to both the rules-based order and the UN system is evident. And framed this way, the rest of the world also has a much clearer stake in the outcome.

2

Power, Power, Power

On October 4, 2019, Houston Rockets General Manager Daryl Morey tweeted: "Fight for Freedom, Stand with Hong Kong." Hong Kong citizens had been demonstrating for months in support of universal suffrage and other less dramatic demands, and Morey joined the fray in their support. The tweet was not out of character for Morey: he frequently used Twitter to address issues of democracy and social justice, although his remarks generally focused on US politics. As Chinese citizens rapidly populated Morey's Twitter feed with angry comments, Morey's boss, Rockets owner Tilman Fertitta, stepped in to try to limit what was quickly becoming a public relations nightmare. In his own tweet later that evening, Fertitta made clear that Morey did "NOT speak for the Houston Rockets" and that the Rockets were "NOT a political organization."[1] Other National Basketball Association (NBA) stalwarts also weighed in. Joe Tsai, the owner of the Brooklyn Nets and co-founder of the internet behemoth Alibaba, published an open letter on Facebook that same evening, cautioning that "there are certain topics that are third-rail issues in certain countries, societies, and communities. Supporting a separatist movement in a Chinese territory is one of those third-rail issues, not only for the Chinese government, but also for all citizens in China."[2] Within 48 hours, Morey tried to step back from his post, tweeting an additional set of carefully crafted comments that acknowledged the complexity of the situation, implied he had since absorbed additional perspectives, and clarified that his tweets were his own and did not reflect the perspective of the Houston Rockets.[3] (Nowhere, however, did Morey state that he had changed his mind or apologize for his original tweet.)

The Chinese government and business community ignored Morey and the NBA's efforts to calm the waters. On October 6, Yao Ming, the head of the Chinese Basketball Association (CBA) and a former longtime Rockets player, announced that the CBA was suspending cooperation with the team. Both state-run China Central Television

(CCTV) and Tencent Holdings, which owned the rights to livestream the NBA games, announced that they would not feature any games with the Rockets.[4] CCTV also canceled plans to broadcast two highly anticipated exhibition games in Shanghai and Shenzhen between the Los Angeles Lakers and the Brooklyn Nets; and several events and a press conference around the Shanghai game – including one to raise money for the Special Olympics – were abandoned.[5] Chinese companies pulled all sponsorship of the Rockets and Rockets merchandise from their stores, a dramatic turn of events given the Rockets' enormous popularity in China: they were second only to San Francisco's Golden State Warriors in the support they commanded from Chinese fans. The estimates of the hit to the Rockets' bottom line was roughly $20 million in revenue from canceled Chinese sponsorship agreements.[6]

As the full financial implications of Morey's tweet became clear, individual basketball players, as well as the NBA leadership, rushed in to try to salvage the situation. Rockets team star James Harden begged China's forgiveness at a press conference, stating, "We apologize. We love China."[7] NBA Commissioner Adam Silver called Morey's tweet "regrettable," and the organization's Chinese website featured an apology to the Chinese people.[8] Yet as debate over China's right to control speech in the United States raged, Silver, a lawyer well versed in freedom of speech issues, had second thoughts. In a statement released two days later in Tokyo before an NBA exhibition game, he offered a stronger commitment to Morey, stating:

> Values of equality, respect, and freedom of expression have long defined the NBA – and will continue to do so. As an American-based basketball league operating globally, among our greatest contributions are these values of the game. . . . In fact, one of the enduring strengths of the NBA is our diversity – of views, backgrounds, ethnicities, genders, and religions . . . with that diversity comes the belief that whatever our differences, we respect and value each other.[9]

Silver later also let it be known that the Chinese government had asked him to fire Morey, a charge Beijing denied.[10]

At stake for the NBA was a Chinese fan base of more than half a billion people and a business valued at over $4 billion. By early 2020, Silver suggested that the NBA had lost as much as $400 million in revenues as a result of the strained relationship. Despite the losses, he reinforced his decision not to fire Morey or otherwise change NBA policy, stating: "We accept the consequences of our system and our values. It's not a position any business wants to be in, but those are the results."[11]

The NBA is not the first international business or foreign government to confront the sharp edge of China's power. Beijing frequently uses its market leverage to try to coerce other countries and foreign businesses to do its bidding. As Tsai alluded to in his NBA statement, Beijing is particularly neuralgic around issues concerning sovereignty: Taiwan, Hong Kong, and the South China Sea. These are regions of the world that the Chinese government claims as its sovereign territory but are, in one way or another, contested by other actors. Beginning in 2012, for example, China extended a ban on the import of bananas from the Philippines, nominally put in place for food safety reasons, to pressure Manila to pull its navy back from the Scarborough Shoal, a contested reef in the South China Sea. The Philippines refused to back down, ultimately taking China to the Permanent Court of Arbitration in the Hague. The Philippines won its case in 2016, but the banana ban was lifted only after newly elected Philippine president Rodrigo Duterte appeared willing to put the court's ruling aside, calling it "just a piece of paper with four corners."[12] The same month as Duterte's remark, the Chinese government announced that it was lifting the ban, and the Chinese Ambassador to the Philippines suggested that China was now interested in importing a wide array of fruits and fish products from the Philippines.[13]

China's willingness to use its economic leverage extends well beyond considerations of sovereignty, however. In 2016–17, it inflicted significant economic costs on South Korean businesses when Seoul agreed to deploy the US-supported Terminal High Altitude and Area Defense (THAAD) missile system. While the system was positioned as a defensive measure against North Korea's missiles, Beijing argued that THAAD's sophisticated radar capabilities could be used to track Chinese missiles.[14] To pressure South Korea into canceling the project, Beijing launched a consumer boycott against the country's Lotte department store chain, which had provided the land for the THAAD system in a land swap arranged by Seoul.[15] Videos appeared online of Chinese schoolchildren singing "Get Lotte out of China! Boycott South Korea products! It starts with me! Boycott THAAD!"[16] Within a year, Lotte, which had operated in China since 2004, announced the closure of its Chinese supermarket chain, and in 2019, it moved to sell its food production facilities. China also cut the number of tourists traveling to South Korea from 8 million to 4.7 million[17] and targeted one of Seoul's most important exports to China: its culture and entertainment industry. Beijing banned Korean television shows, K-pop music videos, and popular Korean celebrities and singers from appearing in China. The Chinese Ministry of Public Security even warned Chinese citizens against watching the popular Korean television drama *Descendants of the Sun*, stating that "Watching Korean dramas could be dangerous and may even lead to legal troubles."[18] The cost to South Korea was an estimated $7.5 billion in 2017 alone.[19] In December 2017, Seoul and Beijing arrived at an agreement in which South Korea would maintain the current THAAD system but not install any new systems or integrate the existing one into a broader US defense network in Asia. China maintained a partial boycott beyond the December agreement, however. South Korea had been the third largest source of foreign video games in China, after Japan and the United States, but it was not until December 2020, three years later, that Beijing finally granted a new game license to a Korean company.[20] China itself has not emerged unscathed. In 2002, public opinion polls revealed that two-thirds of South Koreans had a positive view of China; by 2020, the proportion fell to only one-quarter.[21] Xi Jinping himself fared even worse: 83 percent of South Koreans polled reported they had no faith in the Chinese leader.[22]

While countries such as the Philippines, South Korea, and Australia (in its defiance of China's pandemic-related boycott) demonstrate the political and economic wherewithal to resist China's coercive efforts, multinationals and other non-state actors have fewer resources. In April 2018, the Civil Aviation Administration of China sent a letter to more than 40 international airlines demanding that they refer to Taiwan as China Taiwan or the China Taiwan region and feature Taiwan as part of China on their airline maps.[23] The Chinese government indicated that non-compliance would cost an airline its China routes. While the airlines eventually complied, many achieved a compromise between their principles and China's demands. Japanese airlines, for example, kept Taiwan on their Japanese websites but used China Taiwan on their Chinese-language websites. United Airlines elected to identify all

Chinese cities – those on the mainland and those not – simply by their city name without an identifying country, and it differentiated Taiwan and Hong Kong from the mainland by noting their separate currencies, the New Taiwan dollar and Hong Kong dollar.[24]

In the final analysis, the NBA also appeared to find a "win-win" solution. On October 10, 2020, almost exactly one year to the day of Morey's tweet, CCTV ended its blackout in time to televise the NBA Finals. CCTV's decision was framed as a reward for the generosity that the NBA had demonstrated toward China during the pandemic: "We also have noticed goodwill expressed by the NBA for some time, especially since the beginning of this year, the NBA has been active in helping the Chinese people in fighting the novel coronavirus epidemic."[25] Five days later, however, Daryl Morey resigned from the Houston Rockets. When asked whether his decision had anything to do with his remarks around Hong Kong, Morey at first refused to answer. Later he stated that his resignation had nothing to do with the events of the previous year. Just two weeks later, the Philadelphia 76ers announced that Morey would be their new President of Basketball Operations. Still, CCTV took a moment to gloat: "We reiterate that any words and deeds that attempt to hurt the feelings of the Chinese people will have to pay a price."[26] And as the 2021 season got underway, CCTV reimposed its ban on NBA games, while Tencent livestreamed the Rockets but dropped the 76ers.

Joe Tsai, as well as others, would likely argue that the international community should simply accept China's sensitivities around a few issues such as Taiwan and Hong Kong. However, what China considers to be a sensitive issue can change at any time. A few days after Morey's tweet, CCTV announced, "We believe that any remarks that challenge national sovereignty and social stability are not within the scope of freedom of speech," suggesting that the price of compliance could become even steeper.[27] Four months later, Beijing expelled three *Wall Street Journal* reporters over an opinion piece that described China as the "sick man of Asia." And in June 2020, the city of Beijing proposed a new law that would ban criticism of TCM. Any issue could become a new "red line."

The CCTV comment also raises a broader issue of China's efforts to shape other countries' political values and institutions. In the cases described above, Beijing's demands were clearly and publicly articulated, and the government made access to its market contingent on an identifiable change in the other actor's behavior. China's measures represent a form of coercive economic power that it can deploy in pursuit of its objectives. In other instances, however, Beijing's efforts to shape others' thinking and policy choices may be less binary, more subtle, and more incremental. National Endowment for Democracy (NED) scholars Christopher Walker and Jessica Ludwig have categorized such an approach as "sharp power":[28] an array of tactics that China, as well as other authoritarian governments, uses to manipulate and even undermine the integrity of democratic values and institutions. Former Australian prime minister Malcolm Turnbull, his own country a target of aggressive Chinese sharp power efforts, has described the behavior as "covert, coercive, or corrupting." It is a combination that often makes it difficult to recognize when China has crossed a line or someone has crossed one of China's "red lines."

From Black and White to Technicolor

Chris Fenton didn't believe he was doing anything wrong. The former president of the Motion Picture Group of China-based DMG Entertainment, Fenton had been a successful talent agent in Los Angeles before turning his attention to China. It was the mid-2000s, and, full of energy and enthusiasm, he decided the time was ripe to help develop opportunities for the film industry in China. Not only was there money to be made but he also viewed the work as important to the overall US–China bilateral relationship: even when the two countries' broader political and economic relationship was difficult, he thought, culture could help weather the tensions. As he wrote in his memoir of this time, *Feeding the Dragon*: "I felt a sense of mission that went far beyond box-office numbers. US–China relations were on the line. . . . We were doing more than opening a market or making nice with China. We were bridging a cultural gap, making the world smaller, more stable, less contentious, and much safer."[29] Fenton's determination paid off. His firm broke new ground by co-producing the hits *Looper* and *Iron Man 3*. When I spoke with Fenton in October 2020, he explained to me that co-production of *Looper* with China allowed the film to be released at the same time in China as it was in the United States and to earn a much higher percentage of the film's box office gross. The compromises he had to make didn't seem too significant at the time: persuading the filmmakers to switch out France for China in the script and ensuring that China's image was protected. Still, while selling Chinese officials on a vision of Shanghai as the ultimate city of the future wasn't an insurmountable challenge, finding a way to make a good movie and keep the Chinese officials happy was not as easy. The Chinese objective – to showcase China – ran up against the filmmakers' desire to produce a high-quality, entertaining film. Ultimately, there were two separate cuts of the film: one for the Chinese audience that included a longer celebration of China and another that was for the rest of the world. It was not a solution that pleased Beijing, but Fenton got the access to Chinese financing, development, marketing, and distribution that he wanted. In *Iron Man 3*, Fenton's firm also secured a brief appearance for Chinese star Fan Bingbing in the Chinese version and ensured that the villain was not Chinese. At every turn, Fenton worked hard to accommodate China's desires. In his mind, China's demands were not unreasonable. It was win-win: oblige the market, make money, and promote cultural ties between the United States and China.

When I asked Fenton whether there were lines that he wouldn't cross in accommodating China, he didn't hesitate, but he also didn't talk about the film industry. Instead he raised the Daryl Morey tweet and its aftermath. The Chinese government's response to the tweet, he explained, was a wake-up call for him: he likened it to smoking a pack of cigarettes a day for 20 years because you think it's good for you and then someone tweets that anyone who has been smoking a pack a day is going to die of cancer. For him, the red line was Chinese censorship beyond its borders. Accommodating Chinese preferences for a film cut to be shown inside China was acceptable, he commented, but the Chinese government should not have the right to censor a film distributed globally. He pointed to the controversy over Tom Cruise's flight jacket in *Top Gun 2* as a case in point. In the movie, slated for release in 2021, the jacket originally bore patches with the Japanese and Taiwanese flags. In trailers for the movie, the patches were removed. Speculation is that Paramount's partner on the film, Tencent, objected to the flags. Fenton's solution to the apparent problem is that the film could have removed the Taiwanese and Japanese flags on Cruise's jacket for the mainland market but not for the rest of the world. Fenton also argued that US studios should not refrain from making movies about sensitive Chinese political issues, such as ongoing rights abuses in Xinjiang or Tibet. The problem, as Fenton explained, is that film studios won't make these movies even for a domestic US audience because simply producing such a film would lead the Chinese government to retaliate by going after not only the studio that produced the film but also every person involved in the film.

For US movie studios, the lure of the Chinese box office or the potential for Chinese investment in the US film industry is substantial. Chinese box office revenues are typically second only to those of the United States and are estimated to reach $15.5 billion by 2023.[30] (Chinese revenues surpassed US revenues during the pandemic, however.) University of Virginia professor Aynne Kokas has documented the gravitational pull of the Chinese market, noting that "it is not a coincidence" that three blockbuster films about space in the mid-2010s all featured Sino-US space collaboration.[31] One LA-based US film studio executive with whom I spoke concurs with Kokas's assessment of Chinese market considerations in shaping films' narratives: "If someone is going to be rescued in space, we make sure that the savior is Chinese. Also, we don't have Chinese villains."

Yet there is the danger, as Fenton ultimately came to appreciate, that the integrity of US films and storytelling can be compromised by Chinese influence. China's 2016 Film Industry Promotion Law explicitly encourages the production of films that "transmit the glorious Chinese culture" or "promote core socialist values."[32] As Douglas Larson points out in his study of China's influence in Hollywood, US audiences will be on the receiving end of films that only depict positive images of China. Moreover, the Chinese government's tight control over films for its home box office means that even seemingly innocuous films such as *Christopher Robin* are banned, merely because Xi Jinping is sensitive to memes that portray him as Winnie the Pooh.[33] And succumbing to Chinese pressure can lead to additional problems elsewhere. When the DreamWorks film *Abominable* featured a map of the South China Sea that reflected Chinese sovereignty claims, Vietnam banned the movie, Malaysia censored the scene, and the Philippines called for a boycott. The price of avoiding China's red lines may be crossing those of others.

You Belong to Me

The party and country respect the choice you make. If you decide to return, we will welcome you with open arms. If you decide to stay abroad, we will support you in serving the country in various ways. All of you should remember that wherever you are you are a member of the Chinese family; the country and the people back home always care about their sons and daughters, and your homeland is always a warm spiritual land for you.

Xi Jinping intoned these words before almost 3,000 Chinese scholars and others at the October 2013 100th anniversary celebration of the Western Returned Scholars Association.[34] The association is just one organization of many that is responsible for trying to influence overseas actors' views and policies toward China. It is linked to a much larger enterprise, the UFWD, which the CCP has long utilized to engage Chinese at home and abroad to spread its message and shape international public opinion.

The UFWD, which reports to the CCP's Central Committee (the top 220-odd Communist Party members), is the nerve center of the Party's foreign influence efforts. In 1939, Mao Zedong described United Front work as one of the "magic weapons" that would enable the CCP to defeat the Kuomintang, the ruling party at the time: "[T]he Party is the heroic warrior wielding the two weapons, the United Front and the armed struggle, to storm and shatter the enemy's positions."[35] At the 2015 Central United Front Work Meeting, Xi reiterated Mao's formulation underscoring the importance of UFWD work: "The United Front . . . is an important magic weapon for strengthening the party's ruling position . . . and an important magic weapon for realizing the China Dream of the Great Rejuvenation of the Chinese Nation."[36] Under Xi's leadership, China has constructed a vast UFWD edifice, incorporating the body's work into 18 different central-level Party and government organizations, adding 40,000 new United Front workers,[37] and enhancing the UFWD's reach by including its officials in embassies throughout the world.[38]

According to New Zealand scholar and UFWD expert Anne-Marie Brady, Xi's United Front objectives are fourfold: to use the Chinese diaspora as agents of Chinese foreign policy; to co-opt foreigners to support policy and provide access to strategic information; to advance a pro-PRC strategic communication strategy to suppress criticism of Beijing and its policies; and to support the BRI.[39] The United Front and its various representative organizations might, for example, organize overseas Chinese citizens – businesspeople, students and scholars, and civic organizations – to protest against the Dalai Lama, Taiwan's political autonomy, Hong Kong democracy, and the religious organization Falun Gong,[40] report on Chinese students who deviate from the Party line,[41] and influence local politicians. In December 2017, for example, Sam Dastyari, a rising star in the Australian Labor Party, announced his resignation from the Senate following revelations that he had taken significant donations from a Chinese billionaire. In exchange for the financial contributions, Dastyari publicly supported Chinese policies, including Beijing's claims in the South China Sea, a position that put him at odds with his own party's platform.[42] The Australian government estimated that at least 10 recent candidates for office in Australia were connected to Chinese agencies.[43]

In its efforts to shape the political and economic choices of other countries, the UFWD extends deep into countries' government bureaucracies, business communities, and civil societies, using its economic leverage to incentivize and coerce foreign actors. Over the past several years, the Czech Republic has been the target of extensive UFWD efforts, beginning at the very top of the political pyramid with President Miloš Zeman.

The Dragon Meets the Double-Tailed Lion

In 2015, Miloš Zeman was the only leader of a European Union country to attend Beijing's massive military parade marking the 70th anniversary of the end of World War II. The visit represented the latest sign of a growing closeness between China and the Czech Republic. Chinese conglomerate CEFC China Energy had established its European headquarters in Prague and was in the midst of a shopping spree there, buying up a leading soccer team, travel companies, banks, breweries, and an airline.[44] CEFC's influence was felt throughout the senior-most levels of the Czech government. President Zeman formally adopted the founder of CEFC, Ye Jianming, as a personal advisor, and in 2016, when Zeman welcomed Xi Jinping to Prague, Ye was by his side. A number of former Czech officials, including two former prime ministers and a defense minister, also served as advisors or lobbyists for CEFC.[45]

In his enthusiasm for CEFC and other Chinese ventures, Zeman declared that the Czech Republic would become "an unsinkable aircraft carrier of Chinese investment expansion."[46] Yet the ship soon sank. Billions of dollars in promised investment never materialized, and in 2018, Ye was detained in Beijing on charges of bribery, after a close associate was arrested in the United States and was charged with trying to bribe the president of Chad. Zeman's support for China never wavered, however. In 2019, he transferred a Czech ambassador from China to Armenia for signing a letter penned by foreign diplomats in Beijing that called for improvements in Chinese human rights practices;[47] and the following year, he prevented the Czech foreign ministry from joining a German-led resolution to criticize Beijing's record on human rights. Unsurprisingly, Chinese officials refer to Zeman as an "old friend" of Xi Jinping. Still, by 2019, the cumulative value of China's investment in the Czech Republic was estimated to be relatively modest: between $0.7 and $1.1 billion at most.[48]

CEFC was not Beijing's only source of access into the country's elite circles. The leading Czech firm Home Credit became an important conduit. Beijing granted Home Credit the first foreign license to offer loans within China. Home Credit also provided financial backing for a think tank, Sinoskop, headed by one of President Zeman's translators, whose website featured a pro-Beijing perspective with articles prepared by the same PR firm. And PPF, the parent company of Home Credit, provided financial support to the country's prestigious Charles University, on the condition that it did not harm PPF's interests – which included its extensive financial ties to China. In addition, PFF and Home Credit hired Prague-based public relations firm C&B Reputation Management to improve the Czech–China relationship. Ultimately, an exposé revealed that the company had been "surreptitiously placing pro-Beijing content in mainstream Czech media" and had even developed its own media project that "posed as an independent expert initiative."[49]

The Chinese embassy in Prague played a particularly important role in trying to influence Czech scholarship on China. It funded a course on the benefits of the BRI, which rewarded students who wrote the best essays with an all-paid trip to China.[50] It also funded the university's Czech–Chinese Centre to support conferences that would reflect positively on China.[51] The Centre ultimately closed and several faculty tied to it were fired for establishing a private fund to receive payments from the Chinese embassy. When I asked Martin Hála, a Sinologist and professor at Charles University, for his assessment of Beijing's efforts to shape the Czech discourse, he bluntly stated that the Chinese embassy was "not very effective": "Most of its efforts badly backfired," he said. "They do not appear to understand the local situation very well."

The Chinese embassy also displayed the more overtly coercive wolf warrior face of Chinese diplomacy. In December 2018, the independent Czech National Cyber and Information Security Agency (NÚKIB) indicated that Huawei and ZTE posed a national security threat, triggering a decision by the government to bar central government employees from using the companies' products.[52] The Czech intelligence agency, the Security Information Service (BIS), had also warned as early as 2013 of the potential link between Chinese espionage activities and Huawei and ZTE products. The Chinese ambassador weighed in to criticize the government's decision, later claiming that he had received assurances from the prime minister that the ban was a mistake – a comment that prompted the latter to respond: "I do not know what the ambassador is talking about."[53] According to Hála, the Czech government was caught off guard by NÚKIB's decision to ban Huawei. President Zeman even went on television to criticize NÚKIB's decision and denounce the agency itself. And when the speaker of the Czech Senate announced plans to travel to Taiwan, the Chinese embassy sent a letter to President Zeman threatening retaliation against Czech companies in China, such as Skoda Auto, Home Credit, and Klaviry Petrof.[54] In response, the Czech prime minister called for China to replace its ambassador. The speaker went ahead with the visit to Taipei in August 2020.[55]

President Zeman notwithstanding, the Czech government has adopted an increasingly hard line against Chinese influence efforts. In both 2019 and 2020, the BIS' annual reports warned starkly of Chinese efforts to target the tech, media, education, security, infrastructure, healthcare, economic, and environmental protection sectors to find ways to present a positive image of China. They further noted that China had sent its representatives undercover as diplomats, journalists, and scientists and offered opportunities for travel, as well as investment opportunities, to approach "targeted persons" or to develop a "sense of obligation stemming from Chinese hospitality."[56] The mayor of Prague and members of his opposition Pirate Party dismissed Beijing's demand to eject a Taiwanese official from a conference and canceled a sister city agreement with Beijing that required Prague to support Beijing's position that Taiwan is part of China. (Beijing retaliated by canceling tours by Czech orchestras in China.) Instead, the mayor signed a new cooperative agreement with Taipei.[57] And in October 2020, despite Chinese pressure, the largest Czech network operator, CETIN – covering 99.6 percent of the population – rejected Chinese firms in its 5G rollout, selecting Ericsson instead.[58] The decision may have come as a surprise to Beijing: the parent company of CETIN is PPF.

Beijing continued to seek ways to influence the Czech Republic's China debate. In 2020, the Chinese government investment firm CITIC exercised an option to acquire a majority stake in one of the largest Czech media agencies. An independent watchdog reported that CITIC had plans to grant higher advertising revenues to local media that were more favorably inclined toward China.[59] Such heavy-handed attempts at political influence, however, have cost Beijing support within the populace. A fall 2020 opinion poll revealed that less than 10 percent of Czech citizens trusted China.[60]

Catch More Flies with Honey

The hour-long Zoom call in July 2020 said it all. A prominent Silicon Valley technologist had arranged for a small group of China experts to meet up with an equal number of tech leaders to talk about the United States, China, and technology. The China group led off with a discussion of its concerns around Huawei and its leadership in 5G technology. This transformative technology allows computers and phones to download information as much as 100 times faster than current 4G levels and will be the backbone for the emerging generation of connected devices such as autonomous vehicles and smart home technologies. Huawei is not the only 5G player in town, but it is the fastest off the starting block. The group worried that with its strong ties to the Chinese government, the company would leave countries vulnerable to Chinese cyberattacks. For the group of traditional, security-minded China experts, Huawei meant China would have a significant economic and security advantage globally for decades to come.

But Huawei was not on the minds of the tech crowd. Instead, one of them suggested that TikTok was the real challenge. Until that moment, I hadn't realized that TikTok merited much concern. The hugely popular video sharing app that had been created by the Chinese company ByteDance hardly seemed a significant threat to US technology leadership. However, for several of the West Coast participants, TikTok represented a true breakthrough in the US–China competition over culture and technology. It wasn't simply about ad revenues – although they suggested that those would be substantial – it was about an "impressively creative" new form of communication. In fact, as I later learned, TikTok had accomplished something that no other Chinese company had done: it had created a globally appealing breakthrough social media technology. And it was the first Chinese company to hit No. 1 in Apple's US App store.[61]

The genius of TikTok is its combination of music and a powerful algorithm that allows it to learn what content users like faster than other apps; each user is provided with a unique stream that reflects previously identified preferences. It is creative, engaging, and can build community across international boundaries. By April 2020, the app surpassed 2 billion downloads. ByteDance's founder, Zhang Yiming, stated that he aspired for the company to be a "borderless" company akin to Google. But Zhang was also clear that ByteDance is a uniquely Chinese company: "We are not a copycat of a US company, both in product and technology."[62]

Yet trouble was brewing. India, where downloads from the app had almost reached 700 million – far exceeding any other country – banned the app in April 2020, first for spreading pornography (the judgment was later overturned on appeal), and then for "stealing and surreptitiously transmitting users' data."[63] As chapter 5 explores, the US government raised similar concerns about China's access to users' personal data, as well as ByteDance's ability to control content by banning videos the Chinese government found offensive or elevating ones that supported its policies. Zhang had already run afoul of the CCP a few years earlier, when he had failed to remove "harmful news" from his enormously popular Chinese news aggregator app, Toutiao. He was forced to write a letter of apology that acknowledged his lack of attention to "promoting positive energy" and "grasping the correct direction of public opinion," as well as his "lack of attention to ideology." He also promised to deepen his cooperation with the CCP.[64]

It is unclear whether TikTok can navigate between the CCP's demands for absolute loyalty and other countries' requirements to ensure their citizens' privacy is protected. But the company is only one part of China's tech soft power offensive. Journalist Cláudia Trevisan described to me how, in her home country of Brazil, Chinese technology companies are replacing Silicon Valley stalwarts like Apple and Google in popularity. It is a combination, she said, of the ubiquity of Chinese technology in Latin America, popular Brazilian television shows that promote China as a world leading center of innovation, and the difficulty Brazilians faced in getting visas to travel and study in the United States after the Trump administration entered office in 2017. In addition, she noted, some Chinese companies, such as Huawei, simply gift their technology to other countries. Such efforts do not go unnoticed by governments or their citizens.

TikTok represents something Beijing desperately desires: soft power. In a major foreign policy address in November 2014, Xi Jinping stated, "We should increase China's soft power, give a good Chinese narrative, and better communicate China's messages to the world."[65] A term originally coined by Harvard professor Joseph Nye, soft power deals in a currency of "culture, political values, and foreign policy."[66] Historically, the United States, with its enviable democratic political system, world-class entertainment and sports industries, high-quality brands, and reputation for innovation, has consistently ranked near the top of global soft power ratings. (During the Trump administration's tenure, however, the international community's evaluations of some of these elements, including America's ethical standards, political standards, and trustworthiness, fell precipitously.)[67] China, in contrast, with its authoritarian political system and state control over the media and culture, has typically not fared well in global soft power rankings. Xi, however, has made the development of China's soft power an essential element of his rejuvenation narrative.[68] According to George Washington University professor David Shambaugh, who has studied the country's global outreach, China spends on average $10 billion annually on soft power.[69] (The United States, in contrast, spends just over $1 billion.)[70] Xi Jinping is not the first Chinese leader to emphasize the importance of soft power. His predecessor, Hu Jintao, suggested in a 2007 speech that the rejuvenation of China would be accompanied by the "thriving of Chinese culture."[71] As Xi's speech indicates, his view of soft power is informed by a desire to promote the government's narrative. Yet this very desire for soft power to serve the government constrains Xi's ability to realize his soft power objectives.

Spreading the Word

The Chinese news media represent a core element of Xi's efforts to shape overseas opinion. He has referred to the state media as the "throat and tongue" of the CCP[72] and its mission is to "tell China's story well, spread China's voice well, let the world know a three-dimensional, colorful China, and showcase China's role as a builder of world peace."[73] As China scholar Merriden Varrall has detailed in her study of China Global Television Network (CGTN), Xi is only the latest in a succession of Chinese leaders and senior officials who for decades have argued that China needs to "step up the battle for world opinion."[74] With a network of 72 bureaus and as many as 387 million viewers in 170 countries globally, CGTN seems primed to do just that.[75]

The shortcomings of China's media push, however, are immediately evident in its lack of traction in the United States and other advanced market democracies. *The Point*, an English-language talk show with the highly articulate host Liu Xin, tackles timely issues, such as the China–US security relationship and the coronavirus. Typically, Liu interviews Chinese guests, who present "the Chinese perspective." Her "Headline Buster" segment is designed to counter popular narratives about China or other issues that the CCP wants to refute. In one episode, for example, she explored the issue of forced labor camps in Xinjiang. The program featured interviews with "graduates" from the training programs in Xinjiang who had improved their Chinese and now had jobs.[76] At times, Liu's programming strays into the conspiratorial. For example, she tried to debunk BBC reporting on the Assad regime's use of chemical weapons against civilian non-combatants in Syria and then use her report to claim that Western media have little credibility. Her show, with its strong Chinese government overlay, has yet to find its audience in the United States: the average reported number of viewers is well under 10,000.[77]

Varrall suggests, however, that ultimately CGTN's priority is to influence narratives not in the West but rather in non-Western markets, where countries are not as saturated with content and thus easier to break into.[78] In a 2020 survey of China's impact on the world media conducted by the International Federation of Journalists, some local reporters in Africa indicated that they appreciated the positive Chinese take on their countries, noting that Western media were always seeking to report on African catastrophes.[79] Chinese media partnerships can also serve the interests of local governments to limit dissenting opinions. In Cambodia, for example, the Hun Sen government eliminated 275 publications and revoked licenses for more than 15 radio stations. In their place, it welcomed the Chinese firm NICE Culture Investment Group, which partnered with Cambodia's Interior Ministry to establish NICE TV. The programming now includes shows that are favorable to the Cambodian government and to China.[80]

China's media outreach also includes a popular series of training programs and exchanges for foreign journalists that range from two weeks to ten months. In some cases, the trips are broad introductions to China, while in others, they target specific groups for specific training: for example, taking Muslim journalists on a trip to Xinjiang to undercut Western reports of forced labor and reeducation camps.[81] The editor of a major US foreign policy magazine, who participated in such a trip in the mid-2010s, told me that he found it illuminating. The hosts provided meetings with a wide range of Chinese officials and scholars holding different perspectives. Overall, he did not feel that the trip was an effort to "sell him" on China.

You Are Speaking My Language

In 2004, Beijing established its first Confucius Institutes in South Korea and the United States (at the University of Maryland College Park), after piloting the idea in Uzbekistan. Dedicated to Chinese-language training and cultural activities, the institutes spread like wildfire. Within a decade, China's Ministry of Education established more than 500 CIs in universities and 600 Confucius Classrooms in schools, as well as in institutions, such as the China Institute in New York City. In the United States, CIs found homes in more than 100 institutions. The willingness of the

Hanban, the CIs' headquarters in Beijing, to cover the cost of a significant portion of Chinese-language instruction was immediately attractive to many colleges and universities, even to those without significant financial needs, such as Stanford, Emory, Tufts, and George Washington.

In a 2011 speech before the Hanban, Politburo Standing Committee member Li Changchun stated, "The Confucius Institute is an appealing brand for expanding our culture abroad. It has made an important contribution toward improving our soft power. The 'Confucius' brand has a natural attractiveness. Using the excuse of teaching Chinese language, everything looks reasonable."[82] The Chinese government portrays CIs as the Chinese version of European institutions such as the UK's British Council, Germany's Goethe-Institut, and France's L'Alliance Française. Yet there is a critical difference. While the European institutions are freestanding, CIs are most often embedded in universities and schools and maintain a separate Chinese government governance structure. China's Ministry of Education selects the teachers and the curriculum, and it has often demanded that its contracts with the universities remain secret.

As NED's Christopher Walker has noted, what might be viewed as "soft power" when undertaken by most countries can assume a different form when led by authoritarian states that are determined to "monopolize ideas, suppress alternative narratives, and exploit partner institutions."[83] Within just a few years of Li's speech, many US scholars, as well as the US government, began to have second thoughts about the compatibility of the CIs' governance structure with the principles of US educational institutions. In 2013, University of Chicago anthropology professor Marshall Sahlins published a scathing article in *The Nation* detailing the ways in which CIs contravened established university practices, by requiring, for example, that CI activities conform to the customs, laws, and regulations of China and that the original agreement between the university and the Hanban cannot be made public. Perhaps most damning, Sahlins revealed that CIs in a number of cities had mobilized Chinese students or otherwise worked to prevent talks and activities on campuses related to politically sensitive issues such as Tibet and the Falun Gong.[84] At North Carolina State University, after the director of the CI warned the provost that a visit by the Dalai Lama could hurt the university's relationship with China, the university declined to host the Dalai Lama. The University of California, San Diego, in contrast, ignored similar pressure and faced the consequences when the Chinese government canceled scholarship opportunities for Chinese students to study at the university. Armed with this new understanding of the CIs' activities, more than 100 University of Chicago professors petitioned the university to close its CI, which it did in September 2014.

The Chicago decision helped trigger an avalanche of negative publicity for CIs within the United States. That same year, the American Association of University Professors published a report recommending that universities either close their CIs or renegotiate their contracts to ensure that they addressed concerns over "advancing a state agenda in the recruitment and control of academic staff, in the choice of curriculum, and in the restriction of debate."[85] Members of the US Congress joined senior officials within the Trump administration to pressure universities to close their CIs. Legislation included within the 2018 National Defense Authorization Act forced universities to choose between closing their CIs or jeopardizing funding from the US Defense Department's Chinese Language Flagship program.[86] By early 2021, at least 54 of 100-odd US universities[87] had shut down or were in the process of closing their CIs.[88]

Universities and schools in other countries, including Canada, Australia, the UK, France, Sweden, and Denmark, have also closed their CIs. In early 2020, there were 548 reported CIs globally (of which the United States still had by far the most);[89] by the end of the year, there were 541,[90] leaving the Hanban far short of its target of 1,000 CIs (see Figure 2.1). Recognizing the reputational challenge that CIs are encountering, in June 2020, the Chinese government established a new oversight organization, the Chinese International Education Foundation, which refers to itself as a "non-profit civil organization," despite its backing by several state universities and agencies.[91] As several wealthy market democracies move to shutter their CIs, however, many developing economies continue to welcome them. In Kazakhstan, which maintains five CIs, the leadership is bullish on the prospect of Chinese-sponsored language training. Dariga Nazarbayeva, former deputy prime minister and daughter of a former president, encouraged Kazakh children to learn Chinese, saying, "China is our friend, our trading partner, and the biggest investor in the economy of our country. In the near future, we all need to know Chinese." Despite her enthusiasm, a public opinion survey conducted by the Eurasian Development Bank revealed that only one in

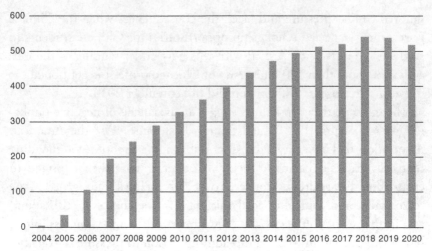

Figure 2.1 Number of Confucius Institutes worldwide from 2004 to 2020
Source: https://web.archive.org/web/20210101041525/http://english.hanban.org/node_10971.htm

six Kazakhs sees China as a "friendly country,"[92] suggesting that China's soft power appeal has yet to take hold. And in Africa, where China has 61 CIs, a survey revealed that 71 percent of citizens believe that English is the most important language for the next generation to learn, while 14 percent selected French, and only 2 percent picked Chinese.[93]

The Iron Fist in a Velvet Glove

In spring 2019, a series of articles in the United States reported that in a war over Taiwan, the United States would lose to China. The assessment was based on the results of war games played at RAND Corporation, a think tank whose primary audience is the US government. According to one of the participants, "If [China's] objective is to overrun Taiwan, that in principle can be accomplished in a finite time period, measured in days to weeks."[94] At the same time, two seasoned China reporters, David Lague and Benjamin Kang Lim, published a special report for Reuters, "How China is replacing America as Asia's military titan," which detailed the dramatic expansion in China's military capabilities under Xi Jinping, noting: "In just over two decades, China has built a force of conventional missiles that rival or outperform those in the US army."[95] Just six months earlier, a blue-ribbon panel had issued a review of the National Defense Strategy "Providing for the Common Defense" that highlighted America's lack of preparedness. The report was filled with dire language. It asserted that "US military superiority is no longer assured" and that the United States might "struggle to win, or perhaps lose," a war against China or Russia.[96]

While policymakers in the United States and elsewhere are increasingly attuned to the importance of Chinese soft and sharp power in shaping the views and decisions of their citizens toward China, ultimately, they are most concerned with Chinese military intentions and capabilities or hard power. Over the course of President Xi Jinping's tenure, China's ambitions have expanded, and its capabilities to realize those ambitions have increased significantly. In some respects, these changes have caught the rest of the world off guard. As former Australian intelligence official Hugh White has stated, "We've underestimated how quickly China's power has grown along with its ambitions to use that power."[97]

Expanding Capabilities

For over 70 years, the United States has commanded the largest, best-equipped, and best-trained military in the world. Increasingly, however, US military officials and security analysts have pointed to China's growing capabilities as challenging that leadership. To begin with, Beijing is spending more on its military than ever before. According to the Stockholm International Peace Research Institute, in 2020, China boasted the world's second largest defense budget: $252 billion. (The United States remained number one at more than $778 billion.)[98] The 2021 Global Firepower index, which looks at 55 data points, also reported that while the United States maintains the world's most powerful military, both China and Russia are closing the gap.

President Xi has placed a priority on building "world-class forces that obey the Party's command, can fight and win, and maintain excellent conduct."[99] Xi's desire in this regard runs deep. In their study of his military reforms, security scholars Joel Wuthnow and Philip Saunders quote him as saying: "A nation's backwardness in military affairs has a profound influence on a nation's security. I often peruse the annals of modern Chinese history and feel heartbroken at the tragic scenes of us being beaten because of our ineptitude."[100] As chairman of the Central Military Commission and head of the Leading Group for National Defense and Military Reform, Xi is the chief architect of China's military modernization strategy. Over the course of his first two terms in office, he has ushered in a set of sweeping reforms, including: the elevation of the air force and navy to a status equal to that of the army; the creation of five joint theater commands; the introduction of a strategic support and joint logistics support force; the reduction of 300,000 military personnel; and a reform of the professional military education system within the People's Liberation Army (PLA).[101] In addition, Xi has cleaned house. Between 2012 and 2017, his anti-corruption campaign netted more than 13,000 military officers. Some were removed exclusively on the grounds of corruption, while others were targeted to make way for Xi's political allies.[102] However, high-profile corruption cases continue to rock the PLA. In 2019, former chief of the joint staff Fang Fenghui was sentenced to life in prison for accepting bribes; more than 70 retired and serving senior officers were also demoted as a result of their association with him.[103]

May the Force Be with You

China has made significant strides in enhancing the quality and preparedness of its military forces. In a report on the trajectory of the country's land-based conventional missile forces, the Center for Strategic and International Studies notes that China has developed the world's "largest and most diverse" arsenal of ground-launched ballistic missiles.[104] Part of its growing capability is directed toward securing its periphery, especially in the Western Pacific. Coupled with air and sea defenses, Beijing's steadily improving anti-ship missile weapons contribute to its ability to impose significant costs on US military forces operating within the first island chain. PLA Rocket Force Brigades also are based in parts of China that enable them to strike South Korea, Japan, and even Guam, where the United States has a critical military base. In addition, China has led the way in developing hypersonic missile technology, which will make its missiles more difficult to track and intercept.[105] And in the Asia Pacific, the tyranny of distance grants China a logistical advantage – the ability to refuel, resupply, and repair – that the United States cannot overcome.

China also maintains the world's third largest nuclear force. In its annual "China Military Power" report to Congress in 2020, the US Defense Department cited the modernization and expansion of China's nuclear capabilities as part of its pursuit of a "nuclear triad," including the development of a nuclear capable air-launched ballistic missile, alongside its ground and sea-based nuclear capabilities.[106] The Pentagon further expects China to double its nuclear warhead stockpile to over 400 in the coming decade – which is still well below the more than 3,800 the United States has stockpiled, however.[107]

The elevation of China's maritime capabilities has been particularly noteworthy. Even before Xi's military reforms, in 2012, then president Hu Jintao asserted the need for China to become a maritime power. A 2015 defense white paper reiterated Hu's call, declaring: "The traditional mentality that land outweighs sea must be abandoned, and great importance has to be attached to managing seas and oceans and protecting maritime rights and interests."[108] To this end, China has developed the largest coast guard in the world. Under the control of the People's Armed Police, the Coast Guard sometimes accompanies Chinese fishing boats as they sail into contested waters in the East and South China Seas. (In 2020, a revised law integrated the Coast Guard into joint drills and operations with other parts of the Chinese military; and in January 2021, Beijing authorized it to use force to prevent threats from foreign vessels.) The fishing boats themselves may be armed – part of the People's Armed Forces Maritime Militia, directly under the control of the PLA and with roots dating before the CCP's rise to power in 1949.[109] These armed fishing boats serve an important role in harassing other countries' vessels and helping secure Chinese sovereignty claims – activities that are often referred to as gray zone aggression. They reflect China's coercive capabilities, which the PLA uses to improve Beijing's negotiating position or salami slice a longstanding problem. And as chapter 6 explores, China is also developing world-class capabilities in building and deploying icebreakers for service in the Arctic – in June 2018 it opened bidding for the country's first nuclear-powered icebreaker – which speaks to ambitions well beyond its backyard.[110]

Singaporean scholars Angela Poh and Weichong Ong suggest that Xi's military reforms differ from previous Chinese military modernization efforts because they also enhance Beijing's ability to compete with the

United States and other adversaries in a "multidimensional manner." In particular, they cite the creation of the Strategic Support Force (SSF) – a fifth part of the PLA that brings together space, cyber, and electronic warfare capabilities – as an important innovation. For China's military, cyberwarfare includes both kinetic attacks, such as an assault on a power grid, and cyber-espionage to gain military advantage: for example, in the design of military hardware. Many US analysts have noted that China's J-20 and J-31 stealth planes appear to be modeled on the US's F-22 and F-35 fighter jets. In addition, the SSF is designed to serve as a coordinating body for military and civilian research and development: nine universities have signed cooperation agreements with it.[111] According to former State Department official Christopher Ford, this military–civil fusion program integrates Beijing's civilian and military innovation and technology planning efforts with infrastructure development, logistics considerations, and industrial capabilities, and enables Beijing to move rapidly and seamlessly from peace to wartime mobilization.[112] Poh and Ong further argue that this form of civil–military integration is "far more directed and comprehensive" than in the United States.[113]

Make New Friends

China's hard power is amplified by its growing ability to draw on the assets of partners outside its borders. While Beijing does not have formal military alliances – save its 1961 pact with North Korea – it has dramatically ramped up its military cooperation with a wide range of countries. In 2019, it participated in 17 joint military exercises with 87 foreign partners and observers.[114] Its closest partners are those in the Shanghai Cooperation Organization (SCO). First established in 1996, as the Shanghai Five, which included China, Russia, Kazakhstan, Kyrgyzstan, and Tajikistan, the group transformed into the SCO in 2001 and has since expanded to include Uzbekistan, Mongolia, Iran, Pakistan, and India. This represents roughly half the world's population and four nuclear weapons states. Along with the Asian Infrastructure Investment Bank (AIIB), the SCO is one of two regional organizations conceived of and headquartered in China.

The SCO was founded to fight against the "three evil forces" of terrorism, separatism, and extremism. In recent years, however, it has evolved to consider issues of collective defense and joint response: for example, serving as a potential mediator of conflicts in Afghanistan, Syria, and Korea.[115] The member countries also undertake joint military exercises: the annual Peace Mission in 2019 involved 3,000 troops. Chinese military scholar Zhou Bo compares the SCO to the North Atlantic Treaty Organization (NATO), commenting, "Both organizations are attractive: on each side, a group of countries is waiting to join."[116] Only Pakistan among the SCO countries, however, is a top recipient of PRC arms sales (see Figure 2.2).

Of the SCO members, Russia has become a particularly important security partner for China, even approaching the level of a military ally. The two countries hold extensive talks and exchanges and conduct joint exercises.[117] They have also engaged in military exercises with third parties, including South Africa and Iran. Russian president Vladimir Putin appeared to presage a new level of Sino-Russian military cooperation in October 2020 when, in discussing a potential military alliance, he commented, "It is possible to imagine anything. We have always believed that our relations have reached such a level of cooperation and trust that it is not necessary, but it is certainly imaginable in theory."[118] He also announced that Russia was helping China to develop a missile attack warning system. The two countries could eventually integrate their missile launch detection systems, which would give them a significant advantage

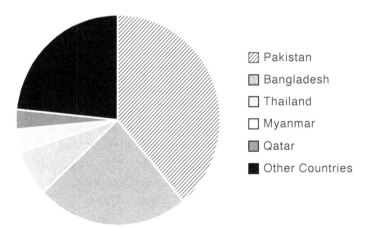

Figure 2.2   Top five recipients of Chinese arms from 2017 to 2019
Source: *https://armstrade.sipri.org/armstrade/page/values.php*

in the case of a US missile strike against one or the other. This level of integration would also be on par with US allied integration.[119] Most notable, however, has been China's support for Russia in the wake of the latter's February 2022 invasion of Ukraine. China has abstained or sided with Russia in UN votes and provided Moscow with an economic lifeline through energy imports and sales of machinery and other critical goods.

Still there are limitations to China's establishment of more formal alliance structures. PKU professor Zhang Xiaoming has noted, for example, that trust among the SCO members is not universal. Beijing's push for greater economic integration among them, including a SCO Bank and free trade agreement, has failed to gain traction. According to Zhang, several member countries are concerned about becoming too economically dependent on China.[120] And conflicts between the members also can cause problems. India, for example, refused to endorse a Chinese BRI project in Pakistan as part of the SCO declaration in 2018,[121] and in 2020 it engaged in a series of violent border disputes with China. Even the relationship with Russia has encountered difficulties. During the Vostok 2018 military exercise, for example, the Kremlin was concerned that China sent a surveillance ship to gather intelligence on Russia's navy.[122] Even more alarming for Russia is China's apparent theft of its IP. In late 2019, the Russian defense industry powerhouse Rostec accused China of copying a wide array of military hardware.[123] In addition, although China has been a significant importer of Russian arms – in 2017, it purchased roughly $15 billion worth – RAND Corporation's Timothy Heath anticipates that China will eventually displace Russia in a number of arms export markets, although both lag well behind the United States. Russia's largest arms recipient is also India, with whom Beijing has an ongoing border conflict (see Table 2.1).[124] Analysts have also noted that Moscow is concerned about China's growing role in Central Asia and the Arctic, both of which Russia considers its backyard.[125] For the time being, the two countries are united in their effort to resist political and military pressure from the United States and its allies and refrain from criticizing the other's aggressive actions, such as Russia's annexation of Crimea, ongoing aggression against Ukraine, and China's island-building efforts in the South China Sea. But as China appears increasingly interested in expanding its arms sales, as well as its military presence, the two countries may find themselves cooperating but also competing for influence in new ways.

Table 2.1 Comparison of arms sales (USD million) from 2017 to 2019

China		Russia		United States	
Recipient	Amount	Recipient	Amount	Recipient	Amount
Pakistan	1,525	India	3,684	Saudi Arabia	9,461
Bangladesh	938	China	3,182	Australia	3,102
Thailand	279	Egypt	2,687	South Korea	2,021
Myanmar	137	Algeria	1,995	UAE	1,902
Qatar	118	Vietnam	939	Japan	1,852
Saudi Arabia	115	Iraq	840	Israel	1,513
Uzbekistan	107	Kazakhstan	735	Qatar	1,474
UAE	95	Belarus	619	United Kingdom	1,084
Indonesia	77	Angola	376	Norway	1,031
Sudan	76	Turkey	280	Afghanistan	959
Others (28)	443	Others (28)	1,902	Others (80)	8,817
Total	**3,910**	**Total**	**17,239**	**Total**	**33,216**

Source: *https://armstrade.sipri.org/armstrade/page/values.php*

Building a New Home

During a break at a January 2019 conference in Beijing, I casually asked two Chinese military scholars how many bases China had planned for the future. "As many as the United States," one said; "More than one hundred," said the other. The organizer of the conference, a former senior diplomat, overhearing our exchange, subsequently announced to the entire conference that China had "no plans to have any bases." Her concern was understandable. The issue of Chinese overseas bases is a politically sensitive one. China has long decried such bases as infringements on other countries' sovereignty. However, the construction of a Chinese military logistics base in Djibouti has given rise to wide speculation over Beijing's longer-term intentions.

In 2010, Fudan University scholar Shen Dingli articulated the case for Chinese overseas bases: protecting people and fortunes, guaranteeing trade, preventing overseas intervention that harms the unity of the country, and defending against foreign invasion. Shen highlighted countering secessionism outside the mainland – meaning Taiwan and Hong Kong – and the need to build troop bases to "face the challenge from other countries" as top priorities.[126]

More than a decade later, Shen's rationale for Chinese overseas bases appears well aligned with Xi Jinping's security priorities. Xi has made explicit his belief that mainland sovereignty over Hong Kong, Taiwan, and the South China Sea is essential to his ambition for the "great rejuvenation of the Chinese nation."[127] And he has voiced his willingness to use force to achieve his goal. China's 2019 defense white paper notes, "We make no promise to renounce the use of force and reserve the option of taking all necessary measures. The PLA will resolutely defeat anyone attempting to separate Taiwan from China and safeguard national unity at all costs."[128]

The Chinese leadership also places a priority on its ability to protect Chinese overseas assets. Naval War College scholar Andrew Erickson has detailed the notion of a "forward edge defense," in which Chinese ambitions move well beyond a focus on active defense of the South China Sea and East China Sea to a "far seas protection" that includes establishing a significant PLA and PLA Navy presence in the Pacific and Indian Oceans as well as the littoral regions of Asia, Africa, Oceania, North America, South America, and Antarctica. All told, as Erickson describes, China's dual Indo-Pacific focus – termed the "Two Oceans region" – includes 71 percent of the global ocean area.[129] In addition, the 13th Five-Year Plan (2016–20) supports China's transformation into a "maritime power" in part to "protect overseas interests and safeguard the legitimate overseas rights and interests of the Chinese citizens."[130] These assets include not only economic assets but also Chinese citizens themselves. During the Arab Spring uprising in 2011, China lacked the capability to evacuate its citizens from Libya and had to rely on other countries, including the United States. By 2015, when China needed to remove its citizens from Yemen, however, it had developed the capability to evacuate not only almost 600 of its own citizens but also 225 from 10 other countries.[131]

In 2017, Beijing established a military logistics base in Djibouti, joining others with bases already there, such as the United States, France, Japan, and Italy. And Chinese military analysts suggest that planning for additional bases is already well underway. As the French scholar Mathieu Duchâtel has reported, Chinese analysts have made a compelling case for bases, including war, diplomatic signaling, building relationships, providing facilities for training, and supporting United Nations Peacekeeping Operations. Renmin University's Li Qingsi and

Chen Chunyu have argued that "building bases on the key maritime transport hubs has already become a strategic choice that increasingly requires urgent action."[132] Other analysts are more explicit, suggesting that China will eventually establish bases in countries, such as Cambodia, Pakistan, the UAE, Sri Lanka, Myanmar, Indonesia, and Kenya.[133]

Importantly for the United States, Xi Jinping's conception of Chinese security also includes a dramatic transformation in the position and role of the US military on the global stage. China's defense minister has crisscrossed the Asia Pacific region with the message that countries "should adhere to the principle that regional issues should be solved by the regional countries through consultation."[134] The United States has important treaty allies dotted throughout the Asia Pacific, including Japan, South Korea, Thailand, the Philippines, and Australia, as well as robust defense partnerships with Vietnam and Taiwan, all of which give China a sense of being encircled. As a former top Chinese diplomat explained to me, the US alliance system is "anachronistic and unfair to China."[135] Some Chinese scholars also assert that the United States is the troublemaker in the region. Fu Mengzi, vice president of the research institute China Institutes of Contemporary International Relations (CICIR), has argued that while the United States has attempted to stoke conflict in the South China Sea, China has worked to reduce tensions through joint economic development and efforts to agree to a South China Sea Code of Conduct.[136]

But the Asia Pacific region is increasingly concerned about China's rising military capabilities.[137] During its chairmanship of the Association of Southeast Asian Nations (ASEAN) in 2020, Vietnam succeeded in advancing a group statement that implicitly criticized China's behavior in the South China Sea. Even NATO, which has traditionally focused on Russia, now cites China's growing influence and international policies as a top priority.[138] In June 2020, NATO Secretary General Jens Stoltenberg asserted, "One thing is clear: China is coming ever closer to Europe's doorstep. NATO allies must face this challenge together."[139] And in laying out his NATO 2030 strategic plan, Stoltenberg underscored the importance of working more closely with countries in Asia, including Australia, Japan, New Zealand, and South Korea, to "defend the global rules and institutions, to set norms and standards in space and in cyberspace, and ultimately to stand up for a world built on freedom and democracy. Not on bullying and coercion."[140] A May 2019 report by the US Defense Department goes so far as to say that if previously the United States was uncertain about Beijing's intentions, such uncertainty has vanished: "In support of the goal to establish a powerful and prosperous China, China's leaders are committed to developing military power commensurate with that of a great power."[141]

Can't Buy Me Love

China's powerful economy is a major asset in helping Beijing realize its ambitions: it enables overseas investment, powers innovation, and funds opportunities for education and training for citizens in other countries. Its economy is also at the heart of China's coercive capabilities. Beijing has successfully used the leverage of its market to force industries, such as international airlines and Hollywood, as well as the NBA, to adopt its policy preferences around issues such as Taiwan and Hong Kong. And it has brought significant economic pressure to bear on countries such as South Korea, the Philippines, and Australia. China's economic wherewithal and innovation strength have combined to make the Chinese military not only the largest in the world but also one of the two or three most powerful across all domains. While China has most often deployed its military power in its own backyard, its capabilities and stated interests signal global reach and ambition.

This combination of soft, sharp, and hard power has not translated into widespread trust in and affinity for China globally. China consistently ranks at the bottom of global soft power ratings. In one of the most well-known soft power polls, the Soft Power 30, it dropped two spots to 27th out of 30 countries in 2019. The report notes that while China displays strengths in culture, education, and business, its foreign policy and human rights issues depress its ranking.[142] This is borne out by 2020 Pew polls. Across major economies in North America, Europe, and Asia, a median of 78 percent said they had no confidence that Xi Jinping would do the right thing with regard to world affairs, and the median of those who held an unfavorable view of China hit 73 percent. There is also a strong correlation between people's views and how well they believe that China has managed the COVID-19 pandemic.[143] This suggests that on balance China's containment of the virus and health diplomacy have not been effective soft power tools.

Trade and investment also are not reliable indicators of soft power. Duke University's Pippa Morgan, who has assessed Chinese economic engagement in Africa, found that while investment and aid generally add to China's soft power, its trade creates overwhelmingly negative perceptions.[144] The popular perception is that trade most often benefits China. Even favorable attitudes toward Chinese investment in many countries do not guarantee an overall positive view of China. A fall 2020 survey of 13 European countries revealed that on average 60 percent of those polled in countries such as Sweden, France, Germany, and the UK had favorable views of Chinese investment; yet these same countries all reported upwards of 60 percent very negative or negative feelings toward China overall.[145] A 2019 poll by the Pew Foundation found that Chinese investment only weakly correlated with a country's overall view of China. For example, in Nigeria, which has received $44 billion in Chinese investment since 2005, 70 percent of the population polled had a favorable view of China; however, in Indonesia, which has received more than $47 billion in capital investment from China during the same time period, only 36 percent of the population polled viewed China favorably.

One possible explanation for the disparity between Nigeria and Indonesia is geography. Overall, countries in the Asia Pacific tend to view Chinese investment with suspicion, while countries in Africa and Latin America are far more positively inclined.[146] These same Asia Pacific countries also report much greater concern over Chinese military aspirations. A survey of Southeast Asian experts and businesspeople found that more than one-third of those polled believed China was a "revisionist power" that intended to turn Southeast Asia into its sphere of influence. Only an average of 1.5 percent believed that China was a benign and benevolent power, and less than 20 percent were confident or very confident that China would "do the right thing." By contrast, an average of more than 61 percent of the interviewees were confident or very confident that Japan would "do the right thing" by contributing to global peace, security, prosperity and governance.[147] (While international perceptions of the United States plummeted during the Trump administration, a median 72 percent in the UK, France, and Germany had confidence that Joe Biden would do the right thing with regard to world affairs.)[148] Perhaps most telling, there is no correlation between the level of Chinese

Table 2.2 Support for China's positions by countries receiving significant BRI investment

Country information		Support for Chinese stances			
Name	Value of Chinese construction contracts since BRI started (USD million)	Hong Kong National Security Law	South China Sea Arbitral Ruling	Xinjiang policies	Huawei 5G
Pakistan	43,950	Yes	Yes	Yes	Yes
Saudi Arabia	32,770	Yes	Yes	Yes	Yes
Indonesia	28,370	No	No	No	Yes
Nigeria	26,520	No	No	No	Yes
Malaysia	25,840	No	No	No	Yes
UAE	25,750	Yes	Yes	Yes	Yes
Algeria	23,850	Yes	Yes	No	Yes
Ethiopia	23,050	No	Yes	No	Yes
Iran	21,840	Yes	No	Yes	Yes
Bangladesh	21,830	Yes	Yes	No	Yes

Sources: https://www.aei.org/china-global-investment-tracker/; https://thediplomat.com/2020/10/ which-countries-support-china-on-hong-kongs-national-security-law/; https://thediplomat. com/2016/07/who-supports-china-in-the-south-china-sea-and-why/; https://thediplomat. com/2020/10/2020-edition-which-countries-are-for-or-against-chinas-xinjiang-policies/; https:// www.npr.org/2019/10/24/759902041/chinas-tech-giant-huawei-spans-much-of-the-globe- despite-u-s-efforts-to-ban-it

BRI investment and support for Chinese policy on contentious issues such as the South China Sea, Xinjiang, or Hong Kong (see Table 2.2).

Conclusion

The objective of China's soft, sharp, and even hard power efforts is to shape the political and economic choices of foreign actors in support of Beijing's values and interests. China wants to prevent companies from identifying Taiwan as a separate entity, universities from inviting the Dalai Lama, and film studios from portraying China in a negative light. As Singapore's former Ministry of Foreign Affairs permanent secretary Bilahari Kausikan cleverly notes, "China doesn't just want you to comply with its wishes, it wants you to think in such a way that you will, of your own volition, do what it wants without being told."[149]

At the same time, the strong hand of the state often undermines Beijing's soft power initiatives or transforms them into sharp power equivalents. As discussed in chapter 1, China's use of PPE as a cudgel to pressure countries to express gratitude to China during the pandemic resulted in significant negative coverage by international media and falling levels of international public approval. In the case of TikTok, the CCP mandate that companies turn over any information the government requests diminishes the founder's ability to operate in major markets and advance China's soft power ambitions. Similarly, the CCP's use of CIs to promote political views and activities on issues such as Taiwan and Tibet has dimmed their prospects in many countries, turning them into objects of suspicion as opposed to celebrations of Chinese language and culture.

Importantly, China's use of soft, sharp, and hard power resonates differently in different contexts. Efforts to "tell a positive story" about China through Chinese media or to deploy CIs are better received in countries where access to a broader range of media and other outlets is more limited. Similarly, with regard to sharp power, most countries withstand Chinese pressure to compromise on issues of core national security or principle, whereas individual private actors are more vulnerable to Chinese coercion and more likely to seek compromise. Beijing's displays of hard power in Asia have also undermined its soft power potential, contributing to high levels of popular distrust in China. For African and Latin American countries, however, military concerns are far less significant. Surprisingly, perhaps, Chinese trade and even investment do not correlate strongly with overall trust and favorability. A broader set of foreign policy and human rights concerns play a more dominant role.

Despite Xi Jinping's stated desire to improve China's image, he demonstrates little inclination to modify Chinese behavior. It is a choice that Chinese public opinion polls appear to support. In December 2020, the *Global Times* – admittedly a news source with strongly nationalistic tendencies – reported that over 70 percent of Chinese citizens polled believe that wolf warrior diplomacy is the "right diplomatic approach," and that China's international image has improved in recent years.[150] Still, in June 2021, Xi called for the creation of a more credible and "loveable" Chinese image, suggesting a rhetorical shift may be underway.[151]

3

Reunifying the Motherland

In late August 2019, I sat down to lunch with a small group of successful businesspeople from mainland China and Hong Kong. The discussion quickly turned to the unrest in Hong Kong. For months, the city had been seized by large-scale demonstrations, in some cases exceeding one million people (see Figure 3.1). The spark for the protests had been an extradition bill proposed by Hong Kong's chief executive Carrie Lam in February 2019 that would allow the government to detain people wanted by Beijing and extradite them to mainland China.[1] Hong Kong citizens feared that Beijing would use the power of the law to target political opponents in Hong Kong and hold them for trial without the basic protection of rule of law. There was reason for concern. Two years earlier, Beijing had secretly abducted a billionaire from his hotel in Hong Kong,[2] and in 2015, several Hong Kong booksellers had been arrested and jailed while visiting mainland China.[3] In the face of the protests, some of which had turned violent, the Hong Kong government appeared paralyzed. Lam tried to slow the demonstrations' momentum by agreeing to suspend the bill – but not withdraw it, as the protestors demanded. Yet even as the government arrested increasing numbers of demonstrators, more joined. And their demands expanded. The rallying cry of the protestors became "five demands, not one less." They called on the Hong Kong government to withdraw the extradition bill, to retract its characterization of the protests as riots, to release all the protestors it had arrested, to conduct an independent inquiry into police brutality, and – the biggest demand – to grant the Hong Kong people universal suffrage.[4]

At stake in the minds of the protestors was the political autonomy guaranteed to Hong Kong in 1997, at the time of the city's handover from the United Kingdom to China. The Joint Declaration signed between the two countries, as well as the Basic Law – Hong Kong's mini-constitution based on the Joint Declaration and adopted by China's legislature, the National People's Congress – had provided for a governance framework

Figure 3.1 Hong Kong pro-democracy protestors on June 16, 2019
Source: Studio Incendo/Flickr/*https://creativecommons.org/licenses/by/2.0/legalcode*

of one country, two systems. In practical terms, one country, two systems agreed to preserve Hong Kong's political, judicial, and economic autonomy, excluding issues of foreign affairs and national security, until 2047. The agreements also allowed that the people of Hong Kong would possess the right to vote directly for their chief executive from a slate of candidates nominated by a representative committee.[5] The extradition bill, in this context, appeared to undermine the agreed-upon governance framework.

My lunch companions sympathized with the protestors' desire to maintain a degree of political autonomy, but all believed the end was preordained. Hong Kong would become "just another mainland city." Over the past several years, the Chinese government had chipped away at the margins of the city's governance framework and moved to integrate Hong Kong more fully into the mainland. A 2014 PRC State Council Information Office white paper affirmed that "The high degree of autonomy of the HKSAR [Hong Kong Special Administration Region] is not full autonomy, nor a decentralized power. It is the power to run local affairs as authorized by the central leadership."[6] In 2017, Beijing assumed jurisdiction over an immigration hall in the West Kowloon train station, prompting some critics to claim that the mainland was infringing on Hong Kong's sovereignty. That same year, a framework agreement for a Greater Bay Area encompassing Shenzhen, Macao, Hong Kong, and Guangdong was signed by the four regions' governments and the central-level National Development and Reform Commission (NDRC). First proposed in 2011 as "The Action Plan for the Bay Area of the Pearl River Estuary," the 2017 version included provisions to abolish work permit requirements for Hong Kong residents and provide them with access to state healthcare and education. While many Hong Kong businesspeople embraced the plan, other Hong Kong citizens worried about the implications for their economic and political autonomy, particularly their robust independent legal system. And most tellingly, in late June, China asserted that the Sino-British Joint Declaration was a "historical document that no longer had any practical significance."[7] Xi Jinping's 2017 speech inaugurating Carrie Lam as Hong Kong's chief executive underscored that the central objective of one country, two systems "first and foremost" was to "realize and uphold national unity."[8] In the eyes of my Chinese lunch companions, steps such as these signaled Beijing's longer-term intent, and, to a person, they believed that the demonstrations would only hasten Xi's resolve to bring Hong Kong more tightly into the fold. The only question remaining in their minds was whether Beijing would resort to force.

A few weeks later, in September 2019, two of Hong Kong's leading democracy activists, Joshua Wong and Brian Leung, offered a much more optimistic take on the situation. The two were fresh off an important political win: Lam had just agreed to withdraw the extradition legislation. But she refused to accede to the other demands, and the two sides were at a stalemate. The protests and violence continued to escalate. Wong and Leung had traveled to the United States to shore up international support for their cause. After a round of meetings in New York, they were headed to Washington, DC, where they were slated to testify before members of Congress and meet with other US officials.

Despite Wong and Leung's relative youth – then 22 and 25 years old, respectively – the two were already veterans of Hong Kong's democracy movement. Both had been leaders of previous protest movements, including the anti-patriotic education campaign – protesting the government's effort in 2012–13 to implement a pro-Beijing curriculum in Hong Kong schools – and the 2014 Umbrella Movement, the city-wide demonstrations in support of universal suffrage, in which the protestors used umbrellas to protect themselves against pepper spray and tear gas. In 2016, Wong had even established a new political party, Demosistō, a combination of Greek and Latin words meaning "people stand," along with two other young activists, Agnes Chow and Nathan Law. That same year, Law became the first member of Demosistō to win a seat in the Legislative Council, Hong Kong's legislature. He was later disqualified from serving for not properly reciting the oath of office.

I had met Wong several times before in Hong Kong and New York and had always been struck by his calm demeanor and long-term outlook, even as he marshaled hundreds of thousands of Hong Kong citizens to protest in support of democracy.[9] On this occasion, however, he appeared battle-hardened. He told me that he had been arrested eight times and had served 120 days in jail. Both he and Leung radiated a tough resolve, expressing a willingness to sacrifice their own futures in order to protect the future of their home. Leung, who had gained prominence when he revealed his face while leading an occupation of Hong Kong's Legislative Council in July 2019, told me that he was committed to the cause of a free and democratic Hong Kong and, with that, he had made a conscious choice to sacrifice his future if necessary. It was a "life choice," as he said. For his part, Wong was only 14 years old when he first took up a protest banner in support of the anti-patriotic education movement. His commitment was complete and his ambition for Hong Kong had only grown over the years. As we chatted, he mentioned several times that the long-term objective of Demosistō and the wider Hong Kong democracy movement was for Hong Kong to become the "master of its own home."

Wong and Leung's trip to Washington was designed to drum up support among US lawmakers for the Hong Kong Human Rights and Democracy Act (HKHRDA). The act, which had languished in Congress for almost five years, would penalize both the mainland and Hong Kong if Beijing encroached on the political autonomy guaranteed to Hong Kong under the Basic Law. The HKHRDA's most dramatic provision called on the United States to withdraw Hong Kong's special economic status, which shielded it from the vagaries of the broader US–China trade and investment relationship. In 1992, the United States had agreed to retain Hong Kong's special status as a unique customs territory even after 1997, as long as China abided by its one country, two systems arrangement. This special status entitled Hong Kong to lower trade tariffs and a separate customs framework, and enabled Hong Kong passport holders to avoid much of the vetting process required for mainland Chinese to visit, study, and work in the United States.[10] Over the years, Hong Kong had become one of the United States' largest export markets and an important conduit for investments flowing in and out of China.[11] Because of its special status, Hong Kong had also avoided the US–China tariff war launched by the Trump administration in early 2018. Growing concern in Congress over Lam's proposed extradition bill and the potential for greater mainland Chinese influence in Hong Kong's domestic political affairs, however, had drawn into question Hong Kong's political autonomy and had renewed US congressional interest in the bill.

Fall 2019 proved to be a high point for Hong Kong's democracy movement. In November, the city held its district council elections, and the democrats won almost 90 percent of the 452 seats with a record 71 percent of the population voting.[12] Lam acknowledged the significance of the vote, stating that the government would "listen to the opinions of members of the public humbly and seriously reflect."[13] And across the Pacific, President Trump signed into law the HKHRDA. Senator Marco Rubio, a sponsor of the HKHRDA, said at the time of the bill's signing that the United States had "new and meaningful tools to deter further influence and interference from Beijing into Hong Kong's internal affairs."[14] Meanwhile, the Chinese state media claimed that "foreign forces" had intervened in the elections and that "patriotic candidates" had been harassed.[15] The CCP also issued a new set of guidelines around patriotic education, designed to ensure a greater patriotic spirit among Hong Kong's residents, particularly the youth. The communiqué called for patriotic education to be integrated into schools, media, and entertainment, with patriotism defined as a love not only of China but also of socialism and the CCP.[16] It was one of the first clear signals of Beijing's intentions.

At the start of the new year, Xi Jinping began to replace mainland officials in charge of Hong Kong affairs with his trusted allies: Luo

Huining helped direct Xi's anti-corruption campaign, and Xia Baolong had overseen a ruthless anti-religion campaign that destroyed Christian churches and toppled more than 1,000 crosses from church roofs in Zhejiang province.[17] Luo, whom Xi appointed to serve as Beijing's top representative in Hong Kong, made his intentions clear early on. He stated that the "unrest has been orchestrated by pro-independence and radical violent forces and has seriously threatened national security and the one country, two systems principle."[18] Luo soon took action. In February, the government arrested several high-profile activists, including the billionaire media tycoon Jimmy Lai. Two months later, police arrested more than a dozen of Hong Kong's most prominent democracy activists. One observer commented at the time that Beijing had decided that the threat posed to national security by the Hong Kong protestors outweighed concerns of retaliation by the United States.[19] In reference to COVID-19, Chinese officials had also begun to refer to the protests as "a political virus of Hong Kong society."[20] By May, the local government had arrested 8,000 Hong Kong citizens.[21]

The most dramatic expression of Beijing's willingness to "make Hong Kong just another Chinese city," however, was its June 30 passage of a sweeping national security law. Article 23 of the Basic Law required Hong Kong to pass national security legislation, and two previous chief executives, C.H. Tung and C.Y. Leung, had tried to do so unsuccessfully in 2003 and 2014, respectively. Beijing was now taking matters into its own hands. The Law of the People's Republic of China on Safeguarding National Security in the Hong Kong Special Administrative Region introduced elements of the mainland's political system into Hong Kong's system. It barred any action Beijing considered directed at secession, subversion, terrorism, or foreign interference in Hong Kong affairs. It also called for tighter control over foreign media and NGOs and reintroduced both patriotic education and Beijing's right to extradite people from Hong Kong.[22] Hong Kong's chief executive would have the power to appoint judges to hear national security cases. Perhaps most important, Beijing, not the Hong Kong judiciary or Legislative Council, would have the power to interpret the law. Despite not being consulted on the new law, Carrie Lam argued that it would not undermine Hong Kong's autonomy and would, in fact, fill a "gaping hole."[23]

Through it all, pro-Beijing Hong Kong officials reiterated their belief that the new law was a welcome intervention by the mainland to help ensure stability. And as Beijing opened its Office for Safeguarding National Security to great ceremony in early July, previous Hong Kong chief executives clapped and smiled. In the wake of the bill's passage, libraries, schools, and universities began to purge pro-democracy books from their shelves.[24] One after another, Hong Kong's well-known democracy activists stepped back from the spotlight. Nathan Law fled to the UK.[25] Brian Leung testified before the US Congress from his graduate student perch at the University of Washington.[26] And Joshua Wong disbanded Demosistō. When the democrats held informal primaries on July 11–12 in advance of the November Legislative Council elections, more than 600,000 voters turned out. In response, Carrie Lam postponed the election for a year, although she cited concerns around COVID-19.[27] At the same time, the Hong Kong government disqualified 12 opposition candidates. Accusations that Beijing had undermined the Sino-British Joint Declaration were met by CCP commentary to the effect that with the 1997 handover, "all the provisions concerning the British side in the Joint Declaration have been fulfilled."[28]

Beijing deployed its new powers swiftly and brutally. In late August, mainland authorities captured 12 Hong Kong citizens who were attempting to travel to Taiwan by boat, labeling them separatists and declaring that they would face criminal charges under the new national security law for attempting to separate Hong Kong from China; Hong Kong police later arrested nine people who assisted them. By November 2020, more than 10,000 Hong Kong citizens had been arrested in conjunction with the democracy protests, and more than 20 percent of those were charged with criminal activities.[29] And in December, 10 of the Hong Kong citizens bound for Taiwan were found guilty and sentenced to prison on the mainland.

The international community condemned what it viewed as an abrogation of China's treaty commitments under the Joint Declaration, and several countries, including Canada, Australia, New Zealand, the UK, and the United States, canceled their extradition treaties with Hong Kong to prevent Beijing using the city as a conduit through which to extradite dissidents living in their countries. On October 6, 2020, the German Ambassador to the United Nations read a statement on behalf of 39 countries stating that they were "gravely concerned" about China's policies toward both Hong Kong and Xinjiang.[30] The Pakistani ambassador to the United Nations, however, responded with a statement of support for China's Hong Kong policy that included 54 countries, primarily from the Middle East and Africa, as well as a few from Latin America and Southeast and South Asia.[31] (A significant subset of these countries had also supported China's policies in the South China Sea in 2016 and Xinjiang in 2019.)[32]

In a speech commemorating the 40th anniversary of the establishment of the Shenzhen Special Economic Zone in October 2020, Xi referred to the "new practice" of one country, two systems, stressing the need for Shenzhen to lead in the development of Guangdong, Hong Kong, and Macao in order to "strengthen their [young people from Hong Kong and Macao] sense of belonging to the motherland."[33] Commentators began discussing how Shenzhen's "transformation from a backwater into a hi-tech metropolis" could "point the way forward for Hong Kong."[34] At the same time, Hong Kong authorities were busy sentencing the young democracy activists, such as Joshua Wong and Agnes Chow, to jail. Hong Kong was, as the businesspeople had predicted, well on its way to becoming just another mainland city.

The Sovereignty Mandate

The Hong Kong protests, which engulfed the city for almost a year until the COVID-19 pandemic and National Security Law dissipated their numbers, directly challenged two of Xi's central policy priorities: selling the China model as an alternative to liberal market democracy and making progress toward the unification of China.[35] The large-scale protests and demands for universal suffrage signaled to Beijing that one country, two systems was producing not a greater sense of unity between the two systems but rather a wider divide.

The notion of sovereignty and the unification of China is at the heart of Xi's ambition to realize the "great rejuvenation of the Chinese nation."[36] Even before assuming leadership of the CCP and the country, Xi stressed the importance of China's sovereignty claims and core interests. During his visit to the United States as vice president of China in February 2012, he noted that if the United States could not respect China's "major interests and core concerns," particularly around Taiwan, the relationship would "be in trouble."[37] And in early 2013, after his selection as CCP General Secretary, he stated, "No country should presume that we will engage in trade involving our core interests or that we will swallow the 'bitter fruit' of harming our sovereignty, security or development interests."[38] Xi frequently reiterates the commitment of the Chinese people to sovereignty: "The Chinese people share a common belief that it is never allowed and it is absolutely impossible to separate any inch of our great country's territory from China."[39] His remarks display a particular urgency around the issue of reunification with Taiwan. In October 2013, Xi stated that disagreements between China and Taiwan "cannot be passed on from generation to generation."[40] And in a January 2019 speech commemorating the 40th anniversary of former Chinese leader Deng Xiaoping's "Message to Compatriots in Taiwan," he made his intentions clear:

> The historical and legal fact, that Taiwan is part of China and the two sides across Taiwan Straits belong to one and the same China, can never be altered by anyone or any force. . . . We make no promise to renounce the use of force and reserve the option of taking all necessary means. . . . This does not target compatriots in Taiwan, but the interference of external forces and the very small number of "Taiwan independence" separatists and their activities. . . . Taiwan independence goes against the trend of history and will lead to a dead end. Taiwan must be unified, will be unified with China.[41]

Unification, Xi asserted, was "a historical conclusion drawn over the 70 years of the development of cross-Strait relations, and a must for the great rejuvenation of the Chinese nation in the new era."[42]

The importance of sovereignty is also deeply imprinted into the national consciousness of the Chinese people. Chinese history books are replete with references to being invaded and occupied during the more than a century between the 1839 Sino-British Opium War and the founding of the PRC in 1949. The period is portrayed as one of a humiliation that can only be rectified when China is unified. While Xi's pronouncements on sovereignty and reunification center on Hong Kong, Taiwan, and the South China Sea, China boasts land and maritime border disputes with as many as 14 different countries.[43] And Xi has not shied away from asserting PRC interests in disputes with several of these countries.

China and India have territorial disputes along several parts of their more than 2,100-mile border. In June 2020, conflict between the two countries resulted in the reported death of 20 Indian and four Chinese soldiers; it was the first fatal border conflict between the two countries in 45 years. Further skirmishes took place in August, September, and October, despite efforts to deescalate the conflict. China also provoked long-dormant political disputes over borders with Bhutan and Nepal. In addition, China and Japan have a longstanding territorial dispute in the East China Sea over the Japanese-administered Diaoyu or Senkaku Islands. (The East China Sea has been identified as "touching" on core interests.) During 2020, China sent ships into waters near the disputed islands for over 100 days straight, the longest streak since 2012.[44]

With the Hong Kong protest movement neutralized, many observers believe that Xi now has Taiwan in his line of sight. As Beihang University professor Tian Feilong noted in an interview, the Hong Kong National Security Law was designed to send a message not only to Hong Kong but also to the United States and Taiwan. According to Tian,

> This bill not only concerns one country, two systems, but also points to Sino-US relations and global governance, and can be applied to the Taiwan issue in the future. . . . If the Chinese government is not afraid of the United States on the Hong Kong issue, it will not be afraid of the Taiwan issue. I believe that the Hong Kong National Security Law can directly change its name and replace some content in the future to become the "Taiwan National Security Law."[45]

Taiwan

The island nation of Taiwan sits less than 100 miles from mainland China. It served as the refuge for Chiang Kai-shek and members of the Kuomintang (KMT), or Nationalist Party, who led mainland China from 1925 until 1949, when they fled to the island after losing the civil war to Mao Zedong and the CCP. In the more than seven decades since that time, Taiwan has transitioned from an authoritarian state into an economically successful and thriving democracy. Despite not possessing formal statehood – it lost its seat in the United Nations to the PRC in 1971 – Taiwan, with a population of almost 24 million, behaves much like a state, with its own constitution, foreign policy, and military. It also maintains diplomatic ties with 14 countries that do not recognize the PRC, as well as with the Holy See. Widely considered a model for many developing countries, Taiwan further burnished its reputation by its effective management of the COVID-19 pandemic.[46]

For China's leadership, Taiwan represents unfinished business. At the 19th Party Congress, Xi declared that reunification with Taiwan was one of the 14 must-do items for China to achieve its "great rejuvenation of the Chinese nation" and realize a "new era" by 2050.[47] Some mainland observers have suggested, however, that Xi does not want to wait until 2050 (at which point, he would be 97 years old).[48] Mainland Chinese leaders have long insisted that Taiwan could not remain an independent entity forever. In the process of gaining diplomatic recognition in the early 1970s, the PRC stipulated that it would not allow the creation of "two Chinas" or "one China, one Taiwan."[49] Successive Chinese leaders have proposed the idea of peaceful reunification, beginning with Mao Zedong, who said that as long as Taiwan was "returned to the motherland," it could retain its own political and economic system and military capabilities; only foreign affairs would be within the purview of the CCP. Deng Xiaoping first coined the phrase "one country, two systems" with regard to Taiwan in January 1979.[50]

In the first years of Xi's tenure, he enjoyed a good working relationship with then Taiwan president Ma Ying-jeou. Ma was born on the mainland and his party, the KMT, supports reunification – in some form, at some point in the future. Ma also accepted the '92 Consensus – a crucial political agreement from Beijing's perspective. The consensus, which was agreed to by officials on both sides of the Taiwan Strait in 1992, maintains that there is only one China and that the mainland and Taiwan belong to that same China. It left open, however, the question of when the two sides might unite and the form of governance that would be in place. Ma devoted himself to advancing stronger economic ties with the mainland, signing an Economic Comprehensive Trade Agreement that resulted in a dramatic increase in business opportunities across the strait. Tourism soared, and the number of students from Taiwan studying on the mainland increased from 7,347 in 2011 to 10,870 in 2015.[51] In addition, Xi and Ma held a historic summit in November 2015 in Singapore. During the meeting, Xi suggested that Taiwan could join the Beijing-led

AIIB (although the two sides ultimately could not agree on the name under which Taiwan would join) as well as the BRI. He also proposed that the two sides establish a hotline to manage crises. Xi concluded the meeting with a flurry of flowery words: "No matter whether it be rain or storm, no power can separate us. We are brothers, and I believe the two sides have the ability and wisdom to resolve our own problems."[52] As a reward for Ma's willingness to advance closer economic integration, China supported Taiwan's participation as an observer in the WHA and the International Civil Aviation Organization (ICAO) and suspended efforts to buy off the island's few remaining formal diplomatic partners.

Despite the overall positive trend in cross-strait relations, however, tensions remained. In 2013, in a conversation with Vincent Siew, who served as Taiwan's vice president from 2008 to 2012, Xi expressed some concern about political trends in Taiwan, noting: "We must increase political trust between the mainland and Taiwan and reinforce the common political foundation of the two sides which are critical for maintaining the peaceful development of cross-strait relations . . . rather than leave them to later generations."[53] In a speech later that year, he drew a red line around any notion of Taiwanese independence, noting: "Forces and activities for 'Taiwan independence' remain a real threat to the peace of the Taiwan Strait. It is therefore incumbent upon us to oppose and contain any rhetoric or move for 'Taiwan independence' without any compromise."[54] Xi's concerns were not without merit. In March 2014, hundreds of students and civil society actors occupied Taiwan's legislature, the Legislative Yuan, to protest a Taiwan–PRC agreement on cross-strait services that would have opened up 64 sectors of Taiwan's economy to PRC investment in areas such as healthcare, environmental services, and finance.[55] The protestors believed that mainland Chinese business would overwhelm Taiwanese businesses and lead to greater mainland Chinese political influence.[56] Even Ma was not an entirely reliable political partner. In 2014, he publicly expressed his support for universal suffrage in Hong Kong and denied that Taiwan would ever succumb to a one country, two systems framework like that of Hong Kong, delivering an address titled "Proud of our Democracy, Proud of Taiwan."[57]

A Rupture in Relations

The 2016 election of Tsai Ing-wen, the Democratic Progressive Party (DPP) candidate, as president of Taiwan signaled that reunification was becoming less rather than more likely. The DPP does not recognize Taiwan as part of China and is committed to maintaining the island's *de facto* independence from the mainland. The mainland media painted Tsai as a radical who was determined to move Taiwan toward *de jure* independence.[58] Yet she evinced few such radical tendencies. Throughout her campaign, she signaled that she did not intend to roll back the agreements made during Ma's tenure.[59] When I met with Tsai soon after her election in a modest campaign office, her demeanor was less firebrand than quiet intellectual. She sat behind a metal desk, with a few young aides in the room, and ticked off a list of priorities for her presidency that was almost entirely domestic. She wanted to ensure that the elderly were cared for, that young people had ample job opportunities and affordable housing, and that Taiwan would develop the capacity to improve its innovation capabilities. There was no talk of advancing an independence agenda; the only nod she gave to the mainland was to suggest that Taiwan needed to diversify its trade away from an overreliance on the PRC, which at the time provided the market for 26 percent of the island's exports (an additional 14 percent went to Hong Kong).

Despite her focus on domestic issues and her low-key approach to relations across the strait, the relationship between Taipei and Beijing deteriorated almost immediately. Once she made clear that she did not plan to support the '92 consensus – asserting that it was "against the will of the people"[60] – the Chinese leadership halted the formal cross-strait dialogue between Taipei's Mainland Affairs Council and Beijing's Taiwan Affairs Office. As a mainland spokesperson stated, "Because the Taiwan side has been unable to recognize the 1992 consensus – the joint political basis for showing the one-China principle – the cross-strait contact and communication mechanism has been suspended."[61] Beijing also adopted additional coercive measures. First, it dramatically reduced the number of Chinese tourists visiting the island. In 2015, the year before Tsai won the presidency, 4.2 million mainlanders visited Taiwan, making up 40 percent of all tourists and providing a substantial contribution to the $44.5 billion tourism industry (equivalent to 8.2 percent of

GDP). In 2017, a year after Tsai's election, Chinese tourists dropped to 2.7 million, and Taiwan's tourism industry shrank to $24.4 billion (only 4.3 percent of GDP).[62] In addition, Beijing demanded that Taiwanese universities issue pro-Beijing statements, suggesting that the education sector – and the enrollment of mainland students who helped fuel it – could be at risk. In 2017, the government granted approval for only 1,000 mainland Chinese students to study in Taiwan, making that year's cohort less than half the size of the previous year's 2,136 students.[63] And in April 2020, Beijing announced that no new mainland students would be allowed to begin studying in Taiwan, although those already there could continue their studies. When one mainland Chinese student asked why this policy had been enacted, the PRC Ministry of Education responded that it was a "national secret," although officially the Chinese government claimed that the decision was a response to the pandemic.[64]

In the wake of Tsai's election, China also leveraged its diplomatic power to curtail Taiwan's space on the international stage. Taiwan's former minister of national defense Lin Chong-pin stated that Beijing was trying to "impoverish Taiwan" by ensuring that other international actors did not recognize it as an independent entity.[65] Beijing denied the Tsai government the opportunity to participate in the ICAO and WHA as an observer. And as chapter 2 illustrated, China took steps to insist that all multinationals doing business in China adhere to its Taiwan protocol. In spring 2018, when Muji, a Japanese retailer with more than 200 stores in China, listed Taiwan as the country of origin on a batch of coat hangers in Shanghai, the Shanghai Administration for Industry and Commerce forced the store to pay a 200,000 yuan fine (about $31,000). Still, although it pulled the hangers, its English-language website continues to identify Taiwan as a separate country or region from China.[66] Even more troubling, China reportedly interfered in Taiwan's 2018 elections by providing funding to preferred politicians and promoting fake news on the internet about government incompetence.[67] Moreover, Beijing renewed its efforts to buy off Taiwan's few remaining allies. Between 2016 and 2020, the number of countries recognizing Taiwan diplomatically fell from 21 to 14.[68] (The Holy See also still recognizes Taiwan but is not a UN-recognized state.) Finally, China also increased the frequency of its hard power demonstrations, such as PLA naval and air force sorties across the median line of the Taiwan Strait[69] and the holding of large-scale military maneuvers around Taiwan. In August 2022, for example, China conducted a week of live-fire drills following the visit to the island by then U.S. Speaker of the House Nancy Pelosi."[70]

Taiwan's enhanced global stature, particularly over the course of the pandemic, as well as the Hong Kong protests, alarmed Beijing and contributed to a vibrant debate on the mainland over the wisdom of invading Taiwan. Professor Tian argued that the Hong Kong protests indicated that one country, two systems had failed and that the political and social trends in Taiwan meant that it would be "impossible to resolve the situation peacefully."[71] Chief of China's joint staff General Li Zoucheng also reportedly stated that China could attack Taiwan to prevent it from becoming independent,[72] and the May 2020 National People's Congress work report failed to include "peaceful" in its reference to unification with Taiwan for the first time in six years. Others, however, urged caution. Chinese historian Deng Tao penned a 5,000-character article describing how the Qing spent 20 years preparing for the invasion and conquest of Taiwan.[73] And retired airforce general Qiao Liang, who in 2004 co-authored a book, *Unrestricted Warfare: China's Master Plan to Destroy America*, nonetheless agreed with Deng, arguing that an invasion of Taiwan would be a "massive economic blow for China," and that Beijing's top priority, in any case, was national rejuvenation, not taking back Taiwan.[74]

Particularly concerning to Beijing are the increasingly strong ties between Taiwan and the United States. The United States maintains a longstanding commitment to Taiwan through the 1979 Taiwan Relations Act (TRA), which guarantees, among other things, that the United States will support political, cultural, and economic ties with Taiwan, as well as provide arms of a defensive nature. While it stops short of committing the United States to defend Taiwan in case of an attack, the TRA does include provisions that the United States provide arms for the adequate defense of Taiwan and retain the capacity to resist the use of force or coercion by the mainland against Taiwan.[75] The United States also supports a robust cultural and economic mission in Taipei, the American Institute in Taiwan.

During the Trump administration, the United States pointedly increased its diplomatic support of Taiwan. The US Congress and the Trump administration passed and signed into law the Taiwan Travel Act in 2017,[76] encouraging senior US officials to meet with their Taiwanese counterparts, as well as the Taiwan Allies International Protection and Enhancement Initiative Act of 2019,[77] which calls on the United States to assist Taiwan in expanding its international presence. During the Biden administration, U.S. allies, including Australia, Japan, and South Korea all voiced increased support for Taiwan, and President Biden, himself, suggested directly that the United States would defend Taiwan in the event of a Chinese invasion.[78] Both the Trump and Biden administrations allowed arms sales to Taiwan on a continuous basis rather a single annual sale, and regularly dispatched US warships to sail through the Taiwan Strait. In addition, Hong Kong's protest movement became a central issue in Taiwan's relationship with the mainland. President Tsai's 2020 reelection campaign adopted the slogan "Hong Kong today, Taiwan tomorrow" to reinforce the notion of threat that a one country, two systems framework posed to Taiwan. Taiwan actively supported the democracy activists in Hong Kong by providing gas masks to the protestors at the height of the demonstrations and offering sanctuary to activists seeking to leave Hong Kong. In the first eight months of 2020, more than 4,500 Hongkongers were granted residency, 1,000 of them on a permanent basis.

President Tsai has responded to Beijing's deployment of both sharp and hard power by trying to reduce Taiwan's reliance on China and expand its ties with outside actors. She revived a decades-old effort to diversify Taiwan's trade away from the mainland, which she termed a "New Southbound" policy. This effort has achieved some success. Taiwan's exports to mainland China decreased by approximately 5 percent from 2018 to 2019, while Taiwan's goods and services exports fell approximately 1 percent overall.[79] In addition, during 2019, the number of tourists traveling from Southeast Asia and elsewhere to Taiwan more than compensated for the loss of mainland Chinese tourists; foreign tourists hit a record 11.84 million, marking a 7 percent increase from 2018.[80] Tsai also launched a successful preferential tax program to encourage Taiwanese businesses to return to Taiwan from the mainland,[81] resulting in $38 billion in Taiwanese investment in the mainland returned to the island.[82] And she has moved to strengthen Taiwan's military capabilities, including the planned construction and deployment of eight new submarines by 2025. Her landslide reelection victory (which was helped by Beijing's repressive measures in Hong Kong) also emboldened her to assert in a post-election interview with the BBC, "We don't have a need to declare ourselves an independent state. . . . We are an independent country already and we call ourselves the Republic of China (Taiwan). . . . We're a successful democracy. . . . We have a separate identity and we're a country of our own."[83] Even the once avidly pro-unification KMT abandoned its support for the '92 consensus, leaving Beijing without a significant political partner in Taiwan.

Beijing, for its part, has not relented but only increased the stridency of its rhetoric and threatening actions. In September 2020, Chinese warplanes crossed the median line of the Taiwan Strait forty times in two days. And on October 10, the PLA undertook a large-scale, multi-force exercise that simulated a successful invasion of Taiwan. CCTV and the nationalist *Global Times* also aired a video version with stirring music.[84] Only the day before, Tsai had reiterated her offer for dialogue with Beijing.[85]

Creating Something from (Almost) Nothing

In his more than three-hour speech at the 19th Party Congress in October 2017, Xi Jinping recited a list of CCP accomplishments during his first term. Included among them was "Construction on islands and reefs in the South China Sea." For almost two years from 2013 to 2015, China dredged and reclaimed land in the South China Sea and created seven artificial features. Other states in the region, such as Vietnam, have dredged land to fortify their claims to reefs and islands in the South China Sea, but in a 15-month period, China reclaimed 17 times as much land as other claimant states combined in the past four decades, reaching a total of 2,900 acres.[86] And, despite a promise by President Xi to US president Obama in 2015 that China would not militarize the features, Beijing proceeded to build airstrips and military structures on them and used them as a base from which to deploy mobile artillery.[87]

Stretching from Sumatra and Borneo in the south to Taiwan and China's Fujian province in the north, the South China Sea encompasses an area of 1,351,000 square miles, more than one-third the size of the United States. Northeast Asia – China, South Korea, and Japan – relies heavily on the flow of energy resources and commerce through the sea's shipping lanes. Fully one-third of global shipping, with an estimated value of $3.5 trillion, travels along these routes. It is also an area with substantial reserves of oil and gas, and, according to wildlife expert Rachael Bale, is "richer in biodiversity than almost any other marine ecosystem on the planet."[88] As a result, the area is awash with thousands of fishing vessels eager to harvest the bounty from a region renowned for its plentiful fish stocks.

Control over these natural resources and fish stocks, as well as over the major island chains in the sea – the Spratlys and the Paracels – is contested by China and five other nations: Brunei, Taiwan, Malaysia, Vietnam, and the Philippines. China's claims, however, are the most expansive. They include almost 80 percent of the area, which the government demarcates on maps with an ill-defined nine-dash line. Chinese officials consider the South China Sea as much an integral part of their territory as Hong Kong and Taiwan. As retired PLA Navy Admiral Wu Shengli dramatically proclaimed: "How would you feel if I cut off your arms and legs? . . . That's how China feels about the South China Sea."[89]

Competition for control of the South China Sea and its island chains began in earnest in the post-World War II period when China (not yet the People's Republic of China and still under the control of the KMT) established a presence on Woody Island in the Paracel Islands, as well as on a few features in the Spratly Islands. During the Allied peace treaty negotiations in August 1951, Chinese premier Zhou Enlai declared China's sovereignty over the Paracel and Spratly Islands. Over the ensuing decades, there were frequent clashes – some deadly – between the fishing boats, coast guard vessels, and other ships that patrolled the waters. At the same time, both international law and regional agreements helped mitigate the potential for broader conflict. China ratified UNCLOS in 1996 and signed a Declaration on the Conduct of Parties in the South China Sea with member nations of ASEAN in 2002 that reaffirmed the parties' "respect for and commitment to the freedom of navigation" in the South China Sea and pledged to resolve territorial and jurisdictional disputes by peaceful means in accordance with universally recognized principles of international law such as UNCLOS.[90] Serious negotiations over a South China Sea Code of Conduct between China and ASEAN have been underway since 2016.[91]

China claims the legal rights around sovereignty that are stipulated in UNCLOS, such as the Exclusive Economic Zone and continental shelf, as well as historical rights within its nine-dash line.[92] To bolster its assertions of historical rights, Beijing cites Chinese references to the Spratlys dating back to the Han Dynasty (206 BC–AD 220). Based on a collection of maps from the Qing Dynasty, China's Foreign Ministry also claims that China held administrative jurisdiction over the Spratlys during the Qing, and has produced an 1868 "Guide to the South China Sea" that reports on Chinese fishermen in the Nansha (Spratly) islands: "The footmarks of fishermen could be found in every isle of the Nansha Islands and some of the fishermen would even live there for a long period of time."[93] Chinese analysts argue that since the Chinese nine-dash line was portrayed on maps prior to the establishment of the modern international legal regime – UNCLOS was adopted and signed in 1982 – current laws should not negate China's earlier prior rights. When maps appear that do not support Beijing's claims, the government quickly removes them. And anyone who publishes or displays maps that "do not comply with national standards" is at risk of prosecution.[94] China has even undertaken archaeological digs to try to find proof of its historical sovereignty over the islands.[95]

Every claimant, however, has its own South China Sea sovereignty story. Tran Duc Anh Son, a well-known Vietnamese historian, for example, asserts that the Nguyen Dynasty (1802–1945) exerted clear sovereignty over the Paracels – even planting trees to warn against ship-wrecks. And there is evidence in history books around the world that a Nguyen-era Vietnamese explorer placed the country's flag on the Paracels in the 1850s.[96] Son also discovered a set of maps from the 1700s at the Harvard-Yenching Library that demonstrate that the Qing Dynasty laid no claim to either of the island chains and considered Hainan Island the southernmost part of the country.[97] In addition to historical ties, Vietnam rests its claims on a 1933 legal annexation document issued by France, which represented a lawful method of territorial acquisition at the time. When Vietnam achieved independence from France, the latter's territorial rights in the Paracels devolved first to South Vietnam and later to the Socialist Republic of Vietnam.[98]

China has been more aggressive than other nations, however, in enforcing its claims. The Australian scholar Andrew Chubb has documented a steady expansion of PRC assertiveness beginning as early as 2006, when Beijing started to use law enforcement ships to control disputed waters, withdrew from UNCLOS' dispute resolution procedures, and started oil and gas production in disputed offshore fields. In this context, Xi Jinping's most notable innovation in PRC strategy was the large-scale dredging and reef reclamation effort he championed in his 19th Party Congress speech.[99] While China has claimed that it developed the features in order to improve marine research, navigational safety, and the living conditions of the personnel stationed there, the outposts have clear military applications.[100]

Troubled Waters

Chinese actions have heightened tensions with several of the other claimants, including Vietnam and, in particular, the Philippines, which launched a two-and-a-half-year lawsuit over Chinese claims with the Permanent Court of Arbitration in the Hague. In July 2016, the tribunal ruled in favor of the Philippines, arguing that Beijing's claims to "historic rights" over the South China Sea encompassed by the nine-dash line could not exceed its maritime rights under the Convention on the Law of the Sea: "Coastal states in the South China Sea are entitled to full 200-nautical mile exclusive economic zones (EEZ's) unencumbered by any Chinese claims."[101] Once China signed on to UNCLOS and its terms for territorial claims, its assertions of "historic rights" were nullified.[102] Even before the judgment, China signaled that it would not abide by the ruling. As noted above, it had stated as early as 2006 that it would not be bound by the court's rulings, and it explicitly announced that it would not participate in the arbitration upon receiving notice of the Philippines' intent to pursue its territorial claims in court. In defense of its position, Beijing rallied 31 countries, primarily from the Middle East and Africa, such as Algeria, Bahrain, Egypt, Kenya, Qatar, and Saudi Arabia, to support its claim that the arbitral ruling was illegitimate.[103] In May 2018, the Chinese Society of International Law issued a 750-page "critical study" detailing why the tribunal was wrong in its judgment. And it attempted to develop new arguments as to why, even if China were not entitled to historic rights, it should be permitted to claim maritime zones from "groups of features" in the South China Sea, rather than from outlying archipelagos. UNCLOS does not recognize the validity of these arguments either.[104]

Despite the legal ruling, Beijing continued to press its claims. In an October 2018 speech before the Southern Theatre Command in Guangdong province, which has responsibility for the South China Sea and Taiwan, Xi Jinping called on all China's military's forces to "step up combat readiness exercises, joint exercises and confrontational exercises to enhance servicemen's capabilities and preparation for war."[105] Shinji Yamaguchi, senior research fellow at Japan's National Institute for Defense Studies, has noted that to support China's claims in the South China Sea, Xi has greatly enhanced coordination among China's various maritime actors on South China Sea activities.[106] Even Chinese fishermen receive basic military training, including exercises to help "safeguard Chinese sovereignty" and to gather information on foreign vessels.[107] Chinese ships rammed and sank Vietnamese fishing boats near the Paracels in 2019 and 2020.[108] And as the COVID-19 pandemic raged, China sent survey ships into areas claimed by Malaysia and Vietnam,[109] created two new municipal districts to govern the Paracel and Spratly Islands, and named more than 80 artificial features, 55 of which are underwater.[110]

In response to Beijing's assertiveness, the other claimants in the South China Sea have alternated between negotiation and retaliation. Neither strategy, however, has deterred China from pursuing its claims. The case of the Philippines is instructive. President Roderigo Duterte, who assumed power less than two weeks before the ruling by the Permanent Court of Arbitration, has vacillated between trying to appease China and pushing back. He initially dismissed the arbitral award in favor of trying to negotiate with Beijing, but discovered there was little room to maneuver. In September 2019, Duterte reported that after he raised the issue of the arbitral award during a meeting with Xi Jinping in Beijing, Xi stated, "You know, our statement was: 'We will not budge.' We don't want to discuss that because it's ours. We own the property. Why should we talk to you?"[111] As a result, in late 2019, the Philippines announced that it would recruit an additional 25,000 officers for its coast guard to be able to respond more effectively to the threat from Chinese coast guard and fishing vessels.[112] And in June 2020, it reversed its decision to terminate the Visiting Forces Agreement with the United States that grants US military aircrafts and ships free entry into the Philippines, noting that the decision had been made "in light of the political and other developments in the region."[113] The next month, Philippine foreign secretary Teodoro Locsin Jr. stated, "The award is non-negotiable. The tribunal authoritatively ruled that China's claim of historic rights to resources within the sea . . . had no basis in law."[114] Along with Hanoi, Manila also criticized Chinese military drills in disputed waters as "highly provocative" and "detrimental" to Beijing's relationship with ASEAN.[115] Such criticism, however, failed to deter Beijing from continued military assertiveness in the region, and the Philippines responded by enhancing its military ties with the United States. By early 2023, the United States had increased its access from five to nine Philippine military bases.

Other ASEAN members have also waded into the conflict. For almost two decades since the signing of the Declaration on a Code of Conduct in 2002, ASEAN has attempted to negotiate a South China Sea Code of Conduct with China. In 2018, it developed a negotiating text for the code of conduct, but many of the critical issues, such as the geographical range, the nature of the dispute resolution process, bans on further land reclamation, and the right of outside actors such as the United States to hold military exercises, have not been resolved.[116] Singapore's ambassador-at-large Bilahari Kausikan has accused China of only superficially engaging with ASEAN, saying that Beijing is negotiating in a "barely convincing way." He notes that "progress has been glacial" and that Chinese diplomats often hold the negotiations hostage until ASEAN adopts positions with which it agrees.[117] Malaysia also adopted a more active stance in pushing back against China's expansive claims. In December 2019, it submitted its own claim to the United Nations Commission on the Limits of the Continental Shelf to establish the outer limits of Malaysia's shelf beyond the 200 nautical mile limit, overlapping with waters claimed by China.[118] The Malaysian auditor general revealed the Chinese PLA Navy and coast guard ships had undertaken 89 incursions into Malaysia maritime waters between 2016 and 2019.[119] And in the spring of 2020, Chinese and Malaysian vessels had an extended standoff in their disputed territory.[120] China's military assertiveness has further triggered rising arms expenditure throughout the region. Overall military spending by ASEAN increased 33 percent between 2009 and 2018.[121]

The X Factor

Underpinning the dynamics of rising tensions, military assertiveness, negotiation, and confrontation in the South China Sea is the diplomatic and military presence of the United States. While not itself a claimant – or even a signatory to UNCLOS – the United States nonetheless takes as its mission preserving freedom of navigation in the South China Sea and globally.[122] In front of a packed audience at the Aspen Strategy Forum in July 2019, then Commander of US Indo-Pacific Command Admiral Philip Davidson described the United States' South China Sea policy as enforcing UNCLOS and continuing with "decades and centuries of defending freedom of navigation." He noted, "We do it all over the globe – we run freedom of navigation on Canada." Davidson made clear that the United States "doesn't do these freedom of navigation operations against China"; they are "demonstrations for all the nations that are indeed down there," although he acknowledged that China protests the operations most vehemently,[123] while Vietnam offers the most vocal support.[124] Over the course of the Trump administration, the number of such operations jumped dramatically from three in 2016 to nine in 2019, earning frequent condemnation from China and assertions that the United States was "seriously threatening China's sovereignty and security . . . and seriously harming regional peace and stability."[125] In addition, the Trump administration, like previous US administrations, encouraged other countries, outside of the claimants, to become engaged in the South China Sea issue. Japan, Australia, the UK, France, and India have all participated in military exercises or other naval activities to demonstrate their support for UNCLOS and the 2016 ruling of the Permanent Court of Arbitration.

The United States historically has taken no sides in the South China Sea dispute, although it has stepped in at various times to support sovereignty rights under UNCLOS and freedom of navigation. In 2012, the Obama administration attempted to broker a deal between China and the Philippines for both countries to withdraw their ships from Scarborough Shoal. (Manila did, while Beijing reneged.) More recently, in June 2019, the United States sent three nuclear-powered aircraft carriers to the South China Sea while the Chinese military was conducting exercises in disputed waters. And in May 2020, it sent three naval ships to patrol the area near Malaysia's coast as a deterrent to the Chinese maritime contingent that had been threatening a Malaysian drillship.[126] In July 2020, the United States issued its clearest statement yet rejecting Chinese claims and supporting the position of the other claimants in the South China Sea. In remarks delivered to the press, then secretary of state Pompeo aligned the US position on the PRC's maritime claims with the decision of the Permanent Court of Arbitration and formally declared that the United States stood with its Southeast Asian allies and partners as well as the international community in defense of freedom of the seas.[127]

For China, Pompeo's remarks were one more demonstration of the United States' interference in China's neighborhood. The Chinese Foreign Ministry spokesman Zhao Lijian stated, "The US is the real destroyer and trouble-maker upsetting peace and stability in the region."[128] Among many Chinese scholars, as well, there is diminishing tolerance for what they believe to be US provocations in China's backyard. CICIR researcher Lou Chunhao, for example, argues that "The South China Sea issue fundamentally is about China and other regional countries' territorial and maritime claims. . . . China has an important role in the South China Sea because it is a regional power. . . . China and ASEAN countries are after all the owners of the South China Sea region."[129] The message is clear: the United States should step back and accept China's interests and new geopolitical realities. Or in common parlance: the United States should pack its bags and head back across the Pacific.

Conclusion

Chinese leaders have historically placed a high priority on sovereignty. The narrative of loss and humiliation dating back to the Qing Dynasty is deeply embedded in the country's political culture, as is the desire to realize long-held territorial claims, whether legally justified or not. While all Chinese leaders since Mao have called for China to realize its sovereignty claims, Xi Jinping has made unification a central condition of his vision of the great rejuvenation of the Chinese nation; and his statements display a strong sense of inevitability and urgency around the realization of Chinese claims, particularly with regard to Taiwan. An important subtext to Xi's reunification campaign is his effort to promote a China model that other countries might emulate. The specter of millions of Hong Kong citizens protesting for democracy and the clear commitment by Taiwan's citizens to their democratic process cast doubt on the credibility of a China model. Moreover, the defeat of pro-Beijing candidates in both Hong Kong and Taiwan's elections represents a very public repudiation of Xi's narrative within territories that Beijing claims as its own. Xi's claim that there is something uniquely Chinese about the path he has set out for mainland China is also undermined by Hong Kong, prior to the National Security Act, and Taiwan.

China's strategy for realizing its sovereignty claims displays elements of soft, sharp, and hard power. With regard to Hong Kong and Taiwan, it demonstrates a high degree of tolerance for the separation of systems and international space for Taiwan as long as it feels confident that its diplomacy is resulting in greater integration. When, however, it perceives that a preponderance of political voices is advocating greater separation from the mainland, and that forces within Hong Kong and Taiwan that supported reunification are weakening, it quickly adopts sharp and hard power tactics. This is particularly evident in the case of Taiwan, where Beijing immediately rolled back the diplomatic and economic wins it had permitted Taiwan under the Ma government as soon as Tsai indicated that she would not support the '92 Consensus. And it introduced a range of sharp power tactics, including reducing the number of Chinese tourists and students and meddling in the mid-term elections. It also has used military action with increasing frequency to discourage Taiwan from taking further action to enhance its independent status.

Similarly, in the South China Sea, although it maintains a process of ongoing diplomatic negotiation, China has expanded both its capability and its willingness to deploy military power. And when other claimants challenge its sovereignty claims, it will respond with coercive economic tools. Only when the claimants accede to Chinese terms will Beijing ease its economic coercion. For example, when the Philippines temporarily dropped its efforts to enforce the decision of the Permanent Court of Arbitration in the Hague, Beijing ended its ban on the import of Philippine bananas and indicated a willingness to increase its imports of a wide range of additional goods. Nonetheless, the Philippine efforts to placate Beijing yielded no accommodation on the actual issue of sovereignty claims.

China also frames its sovereignty quest in the context of US–China relations. The United States is the primary guarantor of regional security and freedom of navigation. It has strong military allies and partners in the region and maintains a legal commitment to support Taiwan's self-defense capabilities. Xi, however, has called explicitly for Asia to be managed by Asians and for the US system of alliances to be dismantled. In this context, China has attempted to use the negotiations over the South China Sea Code of Conduct to prevent the United States from conducting military exercises there. Moreover, Beijing's frequent references to "external forces" as a significant source of unrest and protest in Hong Kong and Taiwan seek to undermine the credibility of domestically derived democracy activism by blaming other countries, in particular the United States, for creating trouble.

China promotes itself as a supporter of the current rules-based order but routinely ignores international law in pursuit of its sovereignty claims. Even before the ruling of the Permanent Court of Arbitration in the Hague, it declared that it would not observe the ruling or participate in the arbitral process. In the case of Hong Kong, China asserted that the Joint Declaration was a historical document with no practical significance, invalidating its legal standing. Beijing ignores widespread international criticism over its disregard for international norms, while successfully rallying countries from Africa and the Middle East to its defense. As Chinese military capabilities continue to grow, it will likely move beyond its focus on Taiwan and the South China Sea to more consistently press its non-core sovereignty claims, such as those against India and Japan.

4

The Dragon's Bite

The economy of Greece was in shambles. Plagued by ballooning debt, levels of unemployment exceeding 25 percent, and widespread street protests, the newly elected leftist government of Alexis Tsipras was desperate. The country's European creditors had been pushing Greece to privatize the country's state assets in order to dig the country out of debt, but the major economies – France, Germany, and the UK – had no interest in investing in those assets. Instead, in 2015, at the height of the crisis, China came calling. The particular suitor was the Chinese government's shipping company China Ocean Shipping Company (COSCO), the world's third largest in number of container ships and container volume. The object of its desire: the Port of Piraeus.

The port had an early distinguished history. Located in the eponymous city of Piraeus, just five miles from Athens and across from the Suez Canal, the port was critical in defending Greece from the Persian invaders in the Battle of Salamis in 480 BC. The popular Greek military commander and politician Themistocles had earlier transferred the Athenian fleet to Piraeus, believing it to be a superior location for the navy. By 471 BC, it had become the permanent navy base. The port was destroyed, however, with the absorption of Greece into the Roman Empire beginning in 86 BC and did not begin to recover until the early 1830s, following the Greek War of Independence from the Ottoman Empire. During World War II, the port again served an important military purpose, allowing British ships to dock there until the port was bombed by the Nazis in 1941. At the end of the war, the Port of Piraeus once more began the process of recovery with the construction of a new container terminal and later addition of a cruise passenger terminal. In 2003, the port listed on the Athens Stock Exchange, with the government as the majority shareholder.[1] Yet despite Greece's world-class shipping industry, the Port of Piraeus failed to thrive economically.

Six years later, at the outset of Greece's financial crisis in 2009, COSCO made its first foray into the port, picking up a 35-year franchise right to two of the port's container terminals.[2] Greek shipowners had encouraged the investment. China was a familiar partner: it had been supplying ships to Greece since 2000, and the Greek merchant fleet, in turn, had been transporting goods to and from China for decades. The Chinese investment in Piraeus soon paid off. Over the following years, the port's ranking jumped from 93rd in 2010 to 44th in 2016.[3] COSCO's continued interest, therefore, was not surprising. In February 2020, I sat down in Athens with Evangelos Kalpadakis, who served as the director of the Diplomatic Office in the Tsipras government. He revealed that even before Tsipras was elected, the Chinese had sent a senior Foreign Ministry official to meet with him. At that time, Tsipras told the official that he was open to cooperating and strengthening relations, but to earn the support of local communities, he would need more from China, such as improved conditions around the port and a wider opening of the Chinese market for Greek agricultural exports, as well as other Chinese investment. But China's bid ran into some difficulty. During his campaign, Tsipras pledged to halt the sale of state assets, and in February 2015, immediately upon assuming office, he announced that there would be no further privatization of Piraeus.

Behind the scenes, however, Greek finance minister Yanis Varoufakis was working to keep Chinese interest in Piraeus alive and attract even more Chinese investment. As he wrote in his memoir *Adults in the Room*, "From a strategic perspective, it struck me as daft to antagonize Beijing at a time when the battle lines against Berlin, Frankfurt, and Brussels were being drawn." Varoufakis had previously published articles in which he supported not only COSCO's involvement in Piraeus but also the sale of Greece's railway system. As he reflected, "Our ports and railways were nineteenth-century museum pieces demanding massive investment that the Greek economy could not (and French and German companies would not) provide." For Varoufakis, China was "the obvious solution." In a meeting with Chinese ambassador Zou Xiaoli on February 25, 2015, Varoufakis proposed – to the surprise of the ambassador, who had anticipated a hostile reception – that China invest in both the three main shipyards, turning them into repair hubs for container ships, as well as the railway. He also suggested that Beijing persuade companies to build assembly facilities in a tech park close to Piraeus, promising a special business tax regimen.[4] Zou realized the opportunity and responded: "[F]rom Beijing's perspective, COSCO is the dragon's jaw. First we must ensure that its teeth bite hard so that the dragon gets in. Once it is in, have no concerns or doubt: the rest of the dragon will follow."[5] At Zou's behest, Varoufakis followed up his dinner with a visit to COSCO's Piraeus operations, bringing along a camera crew to help publicize the partnership. Varoufakis was not COSCO's only champion within the Greek government. Spyros Sagias, a staunch supporter of the privatization effort, who also provided legal counsel to COSCO, received a cabinet appointment just as the company was pushing for control over the port.[6]

The Greek government initially set out a number of conditions, including the purchase of $1.8 billion in Greek treasury bonds. (The EU commissioner had refused to allow Greek banks to purchase the debt as part of a debt rollover effort.) Yet when the Chinese purchase came through, it was only for $238 million. The German government had intervened, telling the Chinese not to purchase the Greek T-bills.[7] Nonetheless, one year later, when Tsipras traveled to China, talks there focused on Piraeus and the terms of privatization. In the end, COSCO purchased a 51 percent stake in the port authority with the ability to acquire a second stake of 16 percent in 2021, if additional investment and payment terms were met. The concession will expire in 2052.[8]

The results have been dramatic. The port's global standing has continued to rise and has given Greece new bragging rights. The port now ranks 26th among the world's 100 largest ports, up from 44th in 2016. As many as 20 million passengers transit through Piraeus annually. It is also Europe's fourth biggest container port, and by 2020, it had surpassed Spain's Valencia as the leading European port in the Mediterranean.

Beijing is also pleased with its investment. It is one of 13 ports in Europe and 97 globally in which China has a significant stake,[9] and it ranks as one of a few clear successes for Xi Jinping's signature foreign policy initiative, the Belt and Road Initiative. The port has paid off in several additional ways as well. In July 2017, a Chinese naval fleet visited the Piraeus port for four days. And in June 2016, Greece, along with Hungary and Croatia – two other recipients of significant Chinese investment – watered down a joint EU statement designed to support the decision of the tribunal at the Permanent Court of Arbitration that backed the Philippines' South China Sea claim against China. Instead of "welcoming" the decision, the EU merely acknowledged it.[10] In 2017, when the European Union sought to issue a statement condemning China's crackdown on political activists and dissidents, Greece, the civilizational cradle of democracy, blocked the resolution. A Greek Foreign Ministry spokesperson referred to the resolution as "unconstructive criticism of China."[11] This marked the first time that the European Union had failed to issue a statement at the annual UN Human Rights Council session in Geneva.[12] And in successive years, as China and Western countries have battled over resolutions around Xinjiang and Hong Kong, Greece's voice has been noticeably absent from the debate.

Despite its overall success, COSCO's investment has not been without its challenges. According to the general secretary of the Piraeus Port Dock Workers' Union, in the early days of the investment, COSCO subcontracted jobs, resulting in a situation in which many of the 1,700 people employed at the port worked for 16 days per month without benefits or job security. Workers were required to urinate in bottles because they were refused breaks. The European Union has also identified Piraeus as a major new entry point for Chinese gangs importing goods and committing wide-scale tax fraud.[13] Two years of negotiations between COSCO and the unions resulted in some improvements. However, in February 2019, the Greek government indicated concern around the company's expansion plans in Piraeus, blocking part of it on environmental and "aesthetic" grounds and opening new discussions on previously approved investments by sending them back to government cultural institutions, including the Ministry of Culture, for reauthorization.[14] The Greek Central Archaeological Council later unanimously voted down COSCO's expansion plans, including a mall next to the new cruise ship terminal. In November 2019, however, despite significant local opposition, China and Greece signed a memorandum of understanding committing both sides to work together to overcome obstacles in COSCO's investment.

Within Greece, views on the value of the port, as well as on China's investment more broadly, differ widely. Plamen Tonchev, one of Greece's foremost China scholars, suggested to me that although the Port of Piraeus is widely considered a success in operational terms, by his estimates, the economic benefit from the port's increased business to Greece is extremely limited. And he is concerned that Greece does not have a clear strategy for assessing the costs and benefits of future Chinese investment. Others are more positive. Tom Ellis, the editor-in-chief of Greece's most widely read English-language newspaper, *Kathimerini*, asserted that Greece will continue to welcome Chinese investment. Greeks, he says, appreciate that the Chinese "invest, they don't just talk," although he also notes: "It is true that decisions by state entities are often based on political or geopolitical calculations, as opposed to private firms, which focus on the financial costs of their investments."

The ongoing debates within Greece over Belt and Road investments are mirrored throughout much of the world as countries grapple with assessing the potential costs and benefits of deeper engagement with China. At stake are the big issues inherent in countries' future development paths: financial sustainability, the environment, sovereignty, national security, and political values. Many countries, like Greece, have also become players in the much larger geostrategic battle between China and the United States. Increasingly, the breadth and depth of a country's BRI engagement has become one measure of its commitment to one or another of these two distinct and often competing worldviews.

The Creation Story

In a set of two speeches in fall 2013 – the first in Astana, Kazakhstan and the second in Jakarta, Indonesia – Xi Jinping announced a new Chinese initiative, One Belt, One Road. The initiative promised massive Chinese investment in infrastructure to promote connectivity from China through Asia, Europe, the Middle East, and Africa. Xi presented the BRI in part as China's contribution to the development needs of the world. And the needs are indeed vast. The Asian Development Bank (ADB) projects that developing Asia alone will have an infrastructure deficit of $26 trillion by 2030.[15] But this hard infrastructure plan was only the first salvo. Since its inception, the BRI has morphed from a relatively straightforward commitment to global connectivity in hard infrastructure, such as ports, railways, and pipelines, to a grand-scale vision for connectivity across multiple platforms, including digital, financial, political, and security. With the growing range of BRI-related projects have come new questions around China's ambitions and the broader strategic implications of Belt and Road.

China has long played a role in designing and constructing overseas infrastructure projects. During the early 1970s, Beijing helped build the Tazara Railway, which stretches 1,155 miles from Dar es Salaam, Tanzania, to Kapiri Mposhi, Zambia. And beginning in 1999, the government-directed "go out strategy" sent hundreds of Chinese firms abroad in search of natural resources to continue to fuel economic growth. Many of the resources that the Chinese companies sought in Africa, Latin America, and Southeast Asia required new infrastructure to transport them to China. Beijing provided the financing, know-how, materials, and labor to make that happen, earning itself a place as a dominant player in both the financing and the construction of the world's global infrastructure.[16]

But Xi Jinping's Belt and Road promised something different. It promised connectivity between China and other countries and among those countries themselves. The BRI would connect some of the lesser-developed, interior regions of China to external markets by building the necessary hard infrastructure. It also would provide a market for Chinese overcapacity. After decades of extraordinary economic expansion, Chinese GDP growth had fallen from double to single digits, and the country's construction, logistics, and energy companies needed new markets. Finally, the BRI would add a political gloss to China's global infrastructure empire. Belt and Road could be promoted as China's contribution to the development needs of the world.

Such ideas had been discussed internally for several years. As the Chinese scholar Jin Ling has pointed out, at least two Chinese economists, Lin Yifu and Xu Shanda, had proposed their versions of a "Chinese Marshall Plan" in 2009, which, while not identical to the BRI, shared some significant similarities.[17] Both plans proposed increasing Chinese infrastructure investment globally as a means of spurring growth in the developing world. Xu, in particular, called for the establishment of a Chinese international assistance and cooperation fund that the government could use to provide loans to domestic enterprises with production surpluses to go global. Xu also saw it as a means of helping internationalize the Chinese currency, the RMB. He termed his idea a "Harmonious World Plan," and suggested $500 billion to provide aid and loans to

Africa, Asia, and Latin America.[18] Lin argued that a global infrastructure initiative would allow China's economy to continue to grow at least 8 percent for two decades. (This target has yet to be met. Instead, growth rates have steadily fallen from 7.5 percent in 2013 to 6.1 percent in 2019 to 3 percent in 2022, as a result of the COVID-19 pandemic.) The Ministry of Foreign Affairs joined the discussion as well, suggesting that Beijing could use the SCO and the ASEAN Plus Three (China, Japan, and South Korea) Framework to support the projects. But it lacked support from other parts of the government.[19] Then Chinese president Hu Jintao also embraced the idea of China spearheading a global infrastructure initiative in his speech at the 2012 Asia-Pacific Economic Cooperation summit, but it was left to his successor, Xi Jinping, to develop and realize the concept.[20]

Lurking beneath the various economic rationales were more blatantly political and security motivations. As early as 2004, almost a decade before Xi's Astana speech, PLA Air Force General Liu Yazhou wrote colorfully that China should stop "hitchhiking" with the United States. Instead, it needed to "develop its Western neighbors," "assume its role as a big country," and "give them a car that they can ride with us in."[21] Jiang Zhida, a Chinese BRI expert, describes the initiative as the "largest and most influential economic initiative in history," and argues that China should use it to increase its regional influence and security.[22] Others have suggested that the goal of the BRI should be to build a stronger alliance between China and the developing world to form a coalition that could counter the US-led Western coalition.[23]

Many observers also credit Chinese scholar Wang Jisi with helping to inspire the initiative.[24] Wang, a longtime professor at PKU, is one of China's most senior and renowned scholars of Chinese foreign policy and US–China relations. With his thick glasses, floppy hair, and unassuming demeanor, he has a balanced perspective that is welcomed equally by Chinese and Western policy communities. And, unusually for a Chinese scholar, he sat on the boards of several Western organizations, including the International Crisis Group and Teach for China. In an April 2011 *Foreign Affairs* article, Wang argued that "a more sophisticated grand strategy" was necessary to "serve China's domestic priorities."[25] Rather than confront the United States and its allies and partners which dominate East and Southeast Asia, he proposed that China should focus on its

Western neighbors and collaborate where possible with the United States. He further developed this idea in a *Global Times* opinion piece, in which he urged the Chinese leadership to "march west," building off of former Chinese leader Jiang Zemin's "Open Up the West" strategy. Articulated in 1999, this strategy encouraged China's wealthier coastal provinces to invest in the natural resource-rich but economically poorer western provinces as a means of improving the living standards in Western China and supporting growth in the coastal provinces. When I met with Wang in New York in October 2019, I asked him whether he deserved the credit for the concept behind the BRI. He modestly declined to answer, noting only that Xi Jinping had indicated that he had read some of his articles, and perhaps they had exerted some influence. Later in our discussion, Wang joked that there was no real political upside in claiming authorship of the initiative – whether a success or not, it would bring too much unwanted attention.

Getting a Piece of the Pie

The actual contours of the BRI have emerged only over time. Although its ambitions are global, the initiative retains a strong domestic rationale. The initial government team overseeing the BRI, the Leading Small Group for Advancing the Development of the "One Belt, One Road," consisted overwhelmingly of domestic experts. Only Yang Jiechi, the senior-most official in charge of foreign policy, had direct responsibility for international relations. The other senior leaders, including Zhang Gaoli, Wang Yang, Wang Huning, and Han Zheng, focused on domestic issues.[26] (One member of the committee, Yang Jing, was demoted and fired from his administrative duties for corruption in 2018.) And the NDRC officials with direct management responsibility, Ou Xiaoli and Xu Shaoshi, were experts in programs such as the development of China's western provinces and the hunt for natural resources.[27]

This domestic focus is unsurprising given the initial impetus to export overcapacity and connect interior regions of the country to external markets. Within China, as international relations scholar Ye Min describes, the BRI has served overwhelmingly as a "mobilization campaign" for state agencies: "Different government agencies inserted their policy ideas [to] make the messages in the strategy more concrete." She notes that despite the official rhetoric around the BRI that stressed a foreign policy strategy or globalization vision, the Ministry of Foreign Affairs and the Ministry of Commerce have played relatively small roles. Instead, the NDRC took the lead through a series of documents, such as "Industrial Capacity Cooperation Three-Year Planning." Ye describes these documents as "vague and non-obligatory" but they ensured that the NDRC's domestic agenda was firmly entrenched in the BRI. In addition, the NDRC directed other ministries and local governments to produce BRI Plans. By the end of 2015, 32 provinces and more than 10 ministries had produced BRI plans that referenced NDRC priorities. For example, the Ministry of Finance proposed reforming energy and financial insurance for outwardly investing companies; the Chinese Customs Bureau adopted over a dozen new measures to improve international trade; and the State Administration of Foreign Exchange pledged to ensure returns on BRI investments and support BRI projects with foreign exchange reserves.[28]

The NDRC initially identified four provinces as priority BRI core areas – Fujian, Xinjiang, Guangxi, and Yunnan – but only Fujian, the wealthiest, appeared in the top five Chinese provinces to participate in the initiative. Some localities were excluded initially and had to spend significant time and energy pushing their way into the plan.[29] In addition, as Lancaster University professor Zeng Jinghan has noted, domestic actors "take advantage of the BRI to advance their own interests rather than the wider geopolitical interests of the entirety of China."[30] Ningbo, a major port city in wealthy Zhejiang province, used its money to sponsor a goods exhibition; and in Wenzhou, another port city in Zhejiang, the local government used its BRI money to host an expo in Europe.[31]

State-owned enterprises (SOEs) such as COSCO, the China Communications Construction Company, and the China Merchants Group were quick to see the benefits of the BRI. In a 2017 poll of 569 SOE and private companies, most Chinese firms praised the BRI's potential for expanding foreign markets and increasing value chain integration. Almost half of the SOEs also thought it would help them export overcapacity. SOEs were clearly more prepared to dive into the BRI than their private enterprise counterparts – about 60 percent of SOE managers said that they were planning to pursue investment opportunities while only 35 percent of non-SOE officials responded the same way – with joint ventures being the most skeptical within that group. Nonetheless, both SOEs and private companies expressed some reservations about their own lack of knowledge about host countries' investment environment, and the potential for political instability in some countries.[32]

Money, Money, Money

In late March 2015, the NDRC, along with the Ministry of Foreign Affairs and the Ministry of Commerce, released an overview of the BRI, "Vision and Actions on Jointly Building the Silk Road Economic Belt and the 21st-Century Maritime Silk Belt," which clarified the initial geographic boundaries of the BRI as stretching from China to the Baltics, the Persian Gulf, the Mediterranean Sea, and the Indian Ocean. The Maritime Silk Road began from China's southern coastal ports and extended through the Indian Ocean, Europe, and the Pacific. There were six land corridors – five extending west and one extending south, including the China–Mongolia–Russia Economic Corridor, the New Eurasian Land Bridge, the China–Central Asia–West Asia Economic Corridor, the China–Indochina Peninsula Economic Corridor, the China–Pakistan Economic Corridor, and the Bangladesh–China–India–Myanmar Economic Corridor, and three sea corridors. Since then, Beijing has added a Polar Silk Road to connect Europe to the Arctic, as well as a Space Information Corridor. Eventually, Xi invited all countries to participate in the BRI. By 2020, 140 countries had signed on in some form to the initiative.

As an economic development initiative, Belt and Road is both more and less than Chinese statements suggest. The World Bank, for example, has noted that if implemented with best practices, the BRI could increase trade by between 2.8 and 9.7 percent for the corridor economies, increase global real income by 0.7–2.9 percent (not including the cost of infrastructure investment), and lift 7.6 million people from extreme poverty (less than $1.90 per day in purchasing power parity) and 32 million people from moderate poverty (a purchasing power parity of less than $3.20 per day).[33]

But an actual accounting of the BRI, including the number of projects and amount of investment, remains challenging. A study by the private consultancy Refinitiv suggests that as of August 2020, there were more than 2,900 projects underway.[34] But many observers have noted that included in such accountings are projects that began before the launch of the BRI or have nothing to do with infrastructure connectivity.[35] For example, the highly touted $4 billion, 460-mile railway from the Port of Djibouti to Addis Ababa, Ethiopia, was inaugurated on January 1, 2018, but actually started in 2011, two years prior to the BRI's establishment. Other projects bear only a tangential relationship to the objectives of the BRI, such as casinos in Cambodia.[36] And still other projects are announced and later canceled.[37]

The actual level of investment by China in the BRI is also a mystery. China has pledged $1 trillion in funding to help address the $26 trillion in developing Asia's infrastructure needs.[38] Many reports, however, conflate Chinese investment and lending. Total announced lending between 2013 and 2020, according to RWR Advisory, totaled $461 billion.[39] The level of investment is much smaller. In early 2020, China's Ministry of Commerce reported that completed BRI infrastructure projects represented $74.61 billion in investment and that its 2019 investment in BRI for the first 11 months totaled $12.78 billion,[40] reflecting approximately 12.9 percent of overall Chinese foreign direct investment (FDI). Chinese Ministry of Commerce data indicate that Chinese non-FDI in BRI countries averaged approximately 13 percent of overall Chinese FDI, peaking in 2016.[41] The majority of Chinese overseas investment is dedicated to acquiring companies with leading-edge technologies and know-how in Europe and the United States.[42]

Bumps in the Road

Speaking at an international emerging markets forum in 2019, senior Ministry of Finance official Zhang Wencai heralded the BRI as an "international public good." Sensitive to the criticism that the initiative is about realizing Chinese economic or security interests, the Chinese government is committed to selling the BRI as a global initiative with global participation.[43] Such a narrative has become particularly important as Belt and Road has become increasingly bumpy. By value, an estimated 32 percent of BRI projects have encountered difficulties with the host countries.[44] The country's lack of transparency in deal-making, rapidly rising levels of debt in some host countries, and problems around

Chinese environmental and labor practices have produced widespread dissatisfaction. The BRI is a vehicle by which China exports its own development model, with its priority on rapid infrastructure development. But alongside that come the externalities of the model as well. The only significant difference is that other countries do not hold their own debt, as China did. Instead, their debt is held by China.

Let Me In

The lack of transparency and broader societal engagement in BRI deal-making often contributes to corruption and efforts to renegotiate or cancel projects when new leaders come to power. In 2018, after reviewing the terms of BRI deals signed by his predecessor, for example, Malaysian prime minister Mahathir Mohamad canceled two BRI pipeline projects: only 13 percent of the construction had been completed while 90 percent of the project had been paid for. But after attempting to cancel the East Coast Rail Link, which is designed to connect the west and east coasts of Peninsular Malaysia, Mahathir announced in April 2019 that the project would resume. Canceling it would have resulted in a $5.3 billion termination penalty – a detail in the original contract that had not been made public.[45] In discussing the projects, Mahathir stated, "Such stupidity has never been seen before in the history of Malaysia."[46] Former Tanzanian president John Magufuli likely would have recognized the sentiment. In 2019, he canceled the construction of the country's first electric railway line and the $10 billion Bagamoyo port project that had been inked during Xi Jinping's 2013 visit to the country. He called the terms of the deals, which had been agreed to by his predecessor, Jakaya Kikwete, "exploitative and awkward" and said they "would only be accepted by mad people." The terms included a 99-year lease, an agreement that Tanzania would not have control over who invested in the port after it became operational, and a ban on any further port development along a significant stretch of the country's coastline.[47]

The lack of transparency can also mask a significant bias in the bidding process in favor of Chinese companies. Despite nominally being open to participation by firms from other countries, BRI projects often rely exclusively on Chinese companies (and Chinese labor). In the construction of BRI infrastructure, for example, 89 percent of the work is done by Chinese firms, 7.6 percent by local firms, and 3.4 percent by international firms. For non-BRI projects, the allocation is radically different: 29 percent is Chinese, 41 percent is local, and 30 percent is international.[48] The World Bank's analysis supports such findings, noting that almost two-thirds of BRI projects are undertaken by Chinese companies.[49] A BRI survey of member companies by the European Union Chamber of Commerce in China released in early 2020 reinforces the sense that inequities are baked into the system. The survey revealed that transparency was the number one challenge the companies confronted. More than half of the companies reported that they were not provided with enough information to make bids, and almost 40 percent said that the procurement systems for BRI projects were not transparent. Importantly, they noted they did not confront these issues of transparency in other international bidding processes.[50]

Paying the Piper

The vast majority of Chinese money flowing through Belt and Road takes the form of loans. China is the world's largest official creditor – larger than the World Bank, the International Monetary Fund (IMF), and the economies of the Organization for Economic Cooperation and Development combined.[51] However, while the large multilateral banks lend at below-market rates, China often charges market or above-market rates and requires collateral such as oil or other resources.[52] Between 2000 and 2017, developing countries' debt to China increased ten-fold from less than $500 billion to more than $5 trillion.[53]

An early report by Moody's revealed that more than 60 percent of BRI partner countries are rated below investment grade or not rated by the ratings agency. And a study by scholars at the Center for Global Development assessed the risk of debt distress in 68 potential BRI borrowers and found roughly half were at risk, and eight were at high risk of debt distress. The problem is compounded when one considers a finding by economists Sebastian Horn, Carmen Reinhart, and Christoph Trebesch that there is a systematic underreporting of Chinese loans, creating a "hidden debt" problem. Since China does not produce an official report detailing its lending, the researchers constructed their own database from publicly available material and found that for the

50 developing country recipients, the average stock of debt owed to China jumped from less than 1 percent of debtor country GDP in 2005 to more than 15 percent in 2017. Twelve countries owe debt of at least 20 percent of their GDP to China.[54] The World Bank, for its part, indicated that 12 of the 43 low- and middle-income countries for which data are available would realize a deterioration in their medium-term outlook for debt sustainability – even if the BRI investment boosted growth.[55]

For some countries, the issue of debt sustainability is not an abstraction. In Montenegro, for example, a highway connecting the Port of Bar to Serbia caused the country's debt-to-GDP ratio to soar to almost 80 percent. A study of 10 BRI projects found six – in Vanuatu, Indonesia, Myanmar, Tajikistan, Pakistan, and Hungary – that would not generate sufficient revenue to justify the cost.[56] Countries such as Mongolia and Azerbaijan also face the prospect of infrastructure projects whose gains will be exceeded by the costs.[57] In a few high-profile cases, countries are forced to transfer resources to service their debt. The most highly publicized case is that of Sri Lanka, in which the country could not service its debt and, instead, granted China a 99-year lease on its Hambantota port. And in Ecuador, a massive BRI dam project is not only environmentally unsustainable but also requires the country to turn over 80 percent of its oil exports to China for at least five years. After amassing almost $20 billion in Chinese loans, the small country began to seek assistance from the international community to pay off or buy out Chinese debt.[58] In Zambia, China's Civil Engineering Construction Corporation has sought to take control over Zambian mining assets as debt collateral.[59] China's demand that the Zambian government give preference to Chinese creditors – who hold approximately one-third of Zambia's debt – by paying arrears owed to them first has made other creditors less inclined to extend additional bailout support to the African country.[60]

The COVID-19 pandemic has further weakened many countries' economies and complicated the financial sustainability of BRI projects. In 2022, the World Bank assessed that of the $35 billion that the world's 74 lowest-income countries will owe in debt service payments, 37 percent is owed to China. Horn, Reinhart, and Trebesch suggest that in order for debt relief to be meaningful for these countries, China must be transparent about the terms of its debt relief and coordinate with the other major debt holders, including the Paris Club governments, the World Bank, the IMF, and private investors, all of whom are already coordinating their responses.[61] A report by Rhodium Group revealed that as of September 2020, 12 countries were attempting to negotiate repayment with Beijing of BRI loans totaling $28 billion. The report further noted that "As many as one in four dollars extended by China through overseas lending to date has come under renegotiation, amounting to $94 billion." Overall, the Rhodium researchers found that Beijing was most prone to defer loans with a grace period, as opposed to forgive them or look for a debt-for-equity swap,[62] as in Zambia. Even when China has forgiven part of a country's debt, the amount is rarely consequential. In South Sudan, for example, China forgave $160 million of debt; the total amount due to it, however, was $6.5 billion.[63] By the end of 2020, reports surfaced that Beijing itself was considering reducing the scale of its BRI lending, due in part to the challenge it confronts in these debt renegotiations.

It's Not Easy Being Green

Xi Jinping has frequently reiterated his commitment to "greening the BRI," and there is some evidence of new thinking along these lines. In November 2020, I participated in a set of discussions with Latin American officials and China experts, in which a Brazilian official relayed that COFCO, China's massive state-owned agriculture and food processing company, was pursuing the development of a process for tracking all soybeans to ensure that they were being grown sustainably. The Brazilian officials were also enthusiastic at the prospect that partnership with China on the environment and innovation could be transformative for both Brazil and the rest of the world on issues like climate change.[64] More often, however, countries report that BRI-related infrastructure projects ignore environmental impacts. According to the World Bank, many BRI corridors pass through ecologically vulnerable areas, and projects may have noticeable negative impacts on pollution, illegal logging, and wildlife trade. According to a 2017 report on Chinese firms engaged in BRI, 58 percent of Chinese companies doing business in BRI countries have never published a corporate social responsibility or sustainability report.[65]

Even as Xi Jinping attempts to position China as a climate leader, as much as 39 percent of China's overseas energy investment in 2019 was in coal projects.[66] Chinese corporations had investments planned or under-way in 102 coal-fired power plants with a price tag of $35.9 billion. The plants are peppered all throughout the BRI corridors, in countries such as Vietnam, South Africa, Pakistan, Mozambique, Brazil, the United Arab Emirates, and Indonesia, among others.

China's zeal for promoting coal plants, however, faced a growing popular backlash in many BRI countries. A 2019 survey by the environmental group E3G revealed that in six countries – Indonesia, Pakistan, the Philippines, South Africa, Turkey, and Vietnam – less than one-third of those polled supported new coal projects, while upwards of 85 percent favored investment in renewables.[67] When Xi Jinping first introduced the BRI in 2013, Kenya had no coal-fired power plants. It relied almost exclusively on renewable energy. Yet in that year, the Kenyan and Chinese governments agreed to construct a $2 billion coal-fired power plant on the island of Lamu, off Kenya's northern coast. The island is a UNESCO World Heritage Site, with both historic architecture and culture and spectacular natural beauty. UNESCO's World Heritage Committee warned Kenya that the plant would threaten the heritage site's status.[68]

The environmental implications were significant. It would have increased Kenya's greenhouse gas emissions by 700 percent, risked the UNESCO site certification, and threatened local fish and wildlife.[69] Acid rain could also harm the stone buildings of Lamu's old town, which date to the 14th century. In addition, the US-based Institute for Energy Economics and Financial Analysis estimated that the cost of the electricity could be as much as 10 times that projected by the project's supporters because the latter underestimated the price of coal imports and operational costs.[70]

Six years later, in July 2019, Kenya's National Environmental Tribunal suspended the project, ruling that the authorities had not undertaken a thorough environmental impact assessment and that the local people had not been adequately consulted. Kenyan and Chinese authorities were understandably unhappy.[71] However, the Chinese ambassador to Kenya pledged to help talk the Chinese partner out of the project if the government did not want to pursue it. At the same time, he sought to place responsibility on the shoulders of the Kenyan government, noting: "We are guests and you [Kenyans] the host. What we can do in a sovereign state like Kenya is only under your request."

Despite funding from the Chinese government, he further claimed that the project was "a private investment."[72] Kenya is not alone in reconsidering its BRI energy commitments. In 2020, Egypt, Bangladesh, and Pakistan all canceled China-funded coal-fired power plants. And there are signs that China is beginning to listen. In 2020, the share of renewable energy (including hydropower) made up 57 percent of China's total energy infrastructure investment.[73] And in September 2021, Xi Jinping announced that China would no longer build coal fired power projects abroad.[74]

Two Steps Forward – One Step Back

China's engagement with Pakistan provides insight into both the promises and the pitfalls of the BRI. The China–Pakistan Economic Corridor (CPEC) is one of Beijing's most important initiatives within Belt and Road. The original CPEC agreement, inked in 2015, represented $46 billion in new infrastructure, including roads, railways, and energy projects that would link China's Xinjiang Uyghur Autonomous Region with Pakistan's Gwadar port, which is strategically located on the Arabian Sea. But by 2020, CPEC's price tag had jumped to $62 billion. Beijing also took on the financing of the $2 billion Gwadar port project after Pakistan failed to raise the required 15 percent contribution.[75] By 2020, $25.5 billion worth of projects had been completed – about one-quarter of the 122 announced projects – 75 percent of which were tied to energy.

After coming to power in August 2018, Prime Minister Imran Khan and his party had promised to improve transparency around CPEC and its financing. A "Committee for Power Sector Audit," for example, found that two Chinese power companies had inflated their bills by more than $200 million.[76] The structure of the deals has also raised concerns. Under the terms of China's energy investment, for instance, Beijing would construct and operate the plants and receive the revenues, with Pakistan guaranteeing uninterrupted payments to Chinese companies. The CPEC projects also required Pakistan to import Chinese machinery and Chinese labor.[77] Moreover, despite the close ties between the two countries, the Export–Import Bank of China's loans provided to Pakistan were at near-commercial rates, well above the rates of the

IMF and World Bank.[78] Consequently, in 2019, Pakistan took out a $6 billion IMF loan package to address its growing fiscal deficits and external loan repayments.[79]

While Prime Minister Khan has maintained public support for CPEC, new projects and implementation of projects already on the books slowed during 2018–19. Pakistani journalist Adnan Aamir reported that in 2019, the government of Pakistan had cut funding for CPEC, including for power generation projects and the New Gwadar International Airport, by 60 percent. Aamir suggests several reasons for the decision by the Pakistani leadership: it was required to cut down government expenditures in order to receive a $6 billion bailout package from the IMF; the Khan government does not share the same enthusiasm for the CPEC as the previous Sharif government; and the share of Pakistani as opposed to Chinese money in the projects has grown well beyond the expectations of the Pakistani government, which understood that China would bear far more of the up-front costs.[80] In a December 2019 interview in the *Financial Times*, Sakib Sherani, former advisor to the Pakistani finance minister, commented on the massive suite of BRI projects to which Pakistan had committed: "There is a disconnect. CPEC-related debt eventually must generate enough exports to be able to deal with the repayments."[81] In addition, some sectors of Pakistani civil society called for the decision-making process and CPEC agreements themselves to be made transparent – something Beijing reportedly resisted.[82]

Concern is also growing on China's side. In 2015, the PLA National Defense University sponsored a symposium in which much of the discussion centered on the importance of the PLA in managing the BRI's security risks. These included risks for Chinese companies involved in BRI projects and broader challenges related to maintaining political and social stability in some BRI countries. Xi Jinping himself has placed a high priority on the role of security, noting in an August 2018 speech to mark the fifth anniversary of the BRI, "High attention must be paid to forestalling risks overseas" and "every effort must be made to comprehensively improve capacity to respond to overseas safety and risks."[83] Such caution is well placed. In Pakistan, for example, the area around the Gwadar port has experienced a number of violent attacks against Chinese workers,[84] prompting the Khan government to deploy a special security division of more than 13,000 troops to protect the port and other CPEC projects.[85]

In January 2021, Beijing called for a joint parliamentary oversight committee to enhance control over CPEC projects. Many observers viewed this move as a sign of Beijing's unhappiness with the continued security issues surrounding the Gwadar Port, the pace and quality of the projects, and the rising level of Pakistani debt.[86] Given Beijing's economic and political investment in CPEC as a flagship BRI project, it cannot afford for it to fail.

Keeping Pakistan in the BRI family also provides China with an important partner in South Asia and a counterweight to India. Moreover, through the port at Gwadar, China gains an outlet to the Arabian Sea and the ability to avoid the Strait of Malacca, a strategic chokepoint. Pakistan has leased the port to the China Overseas Port Holding Company until 2057, and the Chinese firm will earn a 91 percent share of the revenue from the operations of the port.[87] While the economic implications are significant, the real prize for Beijing may be the opportunity in the future to transform Gwadar into a naval base as part of a broader effort to become a dominant naval power in the Indo-Pacific.

Securing Ourselves

In 2004, the American consultancy firm Booz Allen Hamilton predicted that China would seek to expand its military into the Indian Ocean by building maritime civilian infrastructure in the region, the so-called "string of pearls," in order to compete with India and the United States for energy resources and regional dominance. While many observers dismissed this assessment as fanciful, 17 years later, China's Belt and Road has given life to the concept. The PLA has indeed become deeply involved in the development, and in some cases management and ownership, of numerous ports at strategic points around the Indian and Pacific Oceans. While most are commercial ports, several could also serve a military role, raising questions concerning Beijing's ultimate intentions in capitals throughout the world (see Map 4.1).

Few issues associated with the BRI – with the exception of debt sustainability – have stirred as much interest as whether China will use the BRI to develop a system of naval bases in support of the Maritime Silk Road. When China opened its first overseas logistics base in Djibouti in July 2017, it was quick to reassure that it was a "support base," not a

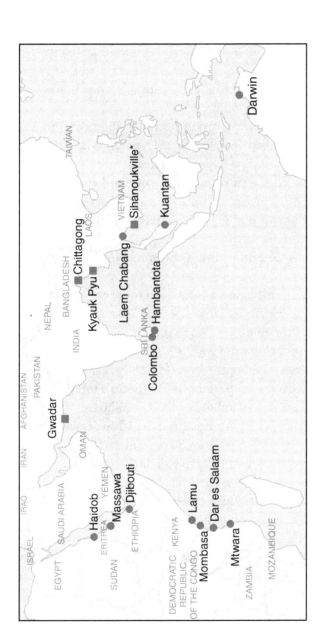

Key

■ Part of the original "string of pearls"   ● Additional ports

*The original "string of pearls" envisioned a canal in Cambodia that would bypass the Strait of Malacca. Sihanoukville is a port.

Map 4.1   China's port construction and investments across the Indian Ocean

Sources: https://merics.org/en/analysis/mapping-belt-and-road-initiative-where-we-stand; http://country.eiu.com/ article.aspx?articleid=1125980496&Country=China&topic=China&topic=Economy&subtopic=Regional%2Bdevelopments& subsubtopic=Investment

"military outpost built to boost the country's military presence."[88] At the same time, once the Djibouti base was in operation, some experts at the PLA Naval Command College stated that the construction of overseas bases would likely provide the "most effective strategic assistance" to China's armed forces in "going out." And they further noted that it was "an inevitable choice in order to realize the dream of a great power and the dream of building a powerful military."[89]

The Djibouti base, along with major port development projects in Kenya, Pakistan, Sri Lanka, Bangladesh, Myanmar, Malaysia, and Cambodia, defines the contours of China's Maritime Silk Road. Senior military officers acknowledge that in order to safeguard the Maritime Silk Road, "the PLA Navy needs to gain the capability to act globally, which means more overseas logistic bases will also be needed." Major General (ret.) Xu Guangyu, for example, has opined that China "will need at least 10 to 20 ports around the world in all oceans and continents."[90]

Beijing is indeed on a port-buying spree. China owns or has a stake in nearly two-thirds of the world's 50 largest ports.[91] Asia security scholar Mohan Malik has detailed Beijing's moves to acquire long-term leases on strategic ports, including Pakistan's Gwadar port for 40 years, Greece's Piraeus port for 35 years, Djibouti's port for 10 years, Sri Lanka's Hambantota port for 99 years, 20 percent of Cambodia's total coastline for 99 years, and the Maldivian island of Feydhoo Finolhu for 50 years.[92] In addition, Beijing is pressuring Myanmar to raise China's stake in the Kyaukpyu port on the Bay of Bengal from 50 percent to 75–85 percent, and to lease it for 99 years, as well in exchange for Myanmar avoiding a $3 billion penalty for reneging on the Myitsone dam deal.[93] Eight of the ports managed by Chinese SOEs are deep-water ports and, of these, Gwadar, Oman's Salalah, and the Seychelles ports could all be converted into naval bases. According to Shanghai Jiaotong University scholar Xue Guifang, "In countries where it enjoys close ties to the host country, China may gradually select some overseas commercial ports for dual use to project power."[94]

Chinese security analysts present an overwhelmingly favorable view of the relationship between China's growing trade and investment networks and its military expansionism. Renmin University scholars Li Qingsi and Chen Chunyu for example, claim that "building bases on the key maritime transport hubs has already become a strategic choice that increasingly requires urgent action." They further note that while US bases "serve hegemonic policies," Chinese bases will serve "defense capacities . . . to prevent terrorist attacks." China will not, they argue, "walk the old road of Western great powers."[95] One of the most overt statements of PRC intentions is voiced by three analysts at the PLA's Institute of Military Transportation, who penned an essay in which they argued: "To protect our ever-growing overseas interests, we will progressively establish in Pakistan, United Arab Emirates, Sri Lanka, Myanmar, Singapore, Indonesia, Kenya and other countries a logistical network based on various means, buying, renting, cooperating, to construct our overseas bases or overseas protection hubs."[96] Chinese objectives are a mix of political, economic, and military, including: war, diplomatic signaling, political change, building relationships, and providing facilities for training.[97] This logistical network will be supported by and in turn support the PLA's ability to launch and sustain overseas missions.[98]

Cambodia is also rumored to be the site of a new Chinese base. Reporting has suggested that China may already be constructing a naval base under a secret agreement.[99] In 2019, then US deputy assistant secretary of defense for South and Southeast Asia Joseph Felter warned of China's intentions after Cambodia requested, accepted, and then rejected American military aid in repairing a naval base.[100] Under the terms of the reported agreement, China would have access to the base for 30 years with automatic renewals every 10 years. Cambodia has authorized China to station military personnel, equipment, and ships at the base. Current construction plans suggest that the port will have one dock for Chinese vessels and one dock for Cambodian vessels. In responding to the report, Cambodian prime minister Hun Sen said it was "distorted news." On July 24, Chinese Defense Ministry spokesman Wu Qian said that China and Cambodia have "always carried out good exchanges and cooperation in military training . . . such cooperation does not target third parties."[101] The following week, China sold an additional $40 million worth of arms to Cambodia on top of a $290 million deal signed earlier.[102] For China, the value of a base in Cambodia would be an additional point of access to the South China Sea and, in particular, greater proximity to Vietnam,[103] which has consistently challenged Beijing's sovereignty claims in the South China Sea.

At the same time, some analysts recognize that political groundwork will need to be laid for others to accept Chinese bases. Xue Guifang and Zhen Hao, law professors at Shanghai Jiaotong University, for example, argue that China must "build an international environment that will accept [its] construction of overseas bases."[104] Xi took some initial steps in early 2019. He called for "a security guarantee system" with China's Belt and Road partners.[105] This includes land as well as maritime partners. In Tajikistan, the Chinese PLA offered to finance and construct 11 border posts and training centers along its border with Afghanistan. It maintains a small base in the Pamir mountains and routinely undertakes patrols.[106] Retired PLA officer Yue Gang has noted that Beijing has also promoted the expansion of private Chinese security firms abroad to protect its investments and workers. They are separate from but affiliated with the PLA; the objective is to avoid "the potential problems it [the PLA] might cause for foreign relations."[107]

I've Got My Eye on You

While the initial impetus for Belt and Road was connectivity via hard infrastructure, in 2015, China's Ministry of Foreign Affairs, NDRC, and Ministry of Commerce published a white paper that set out the concept of a Digital Silk Road (DSR). Speaking at a symposium on cyberspace security and informatization the next year, Xi Jinping stated, "We need to encourage our internet and IT companies to go global, to deepen international exchanges and cooperation, and to participate actively in the Belt and Road Initiative, so as to ensure that IT covers China's national interests wherever they are found."[108] In 2017, at the government's first Belt and Road Forum (BARF), Xi announced that Beijing would construct a "Digital Silk Road of the 21st Century." The concept incorporates China's desire to lead the world in "physical digital infrastructure," such as 5G cellular networks and fiber optic cables; in dual-use systems, such as satellite navigation systems and artificial intelligence; in e-commerce; and in shaping global norms regarding cyber-sovereignty.[109] The DSR signifies the global deployment of Chinese technology, standards, and political values.

Chinese technology companies are more than ready to meet the challenge. As will be explored in chapter 5, more than any other sector, China's internet and telecommunications firms are globally competitive and their brand recognition matches that of their US, Japanese, and EU rivals. Alibaba, Tencent, and Huawei are not only national champions but also global ones. In some areas, they provide technology that is cheaper, faster, and more highly integrated with other technologies than their Western counterparts. They have grown into some of the largest, most profitable corporations in the world, delivering China its first generation of billionaires. Yet despite their status as private companies, they must also be responsive to the demands of the CCP. The Party has taken financial stakes in some firms;[110] placed officials within firms to guide them politically;[111] and in some cases encouraged firms to take stakes in money-losing SOEs to bolster them.[112] In exchange for a heightened level of government intervention, the Party directly supports the companies' efforts to go abroad.[113]

The DSR includes a wide range of Chinese technology products. China is, for example, advancing its financial technology (fintech) products through the DSR. This includes mobile payment systems supported by Alibaba and Tencent, as well as technologies like blockchain and cryptocurrency. China has also piloted its own digital currency, e-CNY, and has plans to take it global to promote the internationalization of its currency. Along with its Cross-Border Interbank Payment System, the e-CNY also has the potential to help enable the Chinese government to avoid the SWIFT-based financial messaging service that the United States uses to enforce economic sanctions.

Beijing has a particular interest in providing 5G technology, which is the backbone of the next generation of critical infrastructure, such as electric grids, and enables the connection of every device with a chip – from phones to smart refrigerators and autonomous vehicles – to a single network. Chinese national champion Huawei is particularly attractive to countries looking to move into the next generation of connectivity because it is decidedly less expensive and more prepared to roll out its technology than its competitors, Ericsson and Nokia.[114] And as with the hard infrastructure component of the BRI, the DSR is a one-stop shop. Huawei is also a global leader in the development of "safe cities," which bring the internet, video surveillance cameras, cell phones with GPS location data, and biometrics into centrally managed data centers. (China began its own safe city program in 2011 with the aim of ensuring that all Chinese cities would possess state-of-the-art public security and safety capabilities by 2022.)[115]

The DSR globalizes the safe city concept and Chinese technology. Huawei claims, for example, that as part of its Safe City initiative, it has contracts with 230 cities worldwide to install software in traffic surveillance equipment and to provide hardware, including cameras and facial recognition devices.[116] (One study, however, found only 73 cities in 52 countries that had deployed the technology.)[117] The safe cities program is not without its detractors. In Pakistan, in 2017, the Punjab Safe Cities Authority in Lahore discovered that Wi-Fi transmitting cards within Huawei's surveillance system enabled Huawei engineers to access the system remotely for "troubleshooting." The cards were ultimately removed. (Other experts made it clear as well that remote access was possible without the cards, through the main network.)[118] As is explored in the following chapter, moreover, the United States argues that deploying Huawei technology will enable China to access critical information and threaten countries' grid security.[119]

Chinese companies are also playing a critical role in developing other aspects of the telecommunications infrastructure through the DSR. In 2018, Beijing granted the Chinese company StarTimes sole rights to its 10,000 Villages Project in Kenya. The project, which Xi Jinping announced in 2015, is designed to bring satellite TV – and with it the Chinese story told by China – to 10,112 villages throughout the country. Pang Xinxing, chairman of StarTimes, first traveled to Africa in 2002, well before the advent of the BRI, and quickly recognized an opportunity to provide access to digital television. By 2007, he had set up operations in Rwanda, providing citizens with more than 30 channels for $3 to $5 per month. Today the company has subsidiaries in 30 African countries and is promoting digital TV throughout the continent. In Kenya, StarTimes has 1.4 million subscribers, roughly half of all Kenya's pay-TV subscriptions. It offers an inexpensive package – just $4 per month – that features only Kenyan and Chinese channels. Kenyan airwaves are filled with kung fu films, dramas about life in China, and documentaries, such as one on Japanese atrocities in World War II, that promote a CCP narrative.[120] Most Kenyans cannot afford the more expensive packages that offer access to other international channels such as the BBC.[121]

Pang's control over both content and delivery offers Beijing an important opportunity to enhance its soft power. According to Pang, many people in Africa like Chinese television because they grew up watching

Chinese movies shown by the local Chinese embassies. His team has dubbed more than 100,000 hours of Chinese programming into local languages. And Chinese content is also becoming more sophisticated. Chinese screenwriters have realized that foreign audiences are not interested in stories about ancient imperial life but instead, as one Chinese television marketing executive noted, "simpler stories about human nature."[122] Longtime Chinese diplomat Fu Ying put it this way:

> It is imperative not only to present a narrative of how our system works, but to tell stories of the Chinese people, their joys and pains, their happiness and grief. More often than not, a simple personal story can make clear a lot of puzzles. With unvarnished accounts of people's ups and downs in life, our stories will more easily strike a chord with audiences, and communication based on Chinese culture will be more approachable and better appreciated.[123]

Or, as Fudan University professor Meng Jian suggested, "The Chinese dream will be more easily accepted by foreign audiences when it is manifested in small and touching stories."[124]

Overall, StarTimes now beams Chinese television to 10 million subscribers in 30 African countries. While much of StarTimes' success in Africa is due to Pang's vision and determination, he also has significant backing from the Chinese government. StarTimes is the only private Chinese company authorized by the Ministry of Commerce to operate in other countries' radio and television sectors.[125]

The impact of China's vast media presence and broader Chinese engagement on the average Kenyan citizen is difficult to gauge. While 65 percent of the Kenyan population viewed China positively in 2020, that reflected a drop from 76 percent in 2015. Moreover, if part of China's soft power push is designed to enhance the image of the China model, only 23 percent believe that China presents the best model for Kenya's development as opposed to 43 percent who aspire to the US model.[126] And in other countries, such as Ghana and Zambia, critics are concerned that their sovereignty has been compromised and that StarTimes could simply "black out" their televisions if it so chose.[127]

Beyond providing countries' digital infrastructure, China also offers training on how to develop laws and regulations to enhance government control over the internet. Beijing conducted a two-week training program in November 2017 for BRI countries on how to manage public opinion, including an early warning system for negative public opinion, "guiding the promotion of positive energy online," and third-party data mining related to online media. Tanzania is a pilot country for BRI capacity building around the internet. After training with Chinese officials, Tanzania began passing restrictions on the internet, closing all unregistered bloggers and websites. The government of Tanzania and the Cyberspace Administration of China also co-hosted a "new media roundtable" at which then Deputy Minister for Communications Edwin Ngonyani confirmed the government's interest in emulating China: "Our Chinese friends have managed to block such media in their country and replaced them with their home-grown sites that are safe, constructive, and popular. We aren't there yet, but while we are still using these platforms, we should guard against their misuse." He further noted that the government wanted to develop the technological skills and capability of tracking cyber criminals. If a person sends an offensive SMS or email, Ngonyani argued, the government should be able to "make arrests and bring them to justice."[128] In 2018, Tanzanian bloggers appealed a set of cyber-regulations around online content that were modeled on those of China: for example, making online forums responsible for deleting any content a regulatory body finds offensive. While many outspoken bloggers closed their sites, some resisted. Those who protested argued that while they would pay the fees for the license required by the new regulations, they would not censor their content.[129]

Other countries have also absorbed both Chinese technological and political know-how. In Uganda, Huawei helped construct a $126 million facial recognition system throughout the country as part of its Safe City initiative, including 11 monitoring centers and a hub to manage the more than 5,000 facial recognition cameras.[130] In 2018, moreover, Huawei provided technical support to Ugandan intelligence officers seeking to surveil a rising opposition politician, Bobi Wine, by helping them break into his WhatsApp group.[131] The Ugandan government was able to disrupt opposition rallies and arrest Wine and many of his supporters.[132] To supplement the technological efforts, the Ugandan government also instituted a social media tax on users of Facebook, Twitter, Instagram, YouTube, and other social media in the hopes of curtailing access to online content and communication among young people and the unemployed, who were the most likely to support Wine in the 2021 election.[133] (Wine, who was openly critical of Chinese treatment of Africans living in China during the COVID-19 epidemic, lost the highly disputed presidential election. Nonetheless, his party won 61 parliamentary seats – the most of any opposition party.) Topics that are considered taboo include the president's family, the oil sector, and presidential term limits.[134] In Zambia, a *Wall Street Journal* investigation revealed that Huawei employees were similarly active in helping the Zambian government monitor opposition groups, activists, and journalists, ultimately resulting in the arrest of pro-opposition bloggers.[135] Nor is such intervention limited to Africa. In the wake of the February 2021 military coup in Myanmar, protestors accused China of providing the military leadership with software and know-how to block the internet.

Not Everyone's a Fan

The BRI remains broadly popular among many officials in low- and middle-income economies, where Chinese investment and technical knowledge help fill a yawning gap between the desire and need for development with the financial and other capabilities available. Yet both in and outside China, three significant sources of opposition to the BRI have emerged. The first are host country citizens and officials who believe that China is taking advantage of them or presents a security risk. In late 2018, I traveled to Riga, the beautiful capital city of Latvia, which is surrounded on one side by the Baltic Sea and the other by Russia and the Republic of Belarus, and encountered a range of perspectives. When I sat down with two senior Foreign Ministry officials, they both expressed their desire for China to consider BRI projects in their country. Latvia was the first Baltic country to sign up to the BRI, and it has pushed for the idea of a final "Northern Corridor" spur to Riga as part of the transportation channel from the Pacific to the Baltic Sea. A train that could travel from the Chinese city of Yiwu to Riga in a 12-day journey in November 2016 was heralded as a milestone in cooperation. In 2016, Riga also had hosted the first 16+1 (now 14+1) Transport Ministers' Meeting, which included an agreement to establish the China–Central and Eastern European Countries secretariat on Logistics Cooperation in Riga.

While the Foreign Ministry officials saw little to no downside in expanding relations with China, other parts of the Latvian government were more skeptical. Although China is one of the top 10 exporters to Latvia, it does not rank within the top 10 destination points for Latvian exports.[136] Some trade officials expressed concern over this lopsided relationship, noting that Latvia exported $150 million to China, whereas China exported $580 million to Latvia. This, they commented, suggested that containers on the train were only full one way. Moreover, officials in Latvia's defense sector voiced disquiet about deeper engagement with China. Latvia is a NATO country, they told me, and China's growing military ties with Russia, particularly naval exercises in the Baltic, were a concern. In 2020, Latvia's Constitution Protection Bureau named China as a cyber and economic espionage threat and recommended that the government avoid "products and services" that were produced there (as well as in Russia, North Korea, and Iran).[137]

China's neighbors also often express a high degree of skepticism regarding Chinese intentions. A poll of more than 1,000 citizens throughout ASEAN member states revealed that 70 percent thought that their governments should be cautious in negotiating BRI projects to avoid unsustainable levels of debt. Less than 10 percent believed that China was a "benign and benevolent power."[138] Concerns in these countries often manifest in protests. For example, in 2019, thousands of people in northern Myanmar protested China's efforts to relaunch the previously canceled Myitsone Dam project, which would displace tens of thousands of Myanmar citizens.[139] In Vietnam, citizens spoke out against a planned BRI North–South Expressway from Hanoi to Can Tho, with critics noting that China's projects use outdated technology, "are of bad quality, don't adhere to safety standards, and create pollution."[140] In Kyrgyzstan, residents protested a long-term lease to China and successfully prevented the construction of a $275 million logistics center.[141] And in Thailand, environmental activists and locals concerned about their livelihood successfully pushed back against a proposed Chinese plan to blast and dredge parts of the Mekong so that it could be used by cargo ships sailing from China's Yunnan province to Thailand, Laos, and the rest of Southeast Asia.[142] As one Thai professor noted, "China has a tendency to make and shape outcomes on the ground as a fait accompli, and then expect others to adjust to them. This is a mistake."[143]

The second source of BRI opposition rests within China itself. Not all Chinese citizens are supportive of the BRI. Sun Wenguang, a retired professor of physics at Shandong University, wrote an open letter in July 2018 criticizing the government for sending billions of RMB and hundreds of thousands of workers abroad while problems abounded at home. His letter attracted attention worldwide.[144] During an interview on the topic with Voice of America, however, he was forcibly removed from his apartment by local public security officials.[145] Other scholars have raised concerns about the wastefulness of the BRI. Tsinghua University law professor Xu Zhangrun pointed out that while over 100 million people were still living in poverty within China, Xi persisted in spending money on countries better off than his own.[146] Such open opposition to government policy earned Xu a suspension from his position, an investigation, and a prohibition against leaving the country.[147] Even scholars who broadly support Belt and Road have raised concerns, however. Renowned scholar Zheng Yongnian cautioned that the government was including everything under the label of BRI, including "singing, calligraphy, and even mathematics." He noted that this "fatal mistake" had caused Western countries to view Belt and Road as China's attempt at global dominance.[148]

Proposed Chinese beneficiaries of the BRI also are sometimes uncertain as to the actual benefits they are receiving. The signature project in the northeast province of Heilongjiang is the two bridges that will cross the Amur River to the Russian Far East. (The bridges belong to that class of projects that had been signed up well before the BRI was launched – almost two decades earlier – but now fall under the BRI umbrella.) Despite the magnitude of the project – it boasts a price tag of $600 million – few Chinese in the area consider the bridges necessary or even support the BRI. In fact, a number of local businesspeople and officials believe that the greater connectivity might benefit national trade but will undermine their position in that trade.[149] This somewhat counterintuitive conclusion is also supported by World Bank findings that there will be significant and changing regional inequities that emerge as BRI projects come to fruition.[150]

And finally, many of the world's advanced economies believe that China's BRI poses challenges to sustainable development within host countries, as well as a competitive threat to their own global standing. The United States, Australia, Japan, and the European Union have all raised concerns about China's expanding economic, political, and military footprint. The United States, in particular, has called out China's financing of Belt and Road projects as "debt-trap diplomacy" and "predatory economics."[151] To that end, the United States established a new institution, the International Development Finance Corporation, to provide financing for multinationals from all countries to undertake high-quality infrastructure projects in the least developed economies[152] and provided $1.5 billion to deepen its political capacity building and military-to-military relations with a broad range of Asian countries through the Asia Reassurance Initiative Act.[153] The European Union, too, has put forward its own "connectivity" program with Asia[154] and expressed growing concern around the then 17+1 Initiative. The European Parliament adopted a resolution in 2018 on the EU–China relationship that called on member states to ensure that their participation in the initiative, particularly as it relates to Belt and Road, falls within the broader EU–China framework, including sensitivity to human rights, transparency, and consideration of long-term strategic EU priorities.[155] Australia and New Zealand, for their part, are concerned about China's growing economic and security footprint in the Pacific Islands and have stepped up their diplomacy and economic outreach. Australia is supporting a $1.39 billion infrastructure financing facility for the Pacific. And Japan, more than any other country, is a peer competitor to China's infrastructure leadership. Its projects in Southeast Asia, for example, total $367 billion, while China's top out at $255 billion.[156] Together, the United States, Japan, and Australia also launched a trilateral infrastructure partnership in the Indo-Pacific region in 2018 and an advisory and certification program to ensure high-quality infrastructure, the Blue Dot Network, in 2019.[157]

Trouble in Paradise

The Chinese government is well aware of the BRI's potential to encounter trouble. In part, Chinese officials worry about problems their businesses might encounter. In January 2015, the State Council's Development and Research Center released its report "One Belt, One Road: Peaceful Development's Economic Link," which identified potential challenges for the BRI, including political instability in BRI partner countries, uncoordinated international trade policies in key BRI regions, lack of funding in partner countries, and a lack of mature investment and financing platforms.[158]

As noted earlier, Chinese officials were also worried initially that the rest of the world would perceive the initiative as designed for the overwhelming benefit of China. Xi tried to assuage others' fears, touting the BRI as "not a one-man show" and not meant to "build China's own backyard."[159] The government barred Chinese scholars from publishing articles that highlighted the "grand implications of the BRI." Instead, they were tasked with focusing on specific projects or economic aspects of the initiative. And in advance of the 2017 BARF, Beijing issued a moratorium on academic conferences on Belt and Road, and a ban on sensitive topics, including highlighting the China-centric nature of the BRI, identifying connections between Muslim countries and Chinese provinces, or describing the BRI as a military plan, a solution to Chinese overcapacity, or an economic rather than a humanitarian mission.[160]

In the early stages of the BRI, Beijing appeared to have largely succeeded in promoting it as a true "win-win" initiative. At the first summit, in 2017, for example, representatives from more than 130 countries attended the forum, including 29 heads of state. Enthusiasm from international participants ran high. Projects were underway, Chinese lending flowed, and the benefits of BRI investment could be seen first-hand in countries such as Kenya and Cambodia. The forum was, from all accounts, a tremendous success.

Two years later at the second BARF, however, the tone was markedly different. Several heads of state who attended the first BARF failed to sign up for the second, including those from Turkey, Poland, Spain, Sri Lanka, Argentina, and Fiji. Moreover, Xi Jinping was on the defensive. His remarks addressed, implicitly, a range of criticisms. For example, he asserted China's commitment to a green Belt and Road, as well as "zero tolerance" for corruption. In response to criticism over the financing of BRI projects, People's Bank of China Governor Yi Gang stated that the government would develop a market-oriented financing and investment system.

According to one participant, the forum was chaotic with many participants disgruntled at their inability to speak. Moreover, Beijing had its own domestically related BRI challenges to address. In the preceding few years, a number of Chinese businesses, particularly in real estate and entertainment, such as Anbang and HNA Group, had used the rationale of the BRI to amass large, often risky holdings that had no direct relevance to the BRI. In the lead-up to the second BARF, Beijing began forcing these companies to divest from their holdings and undertook a larger rationalization of BRI projects, trying to eliminate those that had no direct relationship to the initiative.[161] It was a costly and time-consuming effort that revealed how far the BRI had gone astray.

To address critics of China's BRI debt sustainability model as practiced by the two powerhouse lending institutions behind the BRI, the Export–Import Bank of China and China Development Bank (CDB), the Chinese Ministry of Finance released a debt sustainability framework in late 2019 that was modeled on the World Bank and IMF framework. According to the Center for Global Development's Mark Plant and Scott Morris, however, the Ministry's framework is not sufficiently detailed and does not require Chinese banks to participate.[162] China also proposed a new Multilateral Center for Development Finance with 10 international organizations as partners that would focus on capacity building, project preparation, and information sharing. However, it, too, faced skepticism from outside observers, who wondered whether the initiative would truly engage other organizations.[163] China's third development bank, the AIIB, is well positioned to meet the framework conditions. However, its BRI lending is so small relative to that of CDB and the Export–Import Bank of China (slightly more than $1 billion as of 2018 compared to $100 billion in just one year for the other two banks)[164] that the actual impact of its cooperation with the new framework would be negligible.

The Chickens Come Home to Roost

Four years after the second BARF, there are few indications of real change in China's Belt and Road development and governance practices. Eighty-five percent of the BRI's projects reportedly involve high emissions of the greenhouse gas carbon dioxide (CO_2), and despite an expansion in clean energy projects, there has been no slowdown in the construction of coal-fired power plants.[165] A 2020 poll of over 1,300 Southeast Asian business and public sector elites revealed that almost two-thirds had "little or no confidence" that Beijing's "new approach" would yield anything positive for their countries. Even elites in some of China's closest partners, Laos and Cambodia, were skeptical.[166] Support for the BRI within the grouping of smaller European nations, the 17+1, also diminished. An April 2020 report by the China Observers in Central and Eastern Europe group noted that over the course of the BRI, the trade deficit with China had increased for every member of the 17+1 group. In addition, despite the hype and promise of BRI investment, most countries have received minimal Chinese FDI, with the exception of Hungary, the Czech Republic, Slovakia, and Poland.[167] And even as Beijing continues to strengthen its political ties with the more authoritarian member states, such as Belarus and Hungary, the democratic members of the group are becoming more cautious in their engagement with China, seeking to ensure a balance between Chinese investment and broader political and/or security interests that are more closely aligned with the European Union and United States. The February 2021 17+1 summit was widely regarded as a failure: there was no final consensus document and six member countries failed to send their top leaders. Lithuania exited the framework entirely in June, and one year later, in August 2022, Estonia and Latvia also dropped from the group.

This Is Not the Hotel California

As I sat in the small, non-descript office of Greece's first national security advisor, Vice Admiral Alexandros Diakopoulos, I started to laugh. The vice admiral had graciously agreed to spend some time with me discussing Greece's relationship with China. In response to my question concerning Greece's participation in the 17+1 framework, he responded, "This is not the Hotel California." It was a clever reference to the Eagles' song by the same name, whose lyrics include, "You can check out any time you like, but you can never leave." Diakopoulos, who has since stepped down from his position, pointed out to me that there is no harm in participating in the group: "It commits Greece to nothing, and it [Greece] can always leave. There was no debate over joining; everyone wanted to do it. And the engagement is on our terms. But Greece is a small country, and it needs foreign investment." *Kathimerini*'s Tom Ellis concurs, stating, "Greece needs investment. I would have preferred it to come from Western countries, but as many US and European companies are assessing the prospects, it would be unfair to make Greece wait. Whoever comes is welcome. If it helps their strategic interests, well, that is their business."

In fact, since China's 2016 Piraeus investment, the two countries have expanded their cooperation, albeit in fits and starts. In November 2019, Xi Jinping traveled to Greece to firm up relations with the new prime minister, Kyriakos Mitsotakis, who himself had just returned from a trip to Shanghai, where Xi had suggested that Greece could become a "logistics center for transshipment of western-bound Chinese goods." The conservative government approved $67 million in Chinese investments that had been frozen for 18 months. Together, the Greek and Chinese leaders plan to make Piraeus the biggest port in Europe.[168] Already an estimated 10 percent of Chinese exports to Europe transit through Piraeus. Athens quickly offered its support for COSCO's pledge of new investment, which Xi called "the dragon's head," referencing the comment by Chinese ambassador Zou to Varoufakis several years prior. As much as $660 million will be dedicated to the further development of Piraeus. Yet China's ambitions are much greater. It is looking to expand its investments in energy, transportation, and banking. And Beijing has been careful not to overplay its hand. Unlike in some countries, where the Chinese presence is highly visible, that is not the case in Greece. When I visited the Port of Piraeus, I was struck, above all, at the lack of a Chinese presence. The main port entrance was marked by only a small sign that gave equal weight to COSCO and the Greek port organization.

At one level, Prime Minister Mitsotakis increasingly appears to see Greece's future as tied to that of China. In conversation with COSCO chairman Xu Lirong, he said, "Your company and China as a whole believed and invested in my country when many felt that investment prospects in Greece were nonexistent." And a week later when meeting with Xi Jinping, he said, "Now that our country is developing again, it is regaining a leading role, a leading position, not only in our broader neighborhood but also in Europe as a whole. We are not merely partners. We are broadening our common goals."[169] China has also been particularly effective in its diplomacy. In several of my discussions with Greek officials, they pointed to China's efforts to woo Greece by framing the relationship as one of "two ancient civilizations," a notion that appeals to a small country with great pride in the contributions of its ancient past.

China also sent a highly effective and well-liked ambassador to Greece, Zhang Qiyue, who has avoided the diplomatic firestorms ignited by some of her colleagues in other European countries.

Yet there was also evidence of increasing conflict between the two countries over the Piraeus investment. As the August 2021 deadline for China to realize its increased stake in the port approached, the Greek government asserted that Beijing had not yet secured the appropriate permits to expand the port's capacity as mandated by the 2016 agreement. At the same time, the Mitsotakis government was reportedly reluctant to grant new licenses because of significant public opposition, particularly from Greek workers. An article in *Kathimerini* detailed nine separate issues of contention between COSCO and various Greek actors, such as COSCO's desire to obtain a license to establish and operate a shipyard, which would relegate local shipbuilders to subcontractors. The construction of a new cruise pier also stalled in the face of substantial public opposition.[170] And in March 2022, the Council of State, Greece's highest court, stayed—at least temporarily—China's expansion of the port due to the failure of COSCO to undertake the necessary environmental impact assessment. As China scholar Plamen Tonchev told me, the atmosphere in Piraeus is "toxic," with references to COSCO as "the Chinese emperor."

Mitsotakis's aspirations for Greece as a leader within Europe, particularly within the Balkans, as well as its relationship with the United States, are also contributing to a recalibration of the country's policy toward China. National Security Advisor Diakopoulos made clear to me the importance of Greece's history as a naval power, its position within NATO, and its desire to lead within the Balkans. He pointed out that Greece, not COSCO and China, retained the right to grant the PLA a port visit. And there was no question of Greece's commitment to NATO: "Greece will always have good relations with the United States; the rules-based international order depends on the United States, and Greece is its natural ally." Still, Diakopoulos reiterated, "Greece cannot afford to alienate any major power. It is small and weak. China is very far away, and Greece does not have the same threat perception of China that the United States does."

Kostas Fragogiannis, Greece's deputy minister of foreign affairs for economic diplomacy and openness, stressed to me that while the port had been transformed, it was employing significant numbers of Greeks (not Chinese, as is the case in some countries), and there had been no compromise of either Greece's security or values. A highly successful businessman before assuming the position in the Ministry of Foreign Affairs, Fragogiannis reminded me that democracy was born in Greece. When I asked him about Greece's vote on Xinjiang – in October 2019, Greece again refused to join the majority of European Union member states in condemning China's policies toward the Uyghur Muslim population in Xinjiang[171] – however, he deferred to an assistant and asked her to look into the situation.

He was on firmer ground when I asked him about Greece's inclination concerning the deployment of Huawei technology in the country's 5G network. By February 2020, Huawei already had two 5G pilot programs underway: one in Trikala, in the mountainous area of central Greece, and one in the seaside town of Kalamata. In addition, the company had been deeply invested in Greece for 15 years and held 50 percent of the telecommunications equipment market.[172] Fragogiannis's response was somewhat cryptic. He stated that Greece would never compromise European values or the security of its friends and allies. Yet it was also important to save face for "other parties." In March 2020, Greece's largest telecoms provider, COSMOTE, announced that it had picked Sweden's Ericsson for its 5G network.[173]

The role of Greece's relationship with the United States is increasingly shaping the China–Greece partnership, as the United States ramps up its diplomacy and economic outreach. The US ambassador to Greece Geoff Pyatt, a career diplomat, has been energetic in his efforts to strengthen the bilateral relationship, including ensuring that the United States was the honored country for the 2018 Thessaloniki International Fair. Pyatt developed the American Pavilion, seeking company participation from many of the United States' iconic Silicon Valley firms. The Pavilion featured social influencers from around the world as part of a digital influencers' hub, while another event brought US companies, such as Google, Cisco, Microsoft, and Pfizer, to an innovation hub. Pyatt noted to me that no other country had done anything like that previously. Pyatt has also encouraged a more robust level of engagement among senior Greek and American leaders. Secretary of State Pompeo traveled to Greece in early October 2019 to upgrade military ties between the two NATO allies. The two countries signed a new agreement that permits the United States to expand its deep-water naval base on Crete and to construct facilities for helicopter pilots and bases for drones. In addition, there will be a new naval and air force base in Alexandroupolis. The US Congress further passed the EastMed Act, which will increase US military training for Greek soldiers and funding for military equipment. Moreover, Pompeo supported Greece's claims that Turkish drilling in the Mediterranean and Aegean Seas in waters recognized as Cypriot was "unacceptable." Mitsotakis, in turn, stood by Washington's decision to assassinate Iranian Brigadier General Qasem Soleimani, noting, "We are allies with the US, so we stand by our allies through difficult times."[174]

In September 2020, US officials were back in Greece. This time, US International Development Finance Corporation head Adam Boehler had traveled to meet with the prime minister and signal American interest in investing in Greece's second largest shipyard in Elefsina, a mere eight miles from Piraeus; US companies have also expressed a desire to take controlling stakes in the Alexandroupoli port near the US base. And both China's senior-most foreign affairs official, Yang Jiechi, and Secretary Pompeo paid visits to Greece that same month – Yang to encourage progress on COSCO's effort to expand its stake in Piraeus and Pompeo to sign Greece up to the US-led Clean Network to ensure a trustworthy and secure telecommunications infrastructure,[175] confirming Greece's decision not to work with Huawei and to limit exposure to the broader array of "untrusted" technologies provided by "malign actors, such as the CCP."[176] For its part, Greece is now the proud home to the USS *Hershel Williams*, one of the US Navy's largest warships.

For the moment, Greece, a country of not even 11 million people, seems comfortable being courted and wooed by the world's two superpowers and anxious to avoid choosing sides. One member of parliament seemed to signal that, in the end, Greece's interests lay with the United States: "We appreciate the Chinese investment in Greece ... but of course our relationship with the US is very long, very historic, very important, and multifaceted because it includes a vibrant Greek diaspora in America. Like many other countries in Europe, we have welcomed the Chinese investment but . . . not at the cost of the Atlantic orientation."[177] Nonetheless, as former Tsipras government official Kalpadakis noted, "Piraeus put in the head of the dragon – not only the head but the whole body."

Conclusion

The BRI is an exquisite manifestation of Xi Jinping's dream of the "great rejuvenation of the Chinese nation." It positions China at the center of the international system, with physical, financial, cultural, technological, and political influence flowing out to the rest of the world. It redraws the fine details of the world's map with new railways and bridges, fiber optic cables and 5G, and ports with the potential for military bases. And it is a platform for sharing political values through capacity building on internet governance, safe cities, and media content. China has tried to portray the BRI as a multilateral arrangement and global initiative. Yet the reality is something quite different. It is a collection of often opaque bilateral agreements signed under a Chinese framework notion. The Belt and Road Forums further enhance the impression of Chinese centrality: heads of state travel to China to seek deals as supplicants to China. Even groups such as the 14+1 encourage small and middle-sized countries to compete with each other for Chinese favor rather than to unite around a common negotiating position.

The BRI has the potential to raise incomes globally and to bring much-needed investment to countries that otherwise have found it difficult to modernize their infrastructure. Some countries, such as Pakistan, are being transformed by the BRI, with new energy projects, roads, railways, a massive upgrading of both its Gwadar port and its digital infrastructure. The Port of Piraeus has become one of the top ports in Europe and ranked within the top 50 in the world. Greek officials are understandably bullish on their BRI investments. Officials in Brazil likewise view the BRI as an opportunity to partner with China on a wide range of initiatives, such as infrastructure, innovation, and sustainability. They express an enthusiasm, as well, for China's willingness to "listen" to what countries want and need.

At the same time, BRI host countries often reflect doubts over the externalities that accompany BRI funding: opaque deal-making, rising environmental degradation and pollution, and limited attention to social impact concerns. The lack of transparency in lending ensures that Beijing retains the advantage in negotiations and facilitates corruption. Popular protests have proliferated, particularly around hard infrastructure projects, and new leaders, including those in Malaysia, Pakistan, and

Tanzania, have sought to overturn or renegotiate unfavorable deal terms. At the same time, the BRI has left other countries, such as Pakistan, saddled with projects whose returns will likely never equal the initial investment and seeking additional debt relief from other international lenders. Many Chinese companies and officials themselves are concerned that a lack of understanding of host countries' domestic political and economic situation results in suboptimal outcomes for BRI projects. Despite Beijing's pledges to address these concerns, opinion polls indicate that few countries find China's efforts to change course compelling.

Finally, the BRI has become a significant source of global competition. It has energized other advanced economies in Europe and Asia, as well as the United States, to develop their own infrastructure and connectivity projects to compete with Belt and Road. Australia, India, and the larger European economies have become more attentive to infrastructure needs in their own backyards. Japan, in particular, provides alternatives to Chinese BRI investment in Africa and Southeast Asia, where it has surpassed China as the largest source of infrastructure investment. The United States views the BRI through the lens of geostrategic competition and has been a vocal critic of Chinese BRI governance practices and has sought to persuade other countries not to accept BRI funding. Increasingly, Washington has focused its energy on the Digital Silk Road, where, as the next chapter illuminates, China is poised to play a truly transformative role in creating the infrastructure for the 21st century.

5

From Bricks to Bits

In May 2020, the Chinese government made headlines when it announced a five-year, $1.4 trillion digital infrastructure stimulus initiative. Included in the plan were funds to support China's expanding 5G network, artificial intelligence (AI) and data centers, and Internet of Things applications. Individual cities also jumped on board to announce their own projects, such as building a digital "city brain" that would integrate cities' databases, from traffic to schools to healthcare.[1] China's leading technology companies, including Alibaba, Huawei, and Tencent, would shoulder much of the work. The plan was clear: China's state-directed innovation combined with the country's bountiful entrepreneurial talent would take the country's technology ecosystem to the next level. And if Chinese leaders had their way, these same technologies and technology platforms would be deployed on a global scale. China was ready to set the standard for the world's 21st-century digital infrastructure.

It is a bet that has already paid off. From the conveniences of everyday life to AI-powered autonomous drones, Beijing is forging a path to global technological leadership in which Chinese companies, technologies, and standards establish the rules of the digital road. A young graduate student at PKU shared with me some of the small ways that technology enhances his life. When he receives a package at school, a text appears telling him in what part of the mail processing center he will find the parcel. He then goes to an ATM-like machine, types in his code, and the door of a locker in that area pops open, revealing the package inside. While in class, he orders drinks and snacks from local stores and retrieves them outside during breaks from waiting delivery people. And there is no need to fumble around for his student ID when entering campus – a facial scan takes care of that. Submitting work assignments takes place via WeChat, the messaging service developed by the internet behemoth Tencent, as does everything from making dinner reservations and doctors' appointments to reading the newspaper.

Of course, there is also no need to pull out his real wallet to pay real cash. The e-payment systems of WeChat Pay and Alipay are transforming China into a cashless society. WeChat Pay has over one billion daily commercial payment transactions. The local grocer and street food vendors have QR codes to facilitate mobile payments. And it is not simply China's consumer product and service sectors that are blazing a new technological path. The country's infrastructure is world class. The high-speed train from Beijing to Tianjin provides a smooth, quiet ride, even at speeds that top 200 mph. It is a far cry from the New York to DC trip on Amtrak's high-speed equivalent, the Acela. That ride is neither quiet nor smooth and tops out at 150 mph.

Chinese technology is also going global. Alibaba, Huawei, Xiaomi, Tencent, and now ByteDance, with its winning social media platform TikTok, are becoming known throughout the world's capitals in much the same way as Apple, Google, Microsoft, and Facebook once did. Huawei provides 70 percent of Africa's 4G telecommunications network, and Shenzhen-based Transsion phones are ubiquitous throughout the world's developing economies. Chinese tech companies also follow Chinese consumers around the world. Wherever there are significant overseas Chinese communities, Chinese firms are striking deals to make sure their customers are not left without the convenience of their technology. WeChat Pay and Alibaba's Alipay can be used in the American drugstore chain Walgreens, and Chinese students can use WeChat Pay to pay their tuition at 11 different South Korean universities. Chinese technology companies are also beginning to think about how best to serve foreign citizens. WeChat Pay eliminated the long-standing requirement that foreign citizens use a Chinese bank account to access its services. It now partners with five international credit card companies, including Visa and Mastercard, to enable foreign citizens to link their foreign bank accounts to a WeChat Pay account.[2]

All this convenience comes at a price, however. Lurking just beneath the surface is the Chinese government, whose influence is deeply embedded in every element of these technologies' development and deployment. The level of direct government intrusion into WeChat, which appears to be a private messaging system, can be jarring for foreigners used to at least an illusion of privacy. In one case, an American studying in China posted a message critical of Xi Jinping and was removed from WeChat and WeChat Pay until a "trusted Chinese citizen" would vouch for her. At the same time, a friend of hers was unable to use WeChat Pay because of "suspicious activity" on his account. He suspects that his connection to her caused the disruption in his service. Outside China, the rules are murkier. WeChat is the third most popular social media platform in the world; there are between 100 million and 200 million WeChat users living outside China, 19 million in the United States alone.[3] While censorship only takes place with users registered with a Chinese phone number, an investigation by the University of Toronto's Citizen Lab reveals that WeChat does in fact surveil and collect content from these foreign users, and it uses this information to develop WeChat's capabilities to censor China-registered accounts.[4]

Top to Bottom

Consumer technology is only a small part of Beijing's exploding global technology presence. For the Chinese government, the real prize is the opportunity to build the world's technological backbone. In June 2020, China completed the deployment of its BeiDou "Big Dipper" satellite system – a two-decades-long project that rivals the United States' GPS, Russia's GLONASS, and the EU's Galileo. With over 30 satellites positioned globally, China no longer needs to rely on others' systems. Even before its completion, more than 70 percent of Chinese smartphones and over six million Chinese taxis, buses, and trucks used the BeiDou system. BeiDou is particularly important for Beijing because it allows the PLA, with its precision-guided missiles and advanced communications networks, to operate within an entirely domestically controlled system. It also enables China to jam signals as part of an electronic warfare capability. Other countries, including China's neighbors Thailand, Laos, Pakistan, and Brunei, subscribe to BeiDou – and Pakistan has adopted multiple weapons systems that use the satellite system.[5] Some experts have expressed concern that China could use Beidou to track any Chinese chip-enabled smartphone.[6]

Back on land, China is already recognized as a world leader in the global deployment of 5G technology. Shenzhen, a center of Chinese innovation, is China's first fully 5G enabled city.[7] As part of the May 2020 digital stimulus package, Chinese telecommunications carriers are installing 600,000 5G base stations. This 5G infrastructure, coupled with the BeiDou satellite system, provides a framework within which an entire suite of Chinese infrastructure-related technologies and technology platforms can be embedded. Cities can have their transportation, commerce, telecommunications, security, home appliances, and services integrated through Chinese technologies. It is the 21st-century version of Build, Operate, and Transfer. Robert Blair, who served as the US government's point person on 5G during the waning months of the Trump administration, has pointed out that

> the real value of 5G is not downloading movies faster than you can in 4G LTE. . . . The real value of 5G's going to be felt in four to five years when the true Internet of Things and this truly connected economy's going to happen. . . . It's going to be building out those industrial uses. It's going to be in the transportation sector. It's going to be in the medical sector. It's going to be in the mining sector.[8]

Chinese companies are also globally competitive players in the world of undersea fiber optic cables. Roughly 380 of these cables travel along the ocean seabed, carrying approximately 95 percent of international voice and data traffic.[9] China's first submarine optical cable connected the country with Japan in 1993; today, Huawei Marine commands 24 percent of the undersea cable market.[10] In a 2018 white paper, the Chinese government acknowledged the competition with foreign firms, such as Google, and made explicit that winning the right to build the cables is part of a broader Chinese diplomatic gambit in regions such as Africa.[11] As with China's global deployment of BeiDou and 5G, the United States and other advanced democracies are concerned that Chinese companies will be able to monitor or divert data or even to cut traffic entirely in the event of a conflict.[12]

International assessments of the state of Chinese technology development and deployment are uniformly high. The World Bank's 2019 report "Innovative China" highlights the leadership of Chinese firms such as Alibaba, Didi Chuxing, Huawei, and Tencent in areas like e-commerce and fintech. China also is a top-rated player in high-speed rail, renewable energy, electric cars, and value-added high-tech manufacturing.[13] Yet the Chinese government has plans for scores of additional Chinese technology companies to join their ranks. Huawei's rise as a global 5G powerhouse illuminates some of the ways Beijing plans to make that happen.

Huawei: Def. China Has Promise

Sitting on a Bloomberg News panel in Shenzhen in November 2019, Huawei founder Ren Zhengfei discussed US efforts to constrain Huawei by placing it on the Entity List: the list of companies to which American firms cannot sell without a special license. He likened the US tech sector to sitting at the top of Mount Everest, while China is at the foot of the mountain. "When the snow melts, the water will flow down the mountain and irrigate the crops and pasture," but, he suggests,

> If the US doesn't allow the water to flow down the mountain, people at the foot of the mountain may dig wells to irrigate their crops. . . . In that case, no money will be paid to the US . . . because we have dug many wells at the foot of the Himalayas, and used the water from the wells to irrigate our crops, we believe that we can survive . . . but digging wells is not our ultimate purpose. We want to work with the US to achieve shared success.[14]

Ren has done a good job of watering his crops. In 2020, Huawei achieved a record of over $136.7 billion in revenue, employed more than 194,000 people,[15] and was recognized as the world's leader in the deployment of 5G.

At a time when many Chinese technology CEOs, such as Jack Ma, have stepped back from leading the companies they founded or found themselves trying to navigate an increasingly complex political environment in Beijing, Ren remains in the driver's seat at Huawei. Born in 1944, he grew up in one of China's poorest provinces, Guizhou, the son of schoolteachers. He attended college and then joined the military during the tumultuous Cultural Revolution. While he was in the military, he served in the engineering corps, eventually rising to become a director of the PLA General Staff Department's Information Engineering Academy. He was demobilized in 1983, when the government disbanded the entire engineering corps.[16] He then worked for several years at the state-owned Shenzhen South Sea Oil Corporation before founding Huawei in 1988.

While the details of the company's initial funding are debated, one account reports that Huawei received a government-backed loan of $8.5 million. Ren modeled his firm's organizational structure on that of the Communist Party;[17] even the company's name derives from a patriotic slogan: "*Zhonghua Youwei*" or "China has promise."

Huawei's first business was simply selling switches imported from Hong Kong to mainland customers, mostly hotels and small businesses.[18] In 1993, however, the company produced "the most powerful telephone switch in China" and earned a contract with the PLA.[19] It kept its research in-house, deciding against a joint venture or partnership with a multinational. Still, Ren is quick to acknowledge that he has learned a lot from Western companies. He worked with firms such as IBM and Accenture to improve Huawei's business management processes around its data systems, operating efficiency, and internal controls.[20] In an interview with a British documentary producer, Ren describes transforming his company to reflect the ideas of US politics and business, noting that the only way for Huawei to survive is to learn from the best.[21] His takeaways from the US model are surprisingly political in nature: from the US legal system, he learned to standardize operations and that separation of powers is a good way to avoid putting too much power in the hands of one person. He also said that Apple "is an example we look up to in terms of privacy protection. We will learn from Apple. We would rather shut Huawei down than do anything that would damage the interests of our customers in order to seek our own gains."[22] And when talking about his share in Huawei – slightly over 1 percent – he noted that Apple co-founder Steve Jobs had only a 0.58 percent stake in Apple, which meant to Ren that he should dilute his stake.

Ren's story is also one of courting Chinese officials at the highest level. In 1994, Ren met with Chinese leader Jiang Zemin and urged him to recognize the importance of a domestic telecommunications switch industry; Jiang reportedly agreed.[23] Ren and Huawei soon became the poster child for the Chinese playbook on how to compete with foreign firms. In 1996, Vice Premier Wu Bangguo visited Ren in Shenzhen and offered him millions in loans to "break the monopoly" of foreign firms and develop indigenous Chinese phone technology compatible with the Global System for Mobile Telecommunications (GSM). Ren also received local government support from Shenzhen, which declared

Huawei to be one of its 26 "key development projects." Once Huawei started producing the GSM-equipped components, Wu praised the company: "By breaking the monopoly of Western companies and strengthening the creative capabilities of the Chinese people, Huawei has made a heartening achievement."[24]

Huawei's expansion was rapid and relentless. As writer Jeffrey Melnik has detailed, the company began selling its own wireless network-based products in 1997 and shipped its first mobile handset in 2004 and first smartphone in 2009. Today it is a triple threat with three different businesses: carrier networks and their related wireless technology that provide wireless cellular service; business enterprise that provides hardware and software; and consumer products like smartphones.[25]

The Chinese government stood behind Ren throughout Huawei's rise. To begin with, it restricted foreign competition in China's domestic market – restrictions that Ren himself reportedly urged. Indeed, Ren has stated explicitly that without this protection, "Huawei would no longer exist."[26] Beijing's financial support was also extensive. A European investigation revealed that Huawei may have had access to a $30 billion line of credit from CDB.[27] And the *Wall Street Journal* estimates that Huawei received roughly $75 billion in subsidies between 2008 and 2018. (This compares with $44.5 million that the United States provided to Cisco between 2000 and 2019.)[28] An American company brought a case against Huawei for relying on subsidies but subsequently dropped it for fear of losing market access. This financial support enabled Huawei to expand at home and dramatically underbid competitors abroad.

Ren also expanded Huawei's global presence relatively early in the company's development. In 1999, Huawei established an $8 million overseas software development center in Bangalore, with centers also in Russia, Sweden, and the United States. By 2001, its GSM equipment had been installed in more than 20 Chinese provinces and 10 countries, with 30,000 base stations.[29] Ren has noted that most of Huawei's initial contracts were in Africa because the company's products were not on par with those of Western companies and also because African countries accepted Huawei: "They were in the middle of a war and all the Western companies ran away."[30]

In addition, Ren took advantage of top-flight foreign talent. In 2009, when the famed Canadian telecommunications company Nortel filed for bankruptcy, Huawei wooed the head of the lab, Wen Tong. Tong, who was a star in the world of mobile technology research, brought his entire team to Huawei. Over the next few years, Tong and his group researched – both independently and by pulling together top theoretical innovations from scholars around the world – a particular type of channel coding, polar codes, that mitigates the effects of errors in a communication link.[31] Another outside scholar, Erdal Arikan, whose work provided a seminal breakthrough for Huawei, noted that he had presented his ideas to US firms, such as Qualcomm, but they were not interested. Huawei picked up his work for free just by reading one of his papers. Huawei researchers also attended conferences where top scientists presented their cutting-edge findings. In an interview with *Wired* magazine, UC San Diego engineering professor Alexander Vardy described how he modified Arikan's work and presented it at a conference where Huawei scientists were in the audience. Soon after the conference, he notes, Huawei developed the technology.[32] Huawei's win did not stop there, however. As chapter 6 describes, Huawei proceeded to take the technology and develop it into a global standard for 5G. Now it was a win for China as well.

Not all of Huawei's acquisitions of foreign technology occur legally, however. Over the years, accusations of IP theft have dogged the firm. The US tech giant Cisco filed a lawsuit against Huawei in 2003, claiming that the Chinese firm had copied its software and infringed on several of its patents. Ren admitted that 2 percent of the code in its router software was copied from Cisco, but when Cisco called for Huawei routers to be banned from the United States, Huawei successfully argued to remove the code from subsequent models and software updates instead. Additional cases of IP theft included a Fujitsu circuit board and Motorola cellular network equipment; at one point, a Huawei employee attempted to leave the United States with more than 1,000 internal Motorola documents.[33] In the mid-2010s, T-Mobile and the Anglo-American company Quintel also accused Huawei of IP theft.[34] Most recently, in 2019, a small startup, AKHAN Semiconductor, claimed that after Huawei requested a sample of its Miraj Diamond Glass – a product described as far superior to the traditional Gorilla glass used in smartphones – the Chinese company attempted to reverse engineer the product.[35] Ren has personally denied all the charges, asserting: "The claim of Huawei's stealing of IPR [intellectual property rights] from the West is not possible. . . . Huawei didn't and will never steal, intellectual property. We do have a lot of IPRs and will not use these IPRs as a weapon."[36]

Adding to Huawei's challenges are accusations that it knowingly violated US sanctions on Iran. On December 1, 2018, Canadian officials arrested Ren's daughter Meng Wanzhou, who was also Huawei's chief financial officer, at the request of the United States. The United States sought to extradite Meng on charges of bank and wire fraud, in particular lying to banks such as HSBC about Huawei's relationship with a subsidiary in Iran, Skycom, in order to avoid US sanctions. (In what is widely believed to be a retaliatory measure, China detained two Canadians, Michael Kovrig and Michael Spavor, that same month and held them for 18 months before charging them with espionage in June 2020. They remained in jail until September 2021, when both they and Meng were released.) In May 2019, the United States deemed Huawei's business dealings with Iran a threat to national security and placed the company (and subsequently 114 of its overseas affiliates) on the Entity List; as a result, any American company that wants to sell its chips to Huawei or any of its affiliates has to get a license from the US government to do so. The following year, in May 2020, the Trump administration moved to restrict Huawei's access to US technology or software for designing or manufacturing its semiconductors abroad.[37] Any chip producers who used US semicon-ductor equipment and technology also needed approval before producing chips designed by HiSilicon, Huawei's fabless semiconductor company. As a result, HiSilicon, which had developed an advanced integrated circuit, could not manufacture the chip because it would have to license IP from a UK-based chip designer as well as rely on Taiwan's TSMC for production.

Ren retains his optimistic outlook and fighting spirit. He announced that Huawei would be hiring mathematicians and scientists from Russia and Europe instead of the United States.[38] In July 2020, during a tour of several Chinese universities, he stated, "We real-ized that some politicians in the US wanted us dead. The desire to survive lifted us up and [we] looked for a way to save ourselves."[39] In November 2020, Ren sold Huawei's Honor phone line to a consortium backed by the Shenzhen local government in the hopes of moving the company off the US Entity List. But during 2021 to 2023, the Biden administration only expanded restrictions on U.S. technology exports to, and imports from, Huawei.

The story of Huawei is in the first instance one of Ren Zhengfei's entrepreneurialism and determination to succeed. Yet it also reveals the protective edifice the Chinese government has created to try to promote and protect the success of its companies, including: long-term planning; deep engagement with the country's dynamic entrepreneurs; significant targeted investments in R&D; protecting the Chinese market from foreign competition; and acquiring international talent and technology. It is a playbook that has served China well. But as Huawei's experience also demonstrates, as the Chinese state continues to expand its control over the development of the technology sector at home, it is simultaneously creating new challenges for its ambitions to take Chinese technology global.

China's Digital Playbook

In June 2014, standing before members of the prestigious Chinese Academy of Sciences and Engineering, Xi Jinping delivered a call to action. He exhorted his audience to "make new scientific and technological breakthroughs and gain competitive edges" and to help China "catch up and surpass others" in the global technology race. He also called for China to "hold key technology" in its own hands in order to protect its economic and national security interests. And he suggested that Beijing should not "play games by the established rules," but instead be a rule setter.[40]

The speech is just one of many that Xi has delivered outlining his science and technology ambitions since he came to power in late 2012. The theme is consistent: China's scientific, technological, and business elites must help transform China into a globally competitive innovation powerhouse.[41] For Xi, science and innovation are at the heart of Beijing's international standing, a measurable indicator of Chinese talent, determination, economic competitiveness, and leadership qualities. And over his almost decade in power, he has refined traditional elements of Chinese technology policy and introduced his own ideas to try to accelerate Beijing's rise to the top of the technology leaderboard. First, and above all, innovation should be in service of the state. It should have a "demand orientation," respond to "urgent national needs," and resolve "practical problems." There is room for basic, foundational science, but for Xi, it is a distant second to applied research.[42] Second, Chinese scientists and entrepreneurs should align their efforts and values with those of the CCP. Innovation is not a license to color outside the lines. Xi has relentlessly expanded the power of the CCP to ensure that technology firms' ambitions do not stray from those of the Party. Third, China should avoid over-reliance on others' technology and should instead develop its own capabilities. While the preference for indigenous innovation has been a constant in Chinese technology policy for decades, the country is now more able than ever to realize this goal. Fourth, Chinese universities and companies should access overseas talent and technology to help meet specific needs. As China's economic wherewithal has increased, so too has its capacity to pay for the very best talent. And, fifth, China should set the technology standards for the 21st century. For Beijing, setting standards is the holy grail of its global technology ambition. It offers definitive proof of China's global innovation leadership. These five priorities shape China's technology policy at home and provide it with an impressive platform for expanding its vision abroad. Yet as the government's vision for the future of the global technology landscape becomes clearer, it is also encountering new challenges to its sustainability: domestic resources are increasingly stressed, leading to missed targets in R&D funding, and international actors are increasingly concerned about what Xi's vision means for their firms and their values.

He Ain't Heavy, He's My Brother

In late July 2020, Xi held a closed-door meeting with a group of the country's top entrepreneurs. According to a report from the session, he called on those attending to be patriotic and innovative and to align their business strategies with China's needs. He reminded them that "Marketing knows no borders, but entrepreneurs have a motherland."[43] It is a sentiment that clearly resonates with him. Just a few months later, delivering a speech before a group of scientists and technologists, he altered a few words but reiterated the same point, "Science has no borders, but scientists have motherlands"; and he called on them to be "patriotic scholars."[44]

The relationship between the CCP elites and China's scientific and technology communities, particularly its growing cohort of billionaire tech entrepreneurs – some of whom are CCP members – is a complicated one. More than any other industry in China, technology has individual leaders and firms who are recognizable not only in China but also globally: Jack Ma and Alibaba, Robin Li and Baidu, Ren Zhengfei and Huawei, Pony Ma and Tencent, and now Zhang Yiming and ByteDance (TikTok). The star power of these tech icons at times appears to rival that of Xi Jinping himself. Several of them, like some of their Western counterparts, have a natural ease in the spotlight, sharing their personal stories and occasionally indulging in outrageous public displays. Jack Ma's tribute to Michael Jackson[45] and his comedic kung fu short (starring himself) have significant cross-cultural appeal.[46] It is also easy to appreciate the thoughtful Robin Li discussing his 10 favorite books, including a detailed history of the Long March, a book on plants, and Malcolm Gladwell's collected writings.[47] And who would not like to work for Pony Ma, who led his team on a two-day 32-mile hike through the Gobi Desert?[48] *Fortune* magazine's 2020 Global 500, a ranking of the top 500 companies worldwide by revenue, listed 124 mainland Chinese and Hong Kong companies, including Alibaba, Tencent, and Huawei, along with smartphone company Xiaomi and online retail giants Suning and JD.com.[49] These are companies whose CEOs have amassed levels of personal wealth matched by only a handful of people in the world.

The Chinese government is eager to tap into the creativity and competitive spirit of these companies, many of which are recognized as "national champions" for their global leadership and support of the Party's strategic objectives. This appellation earns them benefits such as subsidies, a protected market, and preference in government contracts.[50] In 2018, Beijing created a list of 17 priority areas for the development of AI and called on Chinese technology firms to join the "national team" in the effort to close the gap with the United States by 2030. The 15 firms that have joined the initiative are a who's who of China's tech world, including stalwarts like Alibaba, Xiaomi, and Huawei.[51]

Yet the broader mandate of these companies and what enables them to be successful beyond China's borders also demands democratizing access to information and finance and innovating in response to the demands of the market. All of these have the potential to threaten Xi's priorities with regard to Communist Party oversight. The 2017 Cybersecurity Law made clear that Chinese companies were required to assist the Chinese government with any inquiry around users' data.[52] And in fall 2019, the local government of Hangzhou, home to Alibaba, surveillance camera maker Hikvision, and more than 100 other technology firms, announced that it would place officials in the companies to help them carry out key projects and ensure alignment between government and company interests.[53] The presence of the Party can be seen everywhere. A gray metal cube sculpture across from Tencent's office in Shenzen, for example, states "Follow our Party, start your business."[54]

Ensuring political orthodoxy in a field that thrives on challenging conventional wisdom and letting the imagination run wild also introduces dissonance into the government's relationship with some of the tech companies. In spring 2018, the Chinese government criticized ByteDance for creating apps that offered news stories that were "opposed to morality" and featured "off-color" jokes. In response, founder Zhang Yiming stated that he would increase the number of censors, develop a list of banned users, and improve monitoring and censorship technology.[55] For a 10-month period during 2018, the government also simply stopped approving new video games amid concerns about gaming addiction,[56] causing Tencent's stock to plummet. When new games were once again permitted, Tencent's offerings promoted Chinese patriotism and socialist values, partnering, for example, with the CCP's newspaper, the *People's Daily*, to put out "Homeland Dream," in which players develop a city, along with policies around poverty alleviation and tax reduction.[57]

Gary Rieschel, head of the venture capital firm Qiming Investments, which has for almost two decades funded tech startups in China, such as Xiaomi, told me tech entrepreneurs "hate" this type of government intervention. And although few say it publicly, quiet comments from some of China's leading entrepreneurs suggest that they agree. Wang Xiaochuan, CEO of the internet search company Sogou, for example, noted in an interview with the Hong Kong-based Phoenix Satellite Television, "If it's in your nature to say, 'I want freedom, I want to sing a tune different from the state's,' then you might suffer, more so than in the past."[58]

Jack Ma has been particularly outspoken in his belief that there should be greater separation between the government and business, suggesting at a 2018 conference: "I personally think that the government has to do what the government should do, and the companies do what companies should do."[59] In October 2020, Ma expanded on this point in an address at the high-profile Bund Finance Summit in Shanghai. He levied a devastating indictment of the government's approach to innovation. The government, he argued, was too focused on "filling the blank spot" – simply ensuring that China possessed whatever Europe and the United States already possessed – as opposed to looking toward the future and creating something new. Ma also underscored his belief that innovation arose from the "marketplace, the grassroots, and young people," implicitly criticizing Xi's state-centered approach. Moreover, a broader crackdown on technology firms ensnared Tencent too, and young billionaire entrepeneurs such as Zhang Yiming and Pinduodo's Huang Zheng have retreated from leading their companies to pursue other activities. The government, Ma asserted, displayed a desire to "manage risk to zero" – an approach that produced a competition of regulatory skills instead of a competition of innovation.[60] The following week, the People's Bank of China and three other Chinese regulatory bodies summoned Ma and other senior officials from his fintech company Ant Group to their offices. Shortly thereafter, the government announced the cancellation of Ant's initial public offering (IPO) slated for later that same week. While Chinese regulators had previously expressed concerns about some of Ant's lending practices, from all accounts these were scheduled to be resolved in the aftermath of the listing. Ma's indiscretion provided skeptics within China's banking and regulatory system with an opportunity to hit the pause button. Reports even suggested that Xi Jinping himself made the decision to cancel the IPO. Ma's disappearance from public view for almost three months following the IPO cancellation further suggested a personal political hit, as opposed to merely a regulatory battle. As a result, Ant will be transformed to operate more like a conventional bank, a potential death blow for a company that thrived by exploiting the weaknesses of China's traditional banking system.[61]

The experiences of Ant Group, ByteDance, and Tencent confirm in the minds of many governments around the world that there is no meaningful separation between the CCP and Chinese technology companies – even if they are primarily privately held – and no check on the power of the Party. As a result, an increasing number of China's most prominent technology companies are encountering new challenges as they seek to do business abroad. In summer 2020, TikTok, with over 700 million users globally, was not only banned in India, as noted in chapter 2 but also ordered by the US government to sell its US operation to an American company and placed under investigation in Australia. For the US government, TikTok raised questions concerning the collection of American users' data – a particular concern given the young age of many TikTok afficionados – and the ability of the company to shape the content users were able to engage with. At one point, for example, TikTok limited posts that displayed what it termed "abnormal body types," which appeared to include heavyset women and people with disabilities;[62] censored content around LGBT rights and the Hong Kong protests;[63] and suspended the account of a US teenager who posted a video informing viewers about the labor and reeducation camps in Xinjiang under the guise of presenting a makeup tutorial.[64]

Concerns about CCP-mandated surveillance and censorship by Chinese technology companies are not limited to citizens outside China. In 2018, the head of Geely Auto, Li Shufu, stated publicly that Tencent's Pony Ma was "definitely looking at our WeChat messages," and that there was no such thing as data privacy in China.[65] Ma issued a sharp denial to Li, but in 2017, Tencent had informed its users that all their personal data, content, and searches were available to the Chinese government. If the Chinese government asks for something, Tencent will comply. Moreover, in a 2019 poll by SinaTech News, 48.7 percent of Chinese citizens polled stated that "collecting user data without permission" was their greatest concern about mobile apps.[66]

Innovation Lifeblood

In a 2016 speech at a scientific event, Xi Jinping stated, "To be the world's major scientific and technological power, the state will have to champion first-class institutes, research-oriented universities, and innovation-oriented enterprises. . . . Our biggest advantage is that we, as a socialist country, can pool resources in a major mission."[67] The mission, as Xi has defined it, is to overtake the United States and other global technology powers, such as Germany and Japan, and to become the global leader in the innovation, manufacturing, and deployment of critical technologies.

State-directed innovation plans have long defined China's approach to technology modernization and global competition. And over decades, the plans and technologies they support reflect an extraordinary degree of consistency. As early as 1963, Premier Zhou Enlai identified science and technology as one of the Four Modernizations, along with agriculture, industry, and defense, necessary for China to develop the economy and society. The disruption and anti-intellectual strain of the Cultural Revolution (1966–76), however, stalled most scientific progress, with a few exceptions, such as the "two bombs, one satellite" program, until after Mao's death in 1976. In the early 1980s, the Four Modernizations again surfaced as a framework for China's overall development strategy. Beijing opened special economic zones to encourage foreign companies to shift production to the mainland in order to help bring technological expertise and know-how to Chinese manufacturing. During the 1980s, China's leaders also developed a brand-new institutional infrastructure to support R&D. They established the Chinese National Natural Science Foundation, the equivalent of the United States' National Science Foundation; launched the 863 Program to encourage Chinese innovation in seven specialized areas – biotechnology, space, information technology, energy, advanced materials, lasers, and automation technology; provided financial support to SOEs in order to purchase know-how and technology from abroad to upgrade their manufacturing capabilities; initiated the Torch Program to support Chinese universities and institutes in commercializing their technologies;[68] and initiated the Key Technologies Research and Development Program, which set priority projects to take from research to commercialization in periods of roughly three years. In 1997, China also established the 973 Program in support of basic research, although much of the funding went to applied research.[69]

By the 2000s, Chinese leaders urged domestic companies to develop their own capabilities and set out more than 400 core technologies for China to master.[70] In 2010, the government announced seven strategic emerging industries that would serve as the engine of Chinese economic and technological development. Several of the technologies mimicked those identified three decades earlier. They included next-generation information technology, biotechnology, energy efficiency and environmental technologies, new materials, new energy vehicles, high-end equipment manufacturing, and new energy. Five years later, these same technologies formed the core of the government's Made in China (MIC)

2025 program. Soon the country's technology landscape was populated by a growing number of strategic initiatives that reinforced the priorities established in MIC 2025, including the 2015 Internet Plus Action Plan, the 2017 New Generation AI Development Plan, and the 2018 China Standards 2035 program.

Underpinning all these programs is a dedicated stream of government investment in R&D. By 2020, Chinese investment represented 23 percent of the world's total, second only to that of the United States. Government money flows to universities, institutes, and companies from a variety of sources: the central government, SOEs, and local governments. In addition, Beijing and local governments directly fund over 1,000 venture capital firms.[71] This impressive funding stream has captured the foreign media's attention, which often compare it favorably to levels of EU or US support.[72]

However, the opaque nature of Chinese government funding makes it difficult to determine exactly how much money is being spent and in what manner. For example, in May 2018, the Tianjin government announced a $16 billion fund for AI, prompting a rash of articles that contrasted the level of Chinese investment with that of Europe ($1.78 billion)[73] and the United States ($1.1 billion).[74] Yet peeling back the curtain just a bit reveals that the Tianjin government itself is only providing $1.5 billion, with the rest to be raised from financial organizations, private enterprises, and other market players, both in China and abroad. An independent study by the Institute for Defense Analysis (IDA) raised additional questions: how much of the Tianjin fund was annualized, derived from the central government, or even focused on R&D? The report noted that the money could support salaries for guards or researchers. The opacity of the Tianjin government's announcement made it difficult to determine. In the end, the IDA report concluded that it was virtually impossible to develop a meaningful comparative metric for US and Chinese AI funding.[75]

The high level of government funding also diminishes the incentive for Chinese firms to invest in their own R&D. Out of the top 50 R&D private investors in the world, 22 are US firms, while only one, Huawei, is Chinese.[76] (On average, China's top 100 internet firms invest only 10 percent of their revenue in R&D, although Alibaba, Tencent, and Baidu invest more than twice that amount.) When compared dollar to dollar, most analysts agree that firms are more efficient than governments at targeting and spending research funding.[77]

Finally, China consistently falls short in realizing its ambitious R&D funding targets. In 2010, government R&D spending accounted for only 1.7 percent of GDP, notably less than the 2.5 percent pledged in the 2006 Medium- and Long-Term Program for the Development of Science and Technology.[78] In 2016, Premier Li Keqiang pledged once again to increase R&D spending to 2.5 percent by 2020 (in fact it reached 2.4 percent by that year).[79] As a result of the pandemic, however, at the government's Two Sessions in May 2020, Beijing instituted a 9 percent cut in R&D funding and called upon local governments to make up some of the difference.[80]

There Is No Room at the Inn

The Chinese government's commanding role in funding and establishing priority areas for research is further bolstered by an array of government policies designed to protect emerging Chinese technologies from foreign competition. Launched by Premier Li Keqiang in 2015, China's MIC 2025 program epitomizes Chinese protectionism and provided an early signal of Beijing's willingness to pursue a broader decoupling of Chinese technology development from that of other countries. The plan and its subsequent roadmap extend to 2030 and even 2049. MIC 2025 seeks to ensure that Chinese companies control the manufacturing and ultimately the domestic market for components in 10 areas of critical technology: new information technology; high-end machine tools and robots; aerospace equipment; ocean engineering equipment and high-end vessels; high-end rail transportation equipment; energy-saving cars and new energy vehicles; electrical equipment; agricultural machinery; new materials and polymers; and high-end medical equipment.[81] And in 2020, Xi announced his dual circulation theory, which elevated the importance of China itself as a closed loop of innovation, manufacturing, and consumption. The country would remain open to the international community – the second circulation process – for selective imports of capital, technology, and know-how, and as a market for Chinese exports. This embedded MIC 2025 in a larger Chinese economic and innovation ecosystem. As one European businessman jokingly remarked, dual circulation represents "foreign technology, foreign money, but not foreign management in charge of it."

Within MIC 2025, not all technologies are created equal. For example, Beijing established a target of 80 percent domestic market share for electric vehicles but a 70 percent share for advanced medical devices.[82] Targets also evolve: in 2017, China increased its target for semiconductors to 80 percent from 70 percent.[83] In some areas, MIC 2025 permits joint ventures, as long as they manufacture in China. In others, the government requires the firms to be Chinese. And in some sectors, such as AI, most of the players will be private Chinese firms, while in sectors such as smart grids or high-speed rail, SOEs will command upwards of 80 percent of the market share.[84] The plan also includes targets for smart equipment usage, and a certain number of patents per 100 million in RMB investment. Different industries also receive different levels of priority. Smart manufacturing and next-generation IT rank at the very top, followed by new materials and new energy vehicles.[85] By mid-2019, the German think tank MERICS reported that there were 445 government documents detailing the measures for implementation, more than 4,000 projects, and 530 smart manufacturing industrial parks focused on big data, new materials, and cloud computing.[86]

A critical element of MIC 2025 is the protection of China's domestic market while its industries work to become competitive globally. For example, in the area of new energy vehicle batteries, regulations around the licensing and production of battery capacity effectively prevent foreign companies from accessing the market and ensure market share for certain domestic firms.[87] China will also out-manufacture other countries' firms, with the objective of capturing global market share, as it did with solar panels and wind turbines: its advanced battery manufacturing is more than triple that planned by the rest of the world.[88] In recent years, the indigenization process has become more aggressive. The northeastern city of Changchun, for example, is in the process of replacing cloud technology by IBM, Oracle, and EMC with that of Digital China.[89]

For some technologies, Beijing simply signals the desired target, leaving local governments to determine how best to realize it. In the case of medical devices, the Chinese government welcomes foreign medical device companies as joint venture partners but excludes these companies from parts of the standards formation process; this results in standards that are aligned with Chinese-made products. In addition, the approval process for medical devices is long and cumbersome, providing time for Chinese firms to capture market share. As Chinese-made medical devices improve in quality, provincial governments are more comfortable establishing regulations that make it more difficult for foreign-made devices to be purchased by hospitals and doctors. In Sichuan province, hospitals are required to use Chinese devices in 15 categories, including respirators and PET-CT scanners.[90] If they do not, they will not be fully reimbursed through insurance for the procedures.[91] And in 2019, a number of provinces and major cities issued new regulations designed to curtail the use of foreign-made medical devices. Ningxia, Suzhou, and Tianjin, for example, called for hospitals to provide justification for foreign medical device imports. Zhejiang province limited state hospital imports of foreign-made medical devices to 232 items,[92] and offered a higher reimbursement rate for hospitals using local products.[93]

The Chinese leadership's drive for technological self-reliance continues to be debated in and outside the country. Former minister of the Ministry of Industry and Information Li Yizhong has argued that China should enhance self-sufficiency and retaliate against the United States' restrictive policies against Chinese technology companies by banning US firms from doing business in China. However, the director of Tsinghua University's Institute of Microelectronics has suggested that China doesn't need to replace all imported technology: "It is impossible to be 100 percent indigenous. Full replacement is for emergencies, not the major thrust of industrial development."[94] Finance Minister Lou Jiwei was ousted in April 2019 for criticizing MIC 2025 as a "waste of taxpayers' money."[95] And the international community has criticized the program for creating an uneven playing field for multinationals by setting targets that advantage Chinese companies and provide subsidies that lead to overproduction and the dumping of cheap products on the global market. In response to the backlash, China removed the name "MIC 2025" from all government documents. Nonetheless, the program continues to be pursued under the more innocuous rubric of "industrial upgrading."[96]

Fishing for Talent

Recruiting scientific talent from abroad to aid China's innovation effort has been a central government policy since the mid-1990s. As University of Nottingham Ningbo professor Cong Cao has described, in 1994, the Chinese Academy of Sciences established a Hundred Talents Program to recruit scientists under the age of 45 from abroad.[97] The recruits were limited to Chinese citizens or others who were willing to renounce their foreign citizenship.[98] Almost 15 years later, in 2008, the Ministry of Education reprised the Hundred Talents Program – in a much expanded form – as the Thousand Talents Plan. Its objective was to recruit 1,000 overseas scientists in 10 years, with 100 of them culled from the very top of their professions.

To recruit scientists to work in or with China, the Thousand Talents Plan offers an impressive array of inducements. The Chinese government, in partnership with a university, will often provide top-flight scientists with their own well-funded labs, living expenses, and very generous stipends. The plan also welcomes both foreign and overseas Chinese scientists, with no requirement to renounce citizenship. By 2019, over 10,000 scientists had participated. As NYU Shanghai assistant professor of physics Tim Byrnes noted, above a certain level, everybody applies to every country in the world: "People cross borders all the time, and eventually they congregate where there is the most money."[99] Despite Byrnes' assessment, however, only 390 non-Chinese scientists and engineers have moved to China to participate in the plan.[100] The vast majority are Chinese citizens or former Chinese citizens who have become citizens of other countries. And even then, it can be difficult to lure the most desired scientists back to China. Between 2014 and 2018, for example, 90 percent of students from China who received a PhD in AI in the United States remained there.[101]

Chinese scientists who study abroad and make their reputations in the world's top labs are particularly prized in the Thousand Talents Plan. They publish more and are more closely integrated into global scientific networks.[102] One of the star returnees was the award-winning scientist Li Chenjian. Li was educated at PKU and the Peking Union Medical College. He traveled to the United States for graduate work, where he received his PhD in Molecular Genetics from Purdue University, and then rose quickly through the ranks of top US university research institutions, from a postdoctoral fellowship at Rockefeller University to a position at Cornell University to an endowed chair at Mount Sinai School of Medicine.

During his time in New York, Li maintained his ties to PKU, serving as the faculty advisor to the PKU Alumni Association in Greater New York and acting as an informal host for delegations of PKU scholars and administrators traveling to the United States. These exchanges offered him the opportunity to share his ideas about educational reform and the value of a liberal arts education with senior PKU officials. Gradually he began to engage more directly with the Chinese educational system, teaching courses at PKU and other Beijing-based universities on a part-time basis. Chinese officials wooed Li with promises of research funding at a much greater level than he had in the United States; they told him he could become a prominent scientific official, president of a university, or start his own company with generous startup funds. Li, however, expressed little interest in the trappings of Chinese officialdom. What interested him, as he told me, was, first, scientific pursuit in its purest form, and even more importantly, educational reform. With this vision in mind, he returned to China in 2013, becoming one of the thousands in the Thousand Talents Plan. There was no fancy package, however. In fact, he jettisoned a 3,600 square foot home in New York City for an old studio in a PKU dorm and took a 40 percent pay cut for the chance to pursue educational reform.

Li was not the only returnee at PKU. During his six years there, the School of Life Sciences recruited 17 new faculty members who had received their PhDs and postdoctoral training in the United States, including two members of the National Academy of Sciences, four chairs of departments or programs, and three professors with endowed chairs. Li, however, soon distinguished himself from other returnee recruits not only by the attention and care he demonstrated toward the students in his lab but also by his radical notions around educational reform. In a succession of administrative positions, from vice provost of PKU to executive dean of Yuanpei College to professor and associate dean of the School of Life Sciences, Li sought to assist China's educational system in its intellectual rebirth through a "long-overdue enlightenment." In his thinking, he wanted to bring about a second "May 4th movement" – a reference to the 1919 movement that grew out of nationalist protests in Beijing and fostered a political and intellectual awakening.[103] His ambition, as he described it to me, was nothing less than to "seek truth, advocate truth, defend truth, love mankind" and bring universal values to China. His course "Critical Thinking of Contemporary Civilization" included writings by Marx but also by John Stuart Mill, Aristotle, Alexis de Tocqueville, Hannah Arendt, and John Locke – not to mention a collection of movies that highlighted the value of a free press, including *The Post* and *Spotlight*. With the support of two forward-leaning university presidents, other administrators, and a small group of like-minded professors, he established a new curriculum within PKU's Yuanpei College that was modeled on Columbia University's core curriculum. The curriculum soon became one of the most popular among incoming undergraduates. Not only was the curriculum different but the educational ethos also prized non-traditional notions such as individuals "making a choice" and acknowledging that there could be more than one right answer. Li's desire to raise the standard of Chinese education and integrate it more fully with that of the rest of the world extended well beyond Yuanpei College. He also played an instrumental role in introducing the Rhodes Scholarship to China and in establishing the Yenching Academy, which brought top students from around the world to study for a Master's degree at PKU.

In March 2018, however, Li made a fateful decision. In the wake of Xi Jinping's successful effort to eliminate the two-term limit on the presidency, Li posted an article on his WeChat account, "Have a straight spine and refuse to be an accomplice," in which he criticized the unwillingness of China's intellectuals and professors to stand up for freedom and to instead "scramble to launch research institutions for the study of Xi Jinping thought." He further noted: "It rarely occurs to people that the primary reason we don't have any notable scientists or masters of liberal arts is our education's systematic nurturing of shrewd liars instead of advocates for truth. This has nothing to do with knowledge. It's all about morality."[104] His article went viral, and he received many emails and messages of support. Censors, however, deleted references to the piece, and the PKU Party secretary threatened disciplinary action against anyone who reposted it. Even though PKU colleagues and some of the PKU leaders defended Li, he was stripped of all his titles, retaining only his position and lab (although he lost most of the funding for this).

After an extended sabbatical in the United States, he returned to PKU in January 2021, determined to continue his scientific research and training of his students.

Li remains convinced that for China to become a world leader in scientific innovation, the system needs fundamental reform. When I suggested that China was already a leader in his own field of biomedical research, he was quick to offer a counter. He pointed to the field of prescription drugs, noting that the world's medical scientists had developed 2,675 small-molecule prescription drugs approved by the Food and Drug Administration, to which China had not yet contributed a first-in-class drug. The first one likely to be approved, he noted, was not a "first-in-class" or even a "me too, me better" drug; instead, he argued, it was just a preexisting drug with a new slow-release delivery regime. And in a later email to me, he pointed out that "In the recent battle against the COVID-19 virus pandemic, whereas Chinese scientists were quite effective in making vaccines by conventional methods, experts in Europe and the United States have already leapfrogged to brand new mRNA vaccine technology."

In lieu of the type of structural reform Li favors, China continues to try to graft the successes of other countries' research onto the Chinese system, and the Thousand Talents Plan remains a favored part of that effort. The Trump administration, however, became increasingly concerned about the darker elements of the plan, particularly the potential for IP theft. In one case, a Thousand Talents Plan recruit, who had been working at the agrochemical company Monsanto for almost a decade, was stopped at the airport on his way back to China with a copy of a proprietary algorithm for an online farming software platform.[105] In another, a Chinese scientist working in a US lab used IP from the lab to file for a US patent under the name of a Chinese company. Several other cases also have involved Chinese scientists in the biomedical field planning to take research from their labs in the United States back to Chinese companies and universities.[106]

Even if scientists are not engaged in IP theft, many scientists awarded Thousand Talents funding maintain one position in China and another in a foreign country but fail to report their dual work status to their non-China-based employers. An investigation by the US National Institutes of Health revealed that 133 researchers had an undisclosed foreign grant and

102 had an undisclosed talent award; of these, 54 had resigned or been fired from their positions. Most cases – 93 percent – involved Chinese funding.[107] Emory University professor Li Xiaojian held simultaneous positions at the university's Department of Human Genetics in the Medical School and in the Chinese Academy of Sciences Institute of Genetics and Developmental Biology; he pursued the same research in both labs.[108]

In 2018, the US Justice Department launched a "China Initiative" designed to counter Chinese national security threats such as economic espionage and cyberattacks. Most of the cases, however, revolved around scholars not reporting their Chinese work affiliation or failing to pay taxes on the income rather than transferring technology. Failure to report Thousand Talents Plan participation and support led to the arrest, for example, of Harvard University professor Charles Lieber in January 2020. Lieber allegedly took more than $1 million in Chinese government money through the plan as a scientist at the Wuhan University of Technology. For his work there, he was paid a monthly salary of $50,000 plus a stipend for living expenses. A prominent scientist and world leader in the field of nanoscience, Lieber failed to disclose to Harvard or the US government (from which he received more than $15 million in grants via the National Institutes of Health and the Department of Defense) his affiliation with the Thousand Talents Plan.[109] In February 2022, the Biden administration ended the program, citing concerns over racial profiling, as well as the need to address the broader threat posed by other countries, such as Iran and Russia.[110]

As with MIC 2025, the negative international publicity around the Thousand Talents Plan has led the Chinese government to delete the term and the names of the participating scientists from various public documents. The term is also censored on Chinese social media. The plan itself, however, continues under a new name: the High-End Foreign Expert Recruitment Program.

Borrow, Buy, Steal

Acquiring technology from abroad can be an important means of advancing a firm's competitive position in a relatively short period. For Beijing, this process is a national priority. In recent years, Chinese firms have gone on a spending spree, taking stakes in and acquiring companies with some of the world's most sophisticated technologies. Many acquisitions are tied to MIC 2025 priority technologies. During 2015–16, alone, for example, China acquired 10 European and US producers of advanced automation equipment[111] – including two crown jewels of Germany's technology industry, Kuka and Midea. Concerned about their countries' competitiveness and national security, politicians sounded alarm bells and looked more closely at proposed Chinese acquisitions. In short order, Australia, Canada, the UK, the United States, and Germany all blocked the sale of technology companies to China on national security grounds – a trend that contributed to Chinese tech mergers and acquisitions peaking in 2016.[112]

China also uses its market leverage to persuade multinationals to transfer highly desired technology. While many multinationals and their governments view this as "coerced" technology transfer, the Chinese government argues that companies can refuse to transfer the technology; as one NDRC official stated,

> Foreign companies seeking access to the Chinese market were required to set up joint ventures and share their technology with domestic partners in China. . . . Actually, American and European companies are not forced, but motivated to invest in China by the expectation that the potential loss from sharing their technology will be far less than the expected gains from getting access to Chinese consumer markets.[113]

The implication of a refusal, however, might well be that the partnership and thus access to the Chinese market will not move forward.[114] In a 2018 report from the American Chamber of Commerce in Shanghai, 21 percent of the more than 400 companies surveyed reported that they felt pressured to transfer technology for market access,[115] and the European Union Chamber of Commerce in China reported almost identical findings: 20 percent of the more than 585 countries surveyed reported that they felt forced to transfer technology.[116] In one case, the Chinese government mandated that any Chinese company in an automobile joint venture had to master one of the three officially designated core new energy vehicle technologies.[117] Soon after, European car companies reported that their Chinese joint venture partners were pressuring them to turn over sensitive technology such as proprietary software codes for electric vehicle technology.[118]

While there is arguably a fine line between coerced and induced, no such ambiguity exists around the issue of IP theft. Companies as disparate as Philips, IBM, Hewlett Packard, American Airlines, Allianz SE, and Deutsche Bank have all reported cyberattacks attributable to Chinese actors.[119] According to a high-level Intellectual Property Commission established by the National Bureau of Asian Research, IP theft has cost the US economy between $225 billion and $600 billion in losses annually, with most of that due to China.[120] A US Department of Justice report estimated that from 2011 to 2018, 90 percent of alleged state-sponsored economic espionage was linked to China.[121] Even more troubling for the US government are the frequent cyber-espionage efforts directed at the US military. China launched a massive attack on the US Navy, for example, to gain undersea warfare technology, including schematics for a supersonic anti-ship missile.[122] During the Obama administration, the US government attempted to negotiate an end to cyber-espionage directed at the private sector. A 2015 agreement stated that "neither country's government will conduct or knowingly support cyber-enabled theft of intellectual property, including trade secrets or other confidential business information, with the intent of providing competitive advantages to companies or commercial sectors."[123] For a brief period after the agreement was signed, the number of cyberattacks declined. However, a report by the congressionally mandated US–China Economic and Security Review Commission concluded that this decline most likely represented a diminution in amateur attacks and a rise in more professional state-backed attacks, which are stealthier and less likely to be discovered.[124]

Standard Setting

Chinese policymakers will occasionally note that "third-tier companies make products, second-tier companies design technology, and first-tier companies set standards." International standards allow products to be used interchangeably across countries and are created by a mix of private companies and industry associations. The companies that own the technology that is adopted for the standard earn the licensing fees.[125] Early on, China occasionally adopted its own standards, for example in telecommunications technologies, such as TD-SCMA and WAPI. These standards failed to gain an international following, however.

Xi Jinping is determined not to repeat these mistakes. In 2018, China began a two-year project, China Standards 2035, to set global standards for emerging technologies, including seven priority areas: integrated circuits; virtual reality; smart health and retirement; 5G; the Internet of Things; information technology; and solar photovoltaics. It advances these standards through the deployment of its technologies as part of the DSR and in international standard setting bodies. As will be discussed in chapter 6, China has also actively promoted its officials to head standard setting bodies. Chinese officials have assumed top leadership positions in both the International Telecommunication Union (ITU) and the International Standards Organization (ISO). In July 2020, Huawei founder Ren Zhengfei was elected president of the 5G Global Standards Association, marking yet another success for both the Chinese government and Ren himself.

Too Much of a Good Thing

The success of the Chinese government's playbook in transforming the country into a global innovation and technology powerhouse is reflected in breakthrough advances in areas as disparate as quantum computing and lung regeneration therapy. But even more striking are the ways in which the playbook facilitates the longer-term development and deployment of Chinese technology to achieve a position of global leadership. The rise of Huawei is indicative of the power of the Chinese model. The firm is a worldwide brand, a global leader in 5G technology and deployment, and now a rule maker. Yet the same symbiotic relationship between the state and the firm that contributed to Huawei's success now threatens to undermine its continued rise. Huawei, like many Chinese technology companies, has become embroiled in a much larger geopolitical battle with China on one side and the United States on the other. It is a fight that engages issues of values, national security, and the very nature of the global economy.

Demands by the Chinese government that Chinese firms, particularly those in the technology sector, be fully responsive to Beijing's interests have begun to limit Huawei's global reach. As former State Department official Christopher Ford noted in September 2019, "Multiple Chinese laws . . . require companies to cooperate unconditionally with the Chinese

Communist Party's security apparatus in order to 'guarantee state security.' The National Intelligence Law, for instance, requires all entities in China to cooperate with its intelligence services, and covers both private companies and state-owned enterprises."[126] Huawei's opaque ownership structure has raised additional questions about the company's ability to act independently of the CCP. While Ren controls 1 percent of the company, the remaining 99 percent is reportedly held by an entity referred to as a "trade union committee." Some American experts have claimed that the trade union committee does not represent members but rather is a government entity, meaning that 99 percent of Huawei is owned by the government.[127] It is a claim that the company, as well as some outside experts, has disputed vehemently.[128] The Trump administration also argued that China's program of military–civil fusion meant that any US engagement with Huawei would ultimately further Chinese military objectives. As Ford commented, "Military–civil fusion also means that it is very difficult and in many cases impossible to engage with China's high-technology sector in a way that does not entangle a foreign entity in supporting ongoing Chinese efforts to develop or otherwise acquire cutting-edge technological capacities for China's armed forces."[129]

Huawei has tried its best to refute claims that it would turn over sensitive user information. Its rotating chairman, Liang Hua, asserted, "Huawei has never received any such requests . . . and even if we received such requests in the future, we would not agree to them. Without any lawful requests, we won't do anything."[130] In May 2019, Huawei commissioned a report from a top Chinese IP lawyer who supported its claim that it could not be forced to spy.[131] Ren himself has tried to reassure countries that the company would not spy, offering to sign "no spy" agreements.[132] Few foreign officials believe, however, that Huawei could or would refuse a Chinese government request. In 2019, Beijing celebrated Ren as one of 100 "Excellent Private Entrepreneurs" who "firmly safeguard the leadership of the Chinese Communist Party."[133] Such accolades, combined with threats by Chinese officials to retaliate economically against countries banning Huawei from their 5G infrastructure,[134] put to rest any lingering doubts that there is a material separation between the company and the Chinese government. As Canadian scholar Margaret McCuaig-Johnston noted, "Private companies do not typically have their governments make dramatic threats on their behalf."[135]

As countries debate whether to use Huawei 5G technology, this inability to separate the interests of the Chinese state from those of the company is a critical issue. In the larger court of global public opinion, the Huawei debate also is enveloped in broader political considerations over how China has managed the pandemic, its treatment of Uyghur Muslims in Xinjiang, and the political crackdown in Hong Kong. Pressure from the United States to ban Huawei further raised the political temperature. By 2021, Australia, Japan, the United States, India, Singapore, Belgium, Denmark, France, Italy, Sweden, the UK, Greece, Germany, and the Czech Republic had all selected Huawei competitors, Nokia or Ericsson, for their 5G providers (see Map 5.1).[136] Some countries banned Huawei outright; others developed technical standards that effectively banned the company; and still other EU members took cover under broader EU guidance.

Other countries, however, continue to welcome Huawei into their networks. In discussing Chinese technology ambitions with Latin American officials and scholars in November 2020, I found broad agreement that the concerns around Huawei and security that prevailed in Europe, North America, and some Asian countries did not resonate in the same way in their part of the world. They did not view Huawei's telecommunications infrastructure as particularly risky. A few voiced concerns

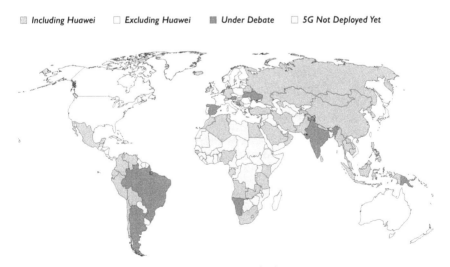

Map 5.1   Huawei 5G deployment
Source: Adapted from *https://tech.newstatesman.com/security/where-every-country-stands-huawei*

over Chinese versions of apps, such as Zoom, that they feared could be used to spy on teachers and students in universities. But overall, the group viewed the interest of China and Chinese technology companies in Latin America as a positive. More broadly, they appreciated that China and Xi Jinping listened to the perspectives of officials in Latin America and genuinely wanted to engage in joint innovation and technology development. The US-led 'national security' imperative was much less appealing and persuasive. I discovered a similar openness to Huawei in a meeting with senior business leaders in New Zealand in summer 2018. The group, all of whom were involved in doing business in China, displayed few qualms about Huawei's ability to use its network to access IP. As one participant stated, "There is no difference to us whether it is the United States or China spying on us." Despite the sanguinity of the businesspeople, however, the New Zealand government ultimately decided not to include Huawei equipment in its 5G infrastructure.

During 2019–20, Huawei came to symbolize the potential for the world's technology ecosystem to splinter into two: one half dominated by Huawei and the other by its European competitors Nokia and Ericsson. Embodied in that choice for some countries was a decision as to whether China posed a value-based and/or national security threat: Huawei was China's avatar. Yet ultimately, the global decoupling dance did not center only on high-flying Huawei and its 5G technology but rather on the less visible semiconductor industry upon which 5G is built.

Creating Something from Nothing

Then Commerce Secretary Penny Pritzker did not mince her words: "Let me state the obvious: this unprecedented state-driven interference would distort the market and undermine the innovation ecosystem. . . . The US government will make clear to China's leaders at every opportunity that we will not accept a $150 billion industrial policy designed to appropriate this industry."[137] Speaking before a crowd of Washington, DC, foreign policy experts and officials, Pritzker was laying out the US government opposition to Beijing's plans to invest $150 billion to create an indigenous semiconductor industry. China's intention to increase its self-sufficiency rate in semiconductors from 9 percent in 2014 to 40 percent by 2020 and 70 percent by 2025[138] had been signaled in 2014 with a national program on integrated circuits and launched formally as part of its MIC 2025 initiative. For the United States, the stakes could not have been higher. At the time, China was the fastest-growing market for semiconductors worldwide and represented 56.6 percent of the global market, worth roughly $170 billion. US firms accounted for half of all worldwide semiconductor sales,[139] and Beijing had just announced that it planned to erase much of that opportunity over the next 10 years.

While the battle over Huawei grabs international headlines, it is only a small part of a tectonic shift underway as China seeks to reshape global technology and capital flows to advantage its domestic firms. As we have seen, China's playbook for global technology leadership reflects an effort to create its own indigenous, self-contained technological ecosystem, with Chinese companies, supply chains, and standards that it can then export globally through the BRI and standard setting bodies. In many respects, China wants to decouple from much of the international community's technology ecosystem before recoupling on Chinese terms – when its firms, technologies, and standards are globally competitive and able to capture global market share. The success of China's effort, however, relies on the rest of the world maintaining consistency in its policies while China engineers its domestic transformation. Pritzker's speech was one of the first indications that the United States and other countries might have something else in mind. Over the next four years, the Trump administration moved to disrupt the Chinese playbook by cutting off the components necessary for China to develop its semiconductor industry. The result has been a significant disruption of Chinese ambitions but also a redoubling of Beijing's commitment.

In 2018, Premier Li Keqiang identified semiconductors as the single top priority among all of China's MIC 2025 industries.[140] Semiconductors are essential to every aspect of technological advancement: data analytics, the Internet of Things, computers, gaming, advanced medical devices, autonomous vehicles, smartphones, laptops, military hardware, robotics, AI and machine learning, surveillance technology, and 5G.[141] But while China is a leader in many technologies that use semiconductors, it lags behind in its ability to design and manufacture semiconductors that will power the next generation of technological advancement. Continued reliance for this critical technology on the outside world, particularly the United States and its allies and partners, had begun to pose a threat to China's plans.

Also known as a microchip, a semiconductor is a material that enables conductivity between an insulator and other materials. The science of the microchip rests primarily in the size of these chips; the most advanced microchips can attain a size of 7 nanometers or smaller. (A nanometer is one billionth of a meter.) There are different types of semiconductors, but the most common are integrated circuits, which contain multiple transistors. According to former Director for Investment of the US Trade Representative Office John VerWey, fabricating semiconductors is among the "most complicated, knowledge-intensive manufacturing processes known."[142] The factories are heavily automated, cost upwards of $10 billion, and require the coordination of up to 16,000 global suppliers.[143] In 2020, global sales of semiconductors hit $439 billion.[144]

China is the world's largest consumer of semiconductors, and chips are the country's largest import in monetary value – even exceeding oil[145] – but the country has not yet developed a fully indigenous capability to produce the most advanced chips. There are several distinct stages in the production process: design, manufacturing, assembly, testing, and packaging. With the exception of Africa, every continent has countries involved in some part of the supply chain. China excels in the lower-end assembly, testing, and packaging part of the chip supply chain. The design element, however, is dominated by the United States, Japan, South Korea, Europe, and Taiwan. Overall, the United States commands 45 percent of global market share, Korea 24 percent, the EU and Japan both 9 percent, Taiwan 6 percent, and China 5 percent.[146] China is overwhelmingly dependent on foreign-made chips. Of all the chips used in China, only 16 percent are made there and only half of those are made by Chinese companies.[147] In a closed-door symposium in July 2020, Chinese officials acknowledged that 90 percent of China's semiconductor manufacturing equipment was imported and its chips were two generations behind that of global leaders.[148]

The relative failure of China's indigenous semiconductor industry to thrive is not for lack of trying. It has represented the largest semiconductor market in the world since 2005, but despite massive investments in the industry since the mid-2000s, it has not managed to develop a world-class chip. Semiconductor Industry Association (SIA) Vice President

Jimmy Goodrich has followed China's semiconductor industry for well over a decade. When I asked him in August 2020 about the state of that industry, he took me back to 2014, when he said China first laid out its most recent semiconductor development plan. Beijing, he said, had determined that semiconductors were too important for national security for it not to have its own capabilities. As noted earlier, as part of its MIC 2025 program, Beijing set targets for the Chinese semiconductor industry to produce 40 percent of all semiconductors it used by 2020 and 70 percent by 2025. It committed $150 billion in public and state-owned funding over 10 years. (While a significant investment, US firms spend more than that.)[149] Beijing first set about trying to buy its way to the top. It bid for US stalwarts such as Fairchild Semiconductor and memory chip maker Micron. It also tried to take an equity stake in disk drive producer Western Digital Corp. State-backed Tsinghua Unigroup chairman and CEO Zhao Weiguo reportedly also attempted to take a stake in Taiwan's world-leading chip maker TSMC, delivering a message to Taiwan's chip industry that its reluctance to open up to Chinese investment was "unwise" and would lead it to a "dead end."[150] In 2015, alone, Chinese firms attempted to acquire 21 foreign chip companies, although with little success.[151]

By 2017, Beijing had determined that it would not be able to build its industry on the backs of foreign acquisitions. Instead, it decided to accelerate plans to build the industry itself. Beijing's 2017 New Generation Artificial Intelligence Development Plan acknowledged that China was "lacking major original results in . . . high end chips" and called for Chinese industry to achieve breakthroughs in "intelligent computing chips and systems," "high energy efficiency, reconfigurable brain-inspired computing chips," and "new-model perception chips."[152] Jimmy Goodrich argues that localizing the semiconductor production chains "runs counter to the DNA that makes up the global value chain." It will, he says, produce something that is "less agile, inefficient, and more expensive."[153]

Part of the Chinese government effort included inducing technology transfer. In a 2017 survey of the integrated circuit design and manufacturing industry, the US Department of Commerce discovered that 25 US companies were required to form joint ventures with or transfer IP to Chinese companies in order to maintain market access.[154] For example,

Qualcomm, a world leader in chip design, which had just settled a major antimonopoly case with the Chinese government, shifted more of its high-end manufacturing to its Chinese partners and upgraded the country's technology capabilities. Advanced Micro Devices and IBM paired with Chinese companies to develop server chips that would compete with their own chips.[155] Still, Goodrich argues that the chip makers were savvy and kept their highest-end chips and technology out of Chinese hands.

The ability of China to pay for top-flight foreign talent, particularly from Taiwan, has also been a significant boon to the country's efforts to scale up its capabilities quickly. Top chip engineers from TSMC now support Chinese firms. In fact, ex-TSMC executives with established reputations in the chip world moved to China to lead two Chinese government-backed chip projects: QXIC in Jinan and the now defunct Wuhan Hongxin Semiconductor Manufacturing (HSMC). Goodrich reveals that China will pay the engineers eight to ten times as much as they would make in Taiwan and pay for them to fly home on the weekends. Taiwan has been relatively helpless to stem the flow; thousands of Taiwanese chip engineers now work for mainland companies.[156]

This relationship has also played a role in mainland Chinese efforts to access foreign IP through illicit means. In 2015, Tsinghua Unigroup signaled interest in buying Idaho-based Micron Technology, a global leader in dynamic random-access memory (DRAM),[157] one option for semiconductor memory that can be used when building a computer.[158] Micron rejected the $23 billion informal bid, indicating that it had little chance of being approved by the US Committee on Foreign Investment in the United States, a government committee that reviews potential foreign investment for national security implications. The failed bid left China without a straightforward path to developing DRAM and NAND (a second type of memory that is used in USB flash drives and other storage devices). The only other global players were Korean powerhouses Samsung and SK Hynix – neither of which was open to acquisition.

The following year, the government of Fujian province, using a $431 million investment from the Chinese government, established Fujian Jinhua Integrated Circuit, with a near-term plan to produce 60,000 chips per month and a longer-term ambition to manufacture 240,000 chips monthly.[159] That same year, Fujian Jinhua also signed a deal with Taiwan's United Microelectronics Corporation (UMC) to invest

$300 million in R&D in exchange for advanced DRAM technology. As Fujian Jinhua began construction of a new $5.65 billion fabrication plant, a UMC engineer recruited two engineers from Micron's Taiwanese office and asked them to steal DRAM IP from Micron for the Fujian Jinhua venture.[160]

Two years later, in November 2018, the US Federal Grand Jury indicted Fujian Jinhua, as well as UMC, on charges of attempting to steal IP from Micron Technology. It also placed Fujian Jinhua on the Entity List, threatening the company's long-term viability. Earlier that year, Fujian Jinhua had taken Micron to court in Fujian on charges of patent infringement; it won the case, and Micron was banned from selling its chips in China. (Micron had no opportunity to present its case in court.)[161]

Despite its best efforts, the Chinese government has yet to deliver the type of strategic autonomy in semiconductor design and manufacturing that Xi Jinping desires. The country's semiconductor national champion SMIC is two or three generations of chip development behind its foreign competitors; and while Huawei's in-house chip design company HiSilicon has had some success, it lacks the capacity to manufacture the chips it has designed.[162] US sanctions against Huawei have also led many of its engineers to move to other firms, and the Trump administration blocked Huawei from accessing the software necessary to design chips, known as electronic design automation (EDA) tools. Two of the three dominant EDA companies, Synopsys and Cadence Design Systems, are American. Germany's Siemens owns the third, but its technology is American as well.[163]

Yet Beijing continues to try to marshal human and financial capital to realize its objectives. It began funding startups that hired executives from Synopsys and Cadence. Synopsys itself established a $100 million strategic investment fund in China, as well as a China semiconductor hub in Nanjing to protect itself against geopolitical tensions.[164] And in October 2019, the Chinese government created a $29 billion fund to support the semiconductor industry;[165] local governments are racing to develop their own champions, such as Fujian Jinhua; and Chinese venture capitalists have turned their attention to chips, doubling investment in the sector to $35.2 billion from 2017 to 2020. Xi has also called on companies such as Alibaba, Baidu, and Huawei to invest in semiconductors. By late 2020, China had more new fabrication facilities under construction than any other country in the world, and all three companies had announced plans to develop or even release chips. Already one-third of the companies listed on the STAR Market by value are semiconductor companies.[166]

Yet there are also signs of inefficiencies and waste in the rush to meet Xi's demands for an indigenous, globally competitive semiconductor industry. According to a report by the *Financial Times*, more than 13,000 enterprises registered as chip companies in the first nine months of 2020. Many had no experience in the industry. Some, for example, came from sectors such as seafood or automobile parts.[167] Chipmaker HSMC claimed it would provide 50,000 jobs, produce US$9.2 billion in output, and rival Chinese chip leader SMIC. The three founders, however, had no semiconductor experience or university education; one had previously sold TCM. The contractor they hired had never built a chip factory.[168] Yet, in the race to produce a chipmaking champion, the Wuhan government invested over $2 billion in the firm. Two and a half years later, in June 2020, the CEO, who had been brought in from TSCM fled, calling the experience "a nightmare." The next month, the Chinese financial media outlet Caixin reported that the company was facing a $16 billion cash shortfall.[169] HSMC declared insolvency in November 2020. No chip was ever produced and the founders disappeared. A $3 billion chip plant under construction by Tacoma Nanjing Semiconductor Technology similarly went bankrupt, and a US-backed manufacturing plant developed in partnership with the Chengdu city government ceased operating after being idle for nearly two years.[170] American semiconductor experts concur that scores of the new semiconductor fabs will be mothballed for failing to meet industry standards.[171]

China has already missed its target of 40 percent self-sufficiency by 2020 and is more than likely to fall short of its 2025 objective of 70 percent; by early 2023, it had achieved about 20 percent.[172] In November 2020, the powerhouse Tsinghua Unigroup, which had received more than $3.2 billion in support from the Chinese government since 2015, ran into trouble. The company had gone on a spending spree, buying up significant global talent, including one of Taiwan's top chip innovators and executives, Charles Kau (who left the firm in October 2020), and defaulted on a $198 million bond. It was a steep fall since Beijing had crowned the firm one of its national champions. In 2017, the firm's chairman said that by 2020 his group would close in on Qualcomm,[173] but the firm failed to develop new technology and expand its market share. Ultimately, some observers have noted, the danger is that China's chip industry will resemble its foray into commercial aviation, with significant sums of money expended, only to deliver products with outdated technology.

The Decoupling Dance

While much of China's problem is home-grown, US policy has introduced significant new obstacles. Washington has passed laws that limit not only the ability of US firms to sell semiconductor technology and manufacturing equipment to China but also the ability of other countries' firms whose equipment relies in some measure on US technology to sell to certain Chinese firms. And in some cases, even when another country's technology had no US component, the Trump administration worked to bar the sale of the technology to China. SIA's Goodrich pointed to the Trump administration's success in persuading the Dutch company ASML not to sell its $120 million photolithography machine, the only one of its type in the world, to China. The technology is necessary to make the most advanced chips – those 3 nanometers and smaller. Without the ASML technology, SMIC cannot advance further unless it develops indigenous technology, which will take years.[174]

The head of global supply chains for one of the United States' top technology companies described to me the decoupling process as being spurred by three events: the increase in labor costs in China; the US–China trade war; and various US government policies seemingly aimed at crippling China's technological rise. Even as he contemplated moving one-third of his business out of China over the next several years to insulate his operations from the increasingly unpredictable dynamic with the United States, he noted that the China market was "too big to ignore," and the company would certainly keep significant assets there to serve it. For American companies such as Qualcomm, the US restrictions are challenging. These firms understand restrictions on chips provided for sensitive technology applications, such as 5G, want to sell chips designated for common devices such as smartphones and watches.[175]

In 2018, Huawei paid US firms such as Qualcomm, Intel, and Micron Technology $11 billion. As much as 60 percent of Qualcomm's revenue came from China, more than 50 percent for Micron, and 45 percent for Broadcom. Veteran China technology expert Scott Kennedy is worried about the US decoupling effort. In 2019, China accounted for $70.5 billion in US semiconductor sales, more than one-third of the total US sales. And as Kennedy notes, the industry employs more than 240,000 Americans in 18 states.[176] Kennedy's fears are well placed: one of Silicon Valley's most innovative chip design firms, Xilinx, was forced to cut over 100 employees as a result of its inability to sell to Huawei.[177]

Within the US government, however, the thinking about technological decoupling is much less about the implications for US business than those for US national security. I asked Matt Turpin, who served in the US government for 25 years, the last few during 2018–19 as the National Security Council's director for China and senior advisor on China to the secretary of commerce, why the United States had targeted Huawei and more broadly the semiconductor industry. I had expected to hear about MIC 2025, Huawei's violations of the US sanctions on Iran, and IP theft. Instead, I received a wide-ranging and instructive education on the imperatives of US national security.

The US initiatives, Turpin explained, were about the Third Offset – a strategy he worked on at the Pentagon with former deputy secretary of defense Robert Work beginning in 2014 to ensure that the United States maintained an innovation edge in military-related technologies and technology platforms. Turpin described a sense of shock when US officials realized how quickly China had developed its own military-technological offset strategy to manage competition with the United States. In order to maintain a deterrent, Turpin explained, the United States needed to be one to two generations ahead of the competition. If you lose that advantage, there is no deterrent. In a world in which China was now the global hub of electronics manufacturing, however, the Chinese, Turpin argued, "were effectively inside the system with the United States" and "it was no longer possible for the United States to 'out-innovate' China and then deny them the fruits of that innovation." Addressing this type of national challenge was not about the Defense Department, it was about global supply chains; and for that, US policy needed to engage with the Commerce and Treasury Departments as well. Huawei mattered, in particular, Turpin indicated, because it was spread across all sectors: hardware, radio access networks, routers, and undersea cables; no other company possessed that type of reach. As a result, the United States sought to deny Huawei critical components, like field-programmable gate arrays, programmable chips that the company needed to build 5G networking equipment (and which have applications from video equipment to military applications, such as electronic warfare, secure communications, and radar).

For Turpin and the broader national security community, the China threat is existential. He is concerned that the burden of proof of malign Chinese intent and activity is too high for many in the US government and that this has prevented the United States, until recently, from responding in a coordinated and effective manner. Moving forward, Turpin suggested, there needs to be public discussion of Chinese intentions and behavior; based on this assessment, the United States then needs to withdraw any assistance or support, political or economic, for Chinese policies that negatively impact US interests. The United States cannot change Chinese behavior, he concluded, but it can change its own.

Conclusion

China's emergence as a world-class technology power capable of setting global standards is a top priority for Xi Jinping and the rest of the Chinese leadership. They have put in place a suite of policies designed to advance this objective, including: a demand-driven model for R&D; significant financial support for individual firms and universities as well as start-ups; the protection of Chinese firms from foreign competition through programs such as MIC 2025; the acquisition of foreign talent and technology through both licit and illicit means; alignment between Chinese government priorities and those of Chinese firms; and pushing Chinese standards through the BRI and international standard setting bodies.

This highly centralized and controlled approach has significant benefits in its ability to link core technology priorities identified in strategic plans such as MIC 2025 with funding initiatives, talent acquisition, and efforts at international standard setting. It has paid off in areas such as 5G, where a Chinese company such as Huawei has driven technological advances and been recognized as a world leader. Chinese government policy provided financing and protected the Chinese market from foreign competition, but the technological advances emerged from an actor that both innovated and acquired technological know-how and possessed an intuitive understanding of the market.

At the same time, the Chinese playbook has created problems for Chinese companies as they seek to expand globally, particularly in advanced market democracies, where there are broader concerns over national security and Chinese government access to countries' information. Xi Jinping's push to deepen the CCP's control over nominally private firms such as Huawei has contributed to their exclusion from some markets. Moreover, Beijing's political repression in Xinjiang and Hong Kong has created a context in which Chinese technology companies are understood as part of a broader Chinese challenge to democratic norms. To the extent that Chinese technology companies underpin this political repression by providing surveillance and censorship technologies, it also impinges on their ability to be treated as separate from the Chinese state and to expand their global market share.

Chinese strategic technology plans, such as MIC 2025 and Dual Circulation, also seek to decouple Chinese technology innovation and manufacturing from the international economy in order to develop and protect an indigenous Chinese technology ecosystem before eventually recoupling. Critical to this process, however, is the continued acquiescence of foreign actors to Chinese terms, such as accessing foreign talent and foreign technology. The decision of the United States to break the pattern by investigating IP theft or other abuses by the Thousand Talents Plan and by placing firms such as Huawei on the Entity List created unforeseen and challenging disruptions to Beijing's strategic plans. Even as firms in each country want access to the other's market, the degree of technology decoupling underway will be difficult to arrest given political concerns and the imperatives of economic and security competition.

Moreover, as the following chapter explores, China is advancing an even broader process of political and ideological decoupling. It is working to transform the global governance system, and in particular norms and values around human rights, internet governance, and economic development, to reflect Chinese values and priorities. Its vision is one in which China's state-centered model of political and economic development is both protected and promulgated.

6

Rewriting the Rules of the Game

It was a steep fall from grace. Meng Hongwei had spent most of his 40-year career in China's criminal justice system. He had moved up through the ranks of China's Public Security Bureau – the country's internal security force – eventually rising to the position of vice minister in 2004. Little known outside China, he achieved international renown in November 2016 when he was elected president of the Paris-based International Police Organization (Interpol), becoming the first Chinese official to hold the position and one of a growing club of Chinese nationals to hold a leading position in an international governmental organization or specialized agency within the United Nations. (Chinese officials already sat at the top of the ITU, the ICAO, the United Nations Industrial Development Organization [UNIDO], and the AIIB: see Table 6.1.) Yet, in September 2018, less than two years after his election, Meng was recalled to Beijing. He managed to send a single WeChat message to his wife, Grace. It advised her to "wait for my call." The only sign of possible trouble was the knife emoji – a euphemism for the CCP's Central Politics and Legal Affairs Commission, which coordinates all law and law enforcement agencies – appended to the brief message.[1] Two weeks later, on October 4, his wife reported him missing, and three days after that, the Chinese government informed Interpol that it was investigating Meng for corruption and "willfulness." Formal charges levied the following year included "abusing his position and power for personal gain" and "disregarding the principles of being a party member."[2]

Meng did not appear in public again for almost nine months. And when he did, he was standing before the Tianjin No. 1 People's Court outfitted in a mustard-colored jumpsuit and confessing to "using various positions" to "help companies and people make illegal gains." He pleaded guilty to accepting bribes totaling over $2 million. As punishment, he was expelled from the Communist Party, stripped of all his positions, fined $290,000, and sentenced to 13 years in prison.[3]

Table 6.1   Chinese leadership in global governance institutions, 2020

UN agencies that China heads		
Name	Leadership term	Function
Food and Agriculture Organization (FAO)	2019–23	Coordinates efforts to end hunger and to assist governments in developing agricultural and water resources
International Telecommunication Union (ITU)	2015–22	Allocates global radio spectrum and satellite orbits, develops information and communications technology (ICT) technical standards, and improves ICT networks in developing nations
United Nations Industrial Development Organization (UNIDO)	2013–21	Assists countries in economic and industrial development in line with UN Sustainable Development Goals
International Civil Aviation Organization (ICAO)	2015–21	Directs the development and standardization of international air transport policies

International organizations that China has created			
Name	Established	Membership	Function
Shanghai Cooperation Organization (SCO)	2003	8 member states, 4 observer states, 6 dialogue partners	Strengthen mutual trust and neighborliness among the member states; promote their effective cooperation in politics, trade, the economy, research, technology, and culture, as well as in education, energy, transport, tourism, environmental protection, and other areas; make joint efforts to maintain and ensure peace, security, and stability in the region; and move toward establishing a democratic, fair, and rational new international political and economic order
Asian Infrastructure Investment Bank (AIIB)	2016	83 member states, 20 prospective member states	Improve social and economic outcomes in Asia; invest in sustainable infrastructure and other productive sectors in Asia and beyond; better connect people, services, and markets

Sources: http://www.fao.org; https://www.itu.int; https://www.unido.org; https://www.icao.int; http://eng.sectsco.org; https://www.aiib.org

At one level, Meng's arrest is a simple story of Chinese president Xi Jinping's determination to root out corruption from within the CCP and government. Almost three million officials have been punished for corruption since Xi came to power in November 2012.[4] At another level, however, Meng's rise and fall is part of a much bigger story concerning Xi's ambition to realign the international system to reflect Chinese values, norms, and policy preferences.

The Global Governance Gambit

Global governance – the institutions, values, and norms that give shape to the international system – matters deeply to China. International institutions' rules and norms help define, for example, what constitutes acceptable behavior for a government's treatment of its own citizens. They also can determine who sits at the table to negotiate the rights to newly accessible resources as the Arctic melts or the standards that will determine which countries' telecommunications technologies are going to dominate the 21st century. And they can establish the rules of international engagement for issues as disparate as trade, maritime rights, and cyberwarfare. Interpol is just one of many global institutions and arrangements that countries have established to help govern themselves.

As both a permanent member of the United Nations Security Council (along with the United States, France, the UK, and Russia) and a self-proclaimed leader of the developing world, China has played a particularly important and unique role in shaping global governance norms and values. It has historically advocated for a set of principles that includes redistribution of global wealth from richer to poorer countries, the ability of every country to determine its own political and economic path, and the primacy of sovereignty or non-interference in other countries' affairs when considering international monitoring, sanctioning, and military action. As China's political and economic priorities have changed at home, however, so too has the relative importance it places on some of these norms. With the expansion of its military ambitions and security needs, for example, its views on UN peacekeeping transformed from outright opposition in the 1970s to limited participation in the 1980s and 1990s to its current position as the largest provider of peacekeeping troops among the permanent members of the Security Council. Behind this change is a set of multiple motivations, including China's desire to be perceived as a great power, to play a constructive role within the developing world, to learn from other countries,[5] and to ensure the safety of its own people, who now live and work in every corner of the world.

More recently, China has advanced itself not simply as a "rules-taker" but as a "rules-maker." In his January 2017 speech before the annual gathering of global elites at Davos, Xi Jinping articulated the case for global governance reform: "The global economic landscape has changed profoundly in the past few decades. However, the global governance system has not embraced those new changes and is therefore inadequate in terms of representation and inclusiveness."[6] And in identifying the system's shortcomings, Xi positioned China as prepared to lead in reforming the system. His call for reform of the international system is also fueled by a sense that the PRC has been disadvantaged in the current system because it was not present at the establishment of important international regimes, treaties, or institutions, such as the IMF. Instead, after World War II, China was represented in the United Nations and other international institutions by the KMT, first as the ruling party of the mainland and then, after its defeat in 1949, as the ruling party of the Republic of China on Taiwan. It was not until 1971, when the UN recognized the PRC government as the sole legitimate government of China, that the seat was transferred. Beijing's absence from the table in drafting many of the international arrangements that exist today does not mean that China has not benefited from the current system. In fact, Chinese officials often assert that because they have benefited from the international system, they do not want to undermine it.[7] Nonetheless, Beijing now seeks to put its stamp on virtually every policy domain – reforming norms and values to advance Chinese interests.

PKU scholar Wang Yong has argued that the global financial crisis was an important inflection point in PRC thinking around the need to reform global governance. Beijing viewed the United States as unwilling to undertake the necessary reform of international economic institutions or share power with emerging economies. (In addition, China objected to the United States' system of alliances that was closed to non-members[8] – most importantly China.) Many Chinese foreign policy elites, like Wang, believe that the world is now in the midst of dramatic shifts that favor China's call for change – one in which global economic, information, and cultural trends are equalizing power among countries, allowing for a plurality of views and contributing to a multipolar world. Xi's proposals for "building a community of shared human destiny, promoting common and cooperative security, maintaining an open world economy, and working cooperatively to maintain the international system"[9] seek to cement these trends by establishing norms and institutions that support a multipolar world, the end of the US-led alliance system, and acceptance of different countries' political systems as equally valid. In such a world, China argues, it is uniquely suited to play "a leadership role."[10]

Many international political and business leaders, as well as the media, have lauded Xi for his willingness to step up and lead on the global stage, particularly as the United States during the Trump administration began to retreat from its traditional leadership role.[11] Whether on the pandemic,[12] climate change,[13] or international development,[14] Xi has claimed the mantle of global leadership. China pursues what Xi calls "big country diplomacy" – a term that signals Beijing's determination to shape its external environment.[15] As French scholar Alice Ekman describes, Xi is masterful at positioning himself as a keynote speaker at international conferences and describing China as a builder of world peace, contributor to global development, and upholder of international order.[16] He also blends Chinese concepts such as "rule by law," in which the CCP stands above the law, with traditionally accepted concepts such as "the rule of law," in which every person and government entity is equal under the law. Over time, Ekman argues, this conflation of PRC discourse with the norms and values embodied in the current rules-based order leads the rest of the international community to believe that China and liberal democracies share a similar approach to global governance, when they in fact do not.[17]

In the context of Xi's big country diplomacy, Meng Hongwei's election as president of Interpol represented a victory for China's broader strategy to place its officials in leadership positions of international organizations. The decision to arrest Meng, therefore, could not have been taken lightly. It removed an important channel through which the Chinese leadership could exert its influence in a prestigious international organization.

During even Meng's brief two-year tenure as president of Interpol, China made significant progress in using the organization to advance its domestic political and security interests. Beijing hosted the 2017 Interpol

General Assembly – a gathering of almost 1,000 officials from more than 150 countries – featuring Xi Jinping as the keynote speaker. In his speech, Xi raised China's desire to help upgrade Interpol's communications network[18] – providing a clear path to advance Chinese technology companies such as Huawei in the process. He also offered to train as many as 5,000 law enforcement officials.[19] Interpol Secretary-General Jürgen Stock attended the second BARF and signed a declaration of strategic cooperation with China's minister of public security, guaranteeing that Interpol would collaborate to help safeguard Beijing's BRI infrastructure projects.[20] According to human rights organizations, even before Meng's appointment, China used Interpol for its own purposes by issuing "Red Notices" – Interpol's system for alerting other countries to wanted criminals – to extradite not only criminals but also political dissidents back to China.[21] And merely by holding a leadership position in Interpol, the Chinese government gained legitimacy at home. A *Beijing Youth Daily* article argued that "a Chinese person has been elected as the head of Interpol . . . which undoubtedly further reflects the recognition that Interpol and the international society give to China's own rule of law."[22]

China's engagement with Interpol provides a glimpse into some of the reasons behind the priority that Beijing places on global governance and the strategies it deploys to advance its interests. While Xi is committed to the broader sweep of global governance reform reflected in multipolarity and sovereignty, he also understands international institutions and arrangements as a set of opportunities to advance narrower PRC economic, political, and strategic interests. Meng's leadership of Interpol offered China the opportunity to use the organization in service of its domestic expansionary program, the Belt and Road; to shape the nature of Interpol police training in ways that could support Chinese interests (e.g. around the issuance of Red Notices); to integrate Chinese technology into a critical international telecommunications infrastructure; and to enhance the legitimacy of its conception of the rule of law within the broader Chinese public. These same motivations of political ambition, domestic legitimacy, economic expansion, and national security drive China to try to reform international norms, values, and institutions across a wide array of issue areas.

Beijing's approach to the four arenas of global governance explored below (the Arctic, human rights, cyber-governance and technology standards, and development finance) reveals yet another playbook for Chinese foreign behavior patterns – in this case designed to transform international institutions and China's role within them. To achieve its strategic objectives, Beijing seeks to place Chinese officials in leadership positions within global governance institutions; flood the institutions' expert committees with its representatives; coordinate all relevant public and private actors to advance its interests; provide financial contributions that are targeted to realizing its domestic priorities; and ensure close integration between its initiatives within international institutions and domestic policy priorities. It is an approach that has yielded several wins but also is incurring growing international opposition.

Let Me In . . . It's Cold Out Here

The Arctic lives in many people's imagination as a vast and mostly untouched icy blue terrain of majestic glaciers and frigid waters, populated by polar bears and reindeer. In reality, it is a region with vast natural resources and economic opportunity. According to the US Geological Survey, the Arctic accounts for 13 percent of the world's undiscovered oil and 30 percent of its undiscovered natural gas.[23] And the region confronts some of today's most pressing global governance challenges, such as climate change. The closest major Chinese city to the Arctic circle, Harbin, sits over 900 miles away. This distance and the fact that China is not an Arctic country, however, have not deterred Beijing from seeking to establish itself as an Arctic power and realize its economic and strategic interests in the region.

A small group of countries that border the Arctic – Russia, Sweden, Norway, Denmark, the United States, Canada, Finland, and Iceland – as well as a representative of the region's indigenous peoples, oversee the management of its resources through the Arctic Council.[24] Founded in 1996, the Arctic Council has spent most of its existence in relative obscurity. Over the past few decades, however, melting polar ice sheets have transformed the geography of the Arctic and, with that, the profile of the council. As the ice melts, previously untapped resources, such as energy and fish, are becoming available. Two new shipping routes are also emerging: the first, the Northern Sea Route, could cut as much as two weeks off the existing Asia-to-Europe route via the Suez Canal and the Strait of Malacca. The second, the Transpolar Sea Route, will traverse the top of the Arctic, eliminating a few additional days of shipping time. Access to these resources and the shipping routes have become a topic of global interest, particularly to China, which is the world's largest trading power and consumer of energy and fish. As the ice melts, China will have access to a route that puts it 4,000 nautical miles closer to Europe. And as the director of the Dalian Maritime University's Research Center for Polar Maritime Studies has commented, "Whoever has control over the Arctic route will control the new passage of world economics and international strategies."[25]

A Boot in the Door

China, under the Nationalist government, was an initial signatory to the Spitsbergen Treaty (known as the Svalbard Treaty as of 1925), which recognized Norway's sovereignty over the archipelago but also protected the rights of all citizens and companies from treaty nations to reside and do business there.[26] China's first foray into Arctic affairs, however, occurred in 1989, when it created the Shanghai-based Polar Research Institute of China. Soon after, it began to establish itself as a center for Arctic research. With a staff of over 200 academic and non-academic workers, the institute forged partnerships with other Arctic research centers throughout the world. In 1992, for example, Beijing organized a five-year scientific research program in the Arctic with two German universities. The Polar Research Institute also established a China–Nordic Arctic Research Center in Shanghai in 2013 to promote collaborative research between nine Nordic and eight Chinese research universities and institutes. The center's broader mission is revealed in its statement of purpose, which includes an effort to "promote cooperation for the sustainable development of the Nordic Arctic and a coherent development of China in a global context."[27] China also constructed a research station on Svalbard, a satellite receiving station in Kiruna, Sweden, a second research center in Iceland, and a third as yet undeveloped in Finland.[28] It jumpstarted its ability to undertake independent research in the Arctic by purchasing an icebreaker from Ukraine in 1994. Named *Xuelong*, or "Snow Dragon," the icebreaker enables China to pursue research in both the Arctic and Antarctica. China brought its own domestically built

Figure 6.1   Chinese icebreaker *Xuelong 2*
Source: Xinhua/Alamy

icebreaker – *Xuelong 2* – on line in 2019 (Figure 6.1). Based on a Finnish design, it is operated by the Polar Research Institute. As a result, China is a leader in Arctic expeditions, having undertaken nine to the Arctic and 28 to Antarctica. As noted in chapter 2, experts believe that China is on its way to building a powerful nuclear-powered heavy icebreaker; only Russia currently possesses such a capacity.[29]

China has also become a leading player in international non-governmental research organizations centered on Arctic issues. It joined the International Arctic Science Committee in 1996 and seeded every one of the working groups with a Chinese official or scholar. And in 2005, China became the first Asian country to host the committee's Arctic Science Summit week, which is recognized as the most important gathering of all organizations engaged in Arctic research.[30]

While China's geographic distance from the Arctic precludes membership in the Arctic Council, it does hold a seat as a Observer. As an observer, China cannot participate directly in decision-making, but it can take part in working groups and propose projects through an Arctic state.[31] China submitted its application to become a Observer in 2007, and in May 2013, the Arctic Council welcomed it, along with Italy, Japan, India, South Korea, and Singapore, as a new observer to the council.[32] China's scientific experts provide one basis for its growing participation in the organization's affairs. Since being elected as an Arctic Council observer, China has become its most active participant. It has submitted an annual observer review report to the organization, participates in working groups and task forces, hosts numerous meetings, and has recommended more than 25 experts to relevant programs, of which eight have been accepted. China was also one of the five Arctic Council Observers to sign an international agreement – the Arctic 5+5 – that banned commercial fishing in the central Arctic.[33] To the extent possible, China uses its status as an observer to make its voice heard at a level equivalent to that of an Arctic Council member.

Kicking the Door Wide Open

China's Arctic interests extend well beyond science-related concerns. A growing strategic interest in the region mirrors the country's broader global ambition in the wake of the 2008 global financial crisis. In 2009, the Polar Research Institute set up an Arctic strategic research department to provide policy support for the Chinese leadership on geopolitical issues around the region.[34] Scholars and officials soon began to articulate a number of rationales for deeper Chinese involvement. One of China's foremost scholars of Arctic politics, Guo Peiqing, stressed the PRC's emergence as a global power: "Being distant from the Arctic should not be the reason for us to be inattentive. China is on the path to becoming a global power from being a regional power. What is happening in the polar region concerns Chinese interests."[35] Others focused on the nature of the issues the Arctic engaged with. As Assistant Minister of Foreign Affairs Hu Zhengyue noted at the time, "Although the Arctic is mainly a regional issue, it is also an interregional issue because of climate change and international shipping."[36] In 2010, then assistant foreign minister (and currently UN under-secretary-general for economic and social affairs) Liu Zhenmin stated, "The issue for Arctic Council members now is how to involve non-Arctic states in relevant research endeavors and discussion at an early stage and in depth."[37] In discussing China's interests in the Arctic, the editors of the *Journal of the Ocean University of China* wrote, "Preparedness ensures success, while unpreparedness spells failure. Only with the development of forward-looking, in-depth research can

[China] possess the right to speak up about future international affairs pertaining to the polar regions."[38]

Guo later made clear his discontent with the Arctic states' control over the decision-making process. The 2011 Nuuk talks on criteria for observers mandates that Arctic Council Observers recognize the sovereignty, sovereign rights, and jurisdiction of the Arctic states over the Arctic. In response to the declaration, Guo stated:

> The "high level official report" marks the emergence of the Arctic edition of the Monroe Doctrine. The Arctic states have declared to the world that the Arctic is the Arctic of "the Arctic states." They oppose the notion that the Arctic is the common heritage of all humankind and hope by means of the Monroe Doctrine to break up interests within their domain and weaken the rights to participation of states outside it.[39]

Shanghai Institute of International Relations scholar Chen Baozhi adopted an even stronger position: "It is unimaginable that non-Arctic states will remain users of Arctic shipping routes and consumers of Arctic energy without playing a role in the decision-making process, and an end to the Arctic States' monopoly of Arctic affairs is now imperative."[40]

In a speech delivered in Hobart, Australia, in 2014, Xi Jinping signaled Beijing's strategic Arctic ambition. He declared that China would soon be "joining the ranks of the polar great powers" and that polar issues had a "unique role" in both its "marine development strategy" and its objective of becoming a "maritime great power."[41] Two years later, China published a guidebook on Northwest Passage shipping that included navigation charts. It also wove the Arctic into the BRI, outlining a vision for a Polar Silk Road and encouraging Chinese companies to contribute to the infrastructure for the new shipping routes and to conduct commercial trial voyages.[42]

Money Talks

Xi's push for China to establish an economic foothold in the Arctic has translated into significant investment. Between 2012 and 2017, Beijing invested or loaned as much as $90 billion toward Arctic development.[43] In Greenland, Chinese companies have taken stakes in several mining projects; their investment between 2012 and 2017 reportedly equaled almost 12 percent of Greenland's GDP.[44] State-owned China National Petroleum Corporation possesses a 20 percent equity stake in Russia's $27 billion Yamal Peninsula liquefied natural gas project and associated port in Sabetta. (This investment is considered part of China's Polar Silk Road, and its Silk Road Fund has an additional 10 percent stake in the plant.)[45] And Iceland has served as a testbed for Huawei's 5G technology, as well as the site of Chinese energy investments, including in a methane company.[46]

One by one, however, the Nordic countries have signaled disquiet over the national security implications of China's investments. Malin Oud, head of the China program for Sweden's Raoul Wallenberg Institute, told me that alarm bells first began to go off in Sweden in 2017 when Hong Kong-based Sunbase International approached the small town of Lysekil, with only 14,000 citizens, to build a deep-water port. The Sunbase CEO had strong ties to the Chinese government, and the plan had the backing of the China Communications and Construction Corporation. The deal was scuttled in early 2018 after an explosion of negative publicity. At the same time, at the January 2018 Defense and Society conference in Sweden – the annual gathering of the Nordic countries' defense ministers – the participants focused their attention for the first time on China, as opposed to only Russia. In 2019, the Swedish Security Service cited Beijing's cyberwarfare, as well as its acquisition of companies, as a threat to Sweden's national security:[47] Chinese companies had invested in 65 Swedish companies between 2002 and 2019, including companies with dual-use technology such as lasers and semiconductors.[48] In response, Sweden announced plans in 2020 to tighten its FDI rules.

Sweden was not alone in rethinking the potential risks posed by Chinese investments. In Iceland, Chinese businessman Huang Nubo attempted to buy a large tract of land, ostensibly for a golf resort. The communities surrounding the proposed land purchase were enthusiastic about the potential injection of Chinese capital. They considered buying the land themselves and then signing a long-term lease with Huang.[49] Iceland's interior minister, Ögmundur Jónasson, who ultimately rejected the deal, worried, however, that the real intent was to build a Chinese-controlled airfield or port.[50] Subsequently, Iceland adopted new laws that limited the ability of foreigners to purchase land, thus stymieing additional efforts by Chinese companies to establish tourism businesses.

Denmark, too, balked at three high-profile Chinese economic initiatives: first, when a Chinese firm attempted to buy a defunct US base in Greenland, which would have provided Beijing with a significant new base for intelligence activities in the Arctic;[51] second, when the Chinese ambassador made a trade deal with Denmark's self-governing Faroe Islands contingent on an agreement to sign a 5G contract with Huawei;[52] and, third, when Beijing attempted to build two airports in Greenland. In its 2019 risk assessment, the Danish Defense Intelligence Service identified Chinese large-scale resource investments in Greenland as a risk given the potential for "political interference and pressure" when "investments in strategic resources" are involved.[53] The intelligence service also assessed China's attempt to "build up Arctic knowledge and capabilities" as a concerted effort between military and civilian actors and described Beijing's participation in the Arctic as a plan to gain influence over the management of the region, in line with its great power ambitions.[54]

A 2019 report commissioned by the Finnish prime minister's office summed up the full range of threats it perceived from deepening its economic partnership with China. These included excessive Chinese influence in the Finnish economy, too much exposure to the Chinese economy, Chinese companies' poor environmental and social responsibility record, Chinese intellectual property theft, and the tendency of Chinese companies to announce high-profile projects – often with substantial enthusiasm from local Finnish actors – that are never realized.[55]

The Arctic Security Dilemma

China denies that its investments are linked to any security aspirations. However, in a 2009 article, Dalian Maritime University academic Li Zhenfu noted that the Arctic had "significant military value" and that the failure of China to have "fundamental information and scientific references to map out its Arctic strategy" limited its ability to advocate for its rights.[56] In late 2016, China opened its Remote Sensing Satellite North Pole Ground Station – its first overseas land satellite receiving station. A wholly Chinese-owned enterprise, it is located in Sweden about 125 miles north of the Arctic Circle. In January 2019, the Swedish

Defense Research Agency warned that even though the station was developed under the auspices of the Chinese Academy of Sciences, the close military–civil relationship in China suggested that it could be used by the PLA for monitoring purposes. It will allow Beijing to collect satellite data anywhere on earth twice as fast as before,[57] and it also enables high-precision satellite navigation and missile positioning. As one Swedish defense analyst noted, "The overall narrative being repeated in Sweden is that we've been naïve."[58]

Concern over Chinese military–civil fusion has also likely shaped the Nordic region's response to Huawei. Although Russia has fully embraced the Chinese company, only one of Iceland's three telecommunication providers, Nova, has selected it for its 5G provider. (The other two selected Ericsson.) The remaining Arctic Council members have barred Huawei 5G technology. And Huawei suffered another hit in its exclusion from the Arctic Connect – the 8,500-mile undersea fiber optic cable that will link Europe and Asia. Although the company had appeared poised to secure the Finnish contract, in summer 2019, when I asked Finnish secretary of state for foreign affairs Matti Anttonen whether China was likely to play a role in the fiber optic cable project, he said there were no such plans.[59] European experts had expressed dismay at the potential for China to use submarine cable projects to assist in its underwater surveillance capabilities.[60] And when the winning companies were finally announced, Huawei was not among them. Instead, the project will be spearheaded by the Finnish company Cinia and the Russian mobile phone provider MegaFon, along with an array of additional Finnish, Japanese, and Norwegian companies.[61]

Military officials in the United States have also voiced concern over Chinese intentions in the Arctic. Former Commandant of the US Coast Guard Karl Schultz highlighted for me Beijing's actions in the South China Sea and its unwillingness to abide by UNCLOS as important indicators of why countries should be apprehensive about China's growing presence in the Arctic. He also stressed his belief that the Arctic is likely to become an arena of future great power competition. In public settings, Schultz has further underscored his concern over China's massive shipbuilding effort, arguing that "presence equals influence"; at the current rate, he notes, China will out-build the United States by 2025, possessing both more capacity and more capability.[62]

As Arctic states grapple with developing an effective response, Beijing has demonstrated no sign of slowing down its activities. In 2018, it released its first Arctic white paper, an effort to develop a compelling narrative of China's rights and interests in the region. The white paper identified China as an "important Arctic stakeholder," which represented a shift from its previous self-proclaimed status as a "near-Arctic state" and a step closer to Xi's dream of China as a great Arctic power.[63] China's terminological twister around its Arctic status earned the ire of then US secretary of state Michael Pompeo, who delivered a speech at the May 2019 Arctic Council gathering in which he stated definitively: "There are only Arctic states and non-Arctic states. No third category exists and claiming otherwise entitles China to exactly nothing."[64]

Perhaps more consequentially, the white paper also reframed Arctic governance in a way that enhanced the role of non-Arctic states and supported Chinese conceptions of a new world order:

> The future of the Arctic concerns the interests of the Arctic States, the wellbeing of non-Arctic States and that of humanity as a whole. The governance of the Arctic requires the participation and contribution of all stakeholders. On the basis of the principles of "respect, cooperation, win-win result, and sustainability," China, as a responsible major country, is ready to cooperate with all relevant parties to seize the historic opportunity in the development of the Arctic, to address the challenges brought by the changes in the region, jointly understand, protect, develop, and participate in the governance of the Arctic, and advance Arctic-related cooperation under the Belt and Road Initiative, so as to build a community with a shared future for mankind and contribute to peace, stability, and sustainable development in the Arctic.[65]

The white paper also argued that non-Arctic states needed to play a role in the region because the impact of Arctic governance goes well beyond the Arctic to include resource exploration and exploitation, shipping routes, scientific research, and the environment. And it offered a subtle but critically important window into Beijing's newfound confidence in asserting its rights: "While pursuing its own interest, China will pay due regard to the interests of other countries." As Guo Peiqing has noted, rather than adopting a neutral position, China has "great strategic interests in the Arctic" and should push for the internationalization of the region.[66] Or as one Chinese university professor proclaimed, China has now become an "indispensable force in Arctic affairs."[67]

Despite its status as an observer rather than full member of the Arctic Council, China's strategy appears designed to earn the right for it to influence the region's policy at a level equivalent to that of council members. Chinese officials refer to China as a "near-Arctic power" and seek to reframe the language around Arctic governance to afford it a greater voice in decision-making. Beijing also attempts to fill the expert committees with Chinese scientists and officials to bring its perspective to bear. It uses its economic leverage to assert its leadership in both scientific exploration and natural resource exploitation, and to gain a foothold for its military and security-related interests through partnership with other countries. And as with its participation in Interpol, Beijing also looks to use the international regime and the region more broadly to cement its BRI and advance the deployment of its 5G technology. This playbook has become China's calling card as it seeks to realize Xi Jinping's call to lead in the reform of the global governance system.

Do the Right Thing

China's Xinjiang Uyghur Autonomous Region is bordered by six Central and South Asian countries, as well as by Mongolia and Russia. Its population of 21 million is roughly half descended from Turkic Muslims and half from Han Chinese, many of whom have been sent there by Beijing over decades to dilute the majority Uyghur Muslims. Over time, the proportion of Han Chinese in Xinjiang has increased from 7 to 40 percent.[68] During the late 2000s through the mid-2010s, violence between the Uyghurs and Han erupted on several occasions, including deadly riots in 2009, a Uyghur-initiated knife attack in 2014 that killed 33 people at the Kunming train station, and suicide car bombers in Urumqi that killed at least 31 people that same year.[69] A small minority of Uyghurs also supported a separatist effort, calling for the establishment of an independent state of East Turkestan.

The Chinese government responded to these events in May 2014 by launching the "Strike Hard Campaign against Violent Terrorism." It was a sweeping campaign designed, as Xinjiang expert Rachel Harris describes, to target all religious expression as opposed to only the small number of Uyghur Muslims who might be susceptible to extremism. In the ensuing years, the campaign has expanded in scope. Beijing has criminalized religion, including daily prayer, beards, and veils,[70] compelled Uyghurs to break the Muslim prohibition on alcohol, and put in place a massive surveillance apparatus, including cameras, biometric data, and apps downloaded onto personal phones that feed information directly to the local public security bureau. It has also adopted modes of traditional Maoist intervention: the "Becoming Family Policy," which included Han Chinese descending into the homes of the Uyghurs to observe and report on their practices and to try to inculcate them with CCP values. Even traveling abroad or having family abroad raises suspicion. Beijing has also established a network of "labor and reeducation" centers that reportedly house upwards of one million Uyghurs.[71] While Beijing insists that the facilities are training centers designed to give Uyghurs new skills, a pattern of secret abductions and forced detentions, the overwhelming security around the camps, and stories of torture and forced sterilization from Uyghurs and other Turkic minorities who have spent time in these training centers suggest otherwise.[72] According to the Australian Strategic Policy Institute, China has constructed as many as 380 detention centers in the region, the largest of which contains nearly 100 buildings.[73] And as much as 17.7 percent of adults in Xinjiang's Turkic and Hui minority population have spent time in one of these detention centers.[74]

There is little to no public outcry by Han Chinese over what is taking place in Xinjiang. In popular representations, Uyghurs are often portrayed as untrustworthy, criminal, and even prone to terrorism. Some discomfort is expressed privately, however.[75] As news first began to leak out about the camps, one Chinese official serving in the United States said to me, "We have no guidance on this issue. I don't know what to tell you." And a prominent Chinese scholar with whom I spoke in fall 2019 shared that his son had married a Uyghur from Xinjiang and still lived there, but that he had "rescued" his granddaughter from the repressive political environment and brought her to study in the coastal province where he lived. In addition, there are reports that Han Chinese living in Xinjiang are leaving because of the difficult conditions.[76] Even some officials appear conflicted over the existence of the camps. One local Xinjiang official was jailed after releasing thousands of inmates from a camp.[77] And Wang Yang, the Politburo Standing Committee member in charge of Xinjiang policy, has hinted at concern over the "dissatisfaction" of officials in the region and stated that "traditional ethnic culture should be protected and the normal religious customs of believers should be ensured."[78]

China also confronts rising criticism from the international community over the human rights situation in Xinjiang. In a statement before the UN General Assembly on October 29, 2019, the UK's ambassador to the United Nations, backed by 23 countries, condemned China for human rights abuses in Xinjiang, citing "credible reports of mass detention, efforts to restrict cultural and religious practices, mass surveillance disproportionately targeting ethnic Uyghurs, and other human rights violations and abuses in the region."[79] But China and its supporters had come prepared. Valentin Rybakov, the permanent representative to the UN from Belarus, representing 54 countries, praised China's "counter-terrorism" efforts in Xinjiang, including the establishment of "vocational education and training centers," and the "return of safety and security to Xinjiang." Rybakov insisted that the "fundamental human rights of people of all ethnic groups there are safeguarded."[80] In 2020, a similar letter raising concerns about the "political re-education camps" was introduced at the United Nations by Germany's UN ambassador with support from 39 countries, a significant increase from the previous year.[81] And although 45 countries supported China's actions in Xinjiang as necessary for "combatting terrorism and deradicalization,"[82] notably absent were the Central Asian countries that had supported China in 2019.

Much of Beijing's support in international institutions derives from a loose coalition of more than 50 developing economies referred to as the "Like-Minded Group of Developing Countries," over which China has shared leadership responsibility at different times with Russia and Egypt (see Table 6.2). In 2015 alone, the group coordinated statements on 15 issues.[83] Surprising to many, however, was that several countries with sizeable Muslim populations (Pakistan, Syria, the United Arab Emirates, and Saudi Arabia) supported China on Xinjiang, while others, such as Indonesia and Malaysia, stood on the sidelines, claiming ignorance of the problem or stating that there were other, more significant challenges to address.[84] For these countries, their growing economic and political relations with China, as well as a desire to protect themselves against criticism of human rights abuses, often contributed to their decision to support Beijing.[85]

Table 6.2 Countries that support China's Xinjiang, Hong Kong, and South China Sea policies

International support for China's Xinjiang policies		
Angola	Eritrea^	Pakistan^
Bahrain^~	Gabon^	Palestine^~
Belarus^	Grenada	Russia
Burundi^	Guinea Bissau^	Saudi Arabia^~
Cambodia^	Iran^	South Sudan^
Cameroon^	Iraq^~	Sri Lanka^
Central African Republic ^	Kiribati	Sudan^~
Comoros^~	Laos^	Syria^~
Congo^	Madagascar	Tanzania
Cuba^	Morocco^~	Togo^~
Democratic Republic of	Mozambique^	Uganda
the Congo	Myanmar^	United Arab Emirates^~
Dominica^	Nepal^	Venezuela^
Egypt^~	Nicaragua^	Yemen^~
Equatorial Guinea^	North Korea^	Zimbabwe^

Legend:
^ = Supported China's Hong Kong policy in 2020.
~ = Supported China's South China Sea policy in 2016.

Sources: *https://jamestown.org/program/the-22-vs-50-diplomatic-split-between-the-west-and-china-over-xinjiang-and-human-rights/*; *https://thediplomat.com/2020/07/which-countries-support-the-new-hong-kong-national-security-law/*; *https://amti.csis.org/arbitration-support-tracker/*

China has worked hard to prevent the issue of its treatment of Uyghurs from taking hold within the United Nations. In some cases, it threatens countries. During March 2018, for example, it warned UN ambassadors in Geneva that "in the interest of our bilateral relations and continued multilateral cooperation," they should not "co-sponsor, participate in or be present at" a panel event that month on human rights violations in Xinjiang sponsored by United States, Canada, Germany, the Netherlands, and the UK.[86] In other cases, Chinese officials have used their leadership positions within the United Nations to attempt to prevent the issue from being discussed. In September 2020, I spoke with President of the World Uyghur Congress Dolkun Isa, one of the world's leading Uyghur activists. Isa argues that 2015–16 marked an inflection point in the CCP's treatment of Uyghurs: "They abandoned bilingual education, closed all the mosques, banned fasting and beards, and set up checkpoints – you needed special permission to travel from one city to the next. It is ethnic cleansing." A student activist in Xinjiang in the late 1980s, he studied in Turkey and Germany after fleeing China for Europe in 1994; in 2006, he became a German citizen. For more than two decades, China used Interpol's Red Notice system to flag Isa as a terrorist and to alert other countries that he should be returned to China. In 2009, he was detained in South Korea and almost sent back to Beijing. German and US officials intervened, however, and he was deported to Germany. Isa suspects that China's financial contribution to Interpol gave it outsized influence. In 2018, after several years of work by Fair Trials, the international criminal justice watchdog organization, a committee of independent experts of Interpol removed Isa's name from the list.

The Chinese government has also repeatedly attempted to block Isa from speaking at the United Nations. In 2017, he was accredited by German NGO the Society for Threatened Peoples and slated to speak at the UN Permanent Forum on Indigenous Issues. Yet as Isa describes, three people physically prevented him from participating, pulled off his badge, and told him not to make any noise. When the Society for Threatened Peoples contacted the United Nations, it received no response. In 2018, Isa applied to speak at the same forum, was initially accredited, and then had his accreditation canceled two days before the meeting. When he went to the United Nations' badge office, he was refused a badge and told not to come again. The head of the United Nations Department of Social and Economic Affairs (UN DESA), Liu Zhenmin, had tried to block Isa by denying standing to the NGO that he represented. Liu accused Isa of sponsoring separatism and terrorism.[87] Still, Isa persisted, and the German and US missions to the UN, along with Human Rights Watch, worked on his behalf. The US ambassador even went with Isa to get a badge, yet he was still refused. Only when they appealed directly to the UN secretary general was Isa allowed entry.

Isa suggests that China uses its position as the second largest contributor to the United Nations to pressure the UN Human Rights Council (UNHRC) to prevent human rights defenders, including Uyghurs, Tibetans, and Taiwanese, from speaking. He told me that, contrary to protocol, staff from the UNHRC will share the names of those on the list to testify with the Chinese mission, giving Chinese officials time to block their appearance. Isa's claims are borne out by the public statement of Wu Hongbo, Liu's predecessor as under-secretary general for UN DESA. In commentary that was televised on CCTV, Wu claimed personal responsibility for blocking Isa's appearance in 2017, noting that he represented Chinese national interests by calling for Isa to be expelled from the forum.[88] Wu stated, "I think being a Chinese diplomat means one can't be careless when it is about protecting China's national interest and safety. We have to strongly defend the motherland's interests."[89]

Despite its best efforts, Beijing, however, has not managed to quell international criticism of its human rights and Xinjiang policies. While China has avoided direct censure by the United Nations for its practices in Xinjiang, in March 2020, several international NGOs questioned Beijing's UN ambassador Zhang Jun about the situation in Xinjiang and requested that UN High Commissioner for Human Rights Michelle Bachelet be permitted unfettered access to the region. The ambassador merely repeated official commentary that the reports of wide-scale human rights abuses and mass surveillance were based on "lies and rumors."[90] And as Chinese foreign minister Wang Yi embarked on a whirlwind tour of five European countries in late August and early September to repair relations that had been damaged by Chinese diplomacy during the pandemic, he announced – to widespread disbelief – that all the trainees in the "education and training program" had "graduated" and "found jobs."[91] In fact, the notion that China is committing genocide in Xinjiang – an understanding that Isa supports – is increasingly finding traction in Western countries, particularly in the wake of reports that Beijing was pursuing forced sterilizations, a condition of genocide formally recognized by the United Nations.[92] By February 2021, more than 180 human rights organizations had called for countries to commit to a diplomatic boycott of the 2022 Winter Olympics in China.[93]

What Is Mine Is Yours

China's engagement in global governance around human rights reflects two distinct, albeit interrelated, ambitions. First, as in the case of Xinjiang, China wants to prevent other countries from criticizing it for its human rights practices. To this end, it has deeply embedded itself in the existing human rights treaties and institutions. It is party to most – six of the nine – UN international human rights treaties, including those that cover discrimination against women, racial discrimination, torture, rights of children, economic, social, and cultural rights, and rights of persons with disabilities. China also signed on to the International Covenant on Civil and Political Rights (ICCPR) on October 5, 1998, although it never ratified the treaty. (As a signatory, it has the obligation to act in good faith and not defeat the purpose of the ICCPR.)[94] Importantly, China has held a seat on the UNHRC since its establishment in 2006, and it was reelected to the council for another three-year term beginning in 2021.

China's position within the UNHRC gives it the ability to shape the council's agenda and debates. For example, in July 2019, the NGOs UN Watch and the Human Rights Foundation invited the popular Hong Kong singer and pro-democracy activist Denise Ho to speak at a meeting of the 41st session of the UNHRC. During her two minutes of remarks, mainland representatives attempted to distract the audience from her statement by invoking two points of order.[95] A 2017 Human Rights Watch report also detailed how the Chinese government has photographed and filmed activists at the United Nations, rejected requests by Chinese activists to travel to the UNHRC meetings in Geneva, and used its position on the Economic and Social Council Committee on Non-Governmental Organizations to prevent accreditation for those NGOs critical of China.[96] In one particularly egregious case detailed in the report, China detained activist Cao Shunli as she attempted to travel to Geneva to participate in a training session on human rights hosted by the UN and, after she died in detention, blocked an NGO's call for a moment of silence dedicated to her at the UNHRC meeting.[97]

China is also engaged in a much larger project to transform the very definition of what constitutes human rights: to legitimize China's notion of state-determined rights as opposed to inalienable and innate rights of the individual, and of economic and social rights as opposed to civil and political rights. Research by Carnegie Endowment scholar Ted Piccone reveals that China has tried to change the discourse around human rights by referring to "human rights with Chinese characteristics" and "emphasizing national sovereignty, calling for quiet dialogue and cooperation rather than investigations and international calls to action, and advocating for the Chinese model of state-led development."[98] Such innocuous language, Piccone argues, undermines the legitimacy of international mechanisms to monitor human rights, as well as the ability to use name and shame tactics. Overall, it "weakens protections for human rights defenders and independent media."[99]

Over the past several years, China has had a number of wins. When it chaired the UNHRC panel tasked with vetting candidates for the position of the UN special rapporteur on freedom of opinion and expression, for example, it advanced the candidacy of Irene Khan, who has supported China's effort to equate development rights with human rights and has argued that the BRI could "contribute to strengthening international rule of law."[100] In June 2017, China also successfully advanced a resolution within the UNHRC which called on UN actors to submit examples of how "development contributes to the enjoyment of all human rights by all."[101] Ma Zhaoxu, China's permanent representative to the United Nations in Geneva, called the resolution "a milestone on the path of breaking the Western monopoly of discourse in human rights and issues."[102] And, together, China and Russia successfully used a budget-cutting exercise to challenge the 2014 UN Human Rights Up Front initiative, which established human rights monitors in peacekeeping efforts, and to eliminate a senior position within the UN secretary general's office that was designed to ensure that human rights considerations are embedded throughout the United Nations.[103]

Still, Beijing's human rights initiatives are not always successful. Between 2016 and 2018, five of China's seven initiatives failed. These included efforts to delegitimize human rights defenders by calling them "individuals, groups, and organs of society engaged in promotion and protection of human rights"; to weaken state obligations to cooperate with the UNHRC; to assert greater control over NGOs by limiting the freedom they have to receive support from external sources; to push respect for territorial sovereignty; and to decrease state cooperation with civil society.[104] Nonetheless, China continues to chip away at the core elements of the human rights regime. And it has taken the fight to the virtual space as well, launching a two-pronged attack to shape both the norms that define the degree of state control over the internet and the standards that will enable that control.

Claiming Space in the Cyber World

"Without cybersecurity, there is no national security, the economy and society will not operate in a stable manner, and the broad popular masses' interests will be difficult to guarantee," Xi Jinping lectured a group of senior CCP officials attending a cyber conference in April 2018.[105] Xi's concerns are not new. Chinese military and security analysts have long argued that internet sovereignty is no different than sovereignty over airspace or the maritime domain; and political analysts have expressed concern that the PRC is vulnerable to an Arab Spring-like internet revolution.[106] To stave off such a challenge, Beijing has pursued a broad strategy of advancing internet sovereignty as an international principle on the global stage, as well as establishing domestic policies around online freedom, privacy, and data localization that are at odds with those of liberal democracies.[107] In 2015, China supplanted Iran as the world's worst abuser of internet freedoms on Freedom House's scorecard. It is a distinction that China has maintained each year since. And since 2019, Freedom House has noted that Beijing's censorship had attained "unprecedented extremes."[108]

China's approach to advancing its norms around cyber-sovereignty is a multi-level game. As discussed in chapter 4, Beijing uses the BRI to provide training sessions and assistance in drafting laws for government officials in other countries on how to manage and censor the internet and to develop their domestic laws to reflect strong state control over it. Beijing also enforces its internet governance preferences through a number of additional avenues: domestic laws that are applied to multinationals; norms established in the UN General Assembly; and, most recently, technical standards advanced in the ITU.

In 2014, Beijing held its first World Internet Conference, an event described as "uniting government and private industry representatives from around the world" to advance ideas around "internet sovereignty," which would allow each country to "choose its own development path and management model of the internet."[109] The principles espoused by China at the conference echoed the country's 2010 white paper on the internet, which defined the limit of freedom of speech as "not being allowed to infringe upon state, social and collective interests or the legitimate freedom and rights of other citizens."[110] While most international actors understand free speech as an inherent individual right with limited state constraints, the China model prioritizes the state's determination of what is acceptable.

China worked hard to get buy-in for its principles. One American business executive who attended the 2014 conference recalled for me the drama surrounding Beijing's efforts to persuade conference attendees to sign a declaration calling for countries to "respect Internet sovereignty of all countries . . . each country's rights to the development, use, and governance of the Internet." Despite being cautioned by international participants that such a joint statement would not be welcomed, when the conference guests returned after midnight from a late-night meeting, they found just such a declaration slipped under their door with a request that it be signed by 8:00 a.m. Later that morning, at a small roundtable with the head of China's Cyber Commission, Lu Wei – later jailed for corruption – foreign conference participants, including senior academic and business executives, explained to China's cyber czar there would never be agreement. Lu Wei himself attempted to laugh off the issue, waving a piece of pink paper and claiming, "I hear some people are a little bit upset. You are all too sensitive." Five minutes later, after consulting with other Chinese officials, Lu backtracked, stating, "I, like you, stumbled into my room. I don't know where this [paper] came from." He then left the meeting. The declaration went no further, but the effort by Beijing to shape norms around internet freedoms continued. At the second Wuzhen summit the following year, Beijing deliberately misrepresented Wikipedia founder Jimmy Wales' address to the conference members on its official website. Wales had argued that "the idea that any one government can control the flow of information of what people know in their territory will become completely antiquated and no longer possible." Chinese conference officials, however, translated and reported his comments as "Probably we will see improved machine translation, which will very much enhance person-to-person communication. And also the government could conduct good analysis on people's communication in various relevant areas."[111]

Despite a clear lack of international support, China pressed forward with its internet sovereignty norms through its 2017 Cybersecurity Law. The law mandates that companies store data inside China and not transfer it to international servers. It also requires that multinationals allow

Chinese officials to test firms' equipment and software at any time. One provision of the law allows Beijing to demand companies' encryption keys, which would undermine the otherwise unbreakable encryption found in apps like Signal.[112] For multinationals, the law increased the risk that information they deemed sensitive could be accessed by the Chinese government, allowing for industrial espionage or tracking individuals for political reasons. Multinationals also confront ongoing demands from the Chinese government to restrict access to information Beijing deems sensitive. In July 2020, for example, Apple censored PopVote, a pro-democracy app that Hong Kong activists had planned to use to select candidates for the September legislative elections. Beijing warned the company that it contravened the new Hong Kong National Security Law. Apple had previously removed virtual private network apps that allowed Chinese citizens to bypass the Great Firewall, the *New York Times'* app, and the emoji of the Taiwanese flag from the iOS keyboard for people in mainland China, Hong Kong, and Macau.[113]

Beijing has also pursued a decade-long strategy in partnership with the SCO to advance its cyber-sovereignty norms within the United Nations. As scholars Sarah McKune and Shazeda Ahmed have documented, SCO members first adopted a cooperative agreement on information security in 2009, and, beginning in 2015, the member countries have conducted anti-cyberterrorism exercises that are designed to locate terrorist organization propaganda on the web, find the posters' identities and locations, and arrest them.[114] In both 2011 and 2015, the SCO submitted for debate a Code of Conduct for Information Security before the UN General Assembly in an effort to build consensus around norms of internet sovereignty. And in 2018, Russia, with the support of China, advanced a resolution within the UN General Assembly to collect countries' views on cybercrime. The following year, in December 2019, the UN General Assembly approved a Russian resolution supported by China that would establish a committee of international experts to draft a "comprehensive international convention on countering the use of information and communications technologies for criminal purposes."[115] The ultimate purpose was to lay the groundwork for a new draft treaty that would allow countries to exert greater control over activities and speech on the internet under the guise of addressing cybercrime.[116]

At the same time, Beijing has resisted any effort to apply existing international law to cyberspace. University of Copenhagen Law professor Anders Henriksen argues that the International Humanitarian Law imposes restrictions which constrain the behavior of potential belligerents,[117] and China does not want to be constrained in its use of cyber tools. Moreover, Beijing's interpretation of UN laws around the right to use force suggests that it would not view a cyberattack as an "armed attack" that would trigger the right to self-defense; and China further does not recognize preemptive self-defense that would allow a state to take measures to disable a cyberattack in advance.[118] This would become relevant, for example, were Beijing to launch or plan to launch a crippling cyberattack on Taiwan. To protect its interests, China has repeatedly argued against international efforts to adopt a more expansive understanding of the applicability of international law to the cyber world. However, it has moved aggressively to use the emerging field of technical standards around Internet governance to advance its preference for cyber-sovereignty.

Beijing's most powerful tool in advancing its political values in international institutions may ultimately derive from an unlikely source: its technological prowess. Over the past decade, China has become a leading force in UN standard setting around technology issues. In part, China's efforts are designed to support its companies. Its leadership in these standard setting bodies, however, can also enable it to redefine understandings around the rights of the state versus the individual in the virtual world.

Let's Get Technical

In early March 2020, after two years of research and meetings, the Chinese government released the basic parameters of its China Standards 2035 strategy. Coordinated among the Chinese Academy of Sciences, the Standardization Administration of China, the National Academy of Engineering, and Chinese technology companies, the strategy is designed to set domestic standards for products and technologies, such as 5G, virtual reality, and the cloud, that Beijing can then internationalize, ensuring interoperability between China's technology backbone and that of the rest of the world. One Chinese official laid out the rationale for the effort as follows: "Industry, technology, and innovation are developing rapidly. Global technical standards are still being formed. This grants China's industry and standards the opportunity to surpass the world's."[119]

Standards possess important economic, political, and security implications. Setting standards that are adopted globally will enable Chinese firms to derive significant new economic benefits: other countries will become markets for Chinese technologies and services, and instead of China paying fees to foreign multinationals to license technology, others will pay fees to license Chinese technologies.[120] As research by Emily de La Bruyère and Nathan Picarsic indicates, the China Standards 2035 program targets many of the same technologies included in Made in China 2025, such as new energy and autonomous vehicles, environmental technologies, medical equipment, new materials, high-end equipment and manufacturing, and others; and its ambitions extend through the entire supply chain for these technologies. For example, with regard to smart vehicles, Chinese standards will apply to "automotive information security, operating systems, communications, wireless charging, high power charging, fuel cell and battery recycling, and other related standards." The strategy also seeks to advance the proliferation of standards around Chinese platforms such as the social credit system, as well as e-commerce, finance, and logistics.[121] Moreover, the China Standards 2035 strategic outline also calls for China to engage deeply with preexisting international standards organizations, to develop new ones, where necessary, and to improve the country's ability to lead the organizations.

China has articulated a dedicated strategy to become a leader in setting technology standards. In 2015, it set several objectives: participating in at least half of all standard setting efforts in recognized international standard setting bodies; increasing the number of Chinese officials in leadership positions; and establishing China as a "standards power" by 2020. According to a report by the US–China Business Council, from 2011 to 2020, the number of Chinese in secretariat positions in technical committees or subcommittees increased by 73 percent in the ISO. And the number of Chinese companies participating in the Third Generation Partnership Project, which is responsible for setting 5G standards, has more than doubled to 110, more than twice the 53 US voting members.[122]

Two overarching standard setting bodies were headed by Chinese officials: the ITU was headed by Zhao Houlin, who was previously its deputy secretary general (he was reelected to a second four-year term as secretary general in 2018) and an official of China's Ministry of Posts and Telecommunications; and the International Electrotechnical Commission (IEC), which sets standards for power generation and transmission, home appliances, semiconductors, fiber optics, batteries, nanotechnology, and other technologies, was headed by Shu Yinbiao, chairman of China Huaneng, the Chinese state-owned energy and electric grid company. Zhao used his position to champion the BRI, signing a memorandum of understanding with China on assisting countries in strengthening their communications networks in 2017 and vowing in 2019 that the ITU would join hands with China: "It's the grand guide and platform for China's foreign aid plans. It's an express train that once you get on, you can join forces with China and develop along with the country." He also announced plans to sign a deal with the Export–Import Bank of China to facilitate the implementation of more ICT projects.[123]

Other countries' multinationals have raised concerns about China's growing dominance in standard setting bodies, noting that Chinese officials may use their position to promote Chinese-led proposals, and Chinese companies may be pressured into voting as a bloc in support of Beijing's objectives.[124] In a widely reported case, the Chinese firm Lenovo supported a standard for encoding information and correcting errors in data transmission that had been proposed by the American firm Qualcomm as opposed to the one advanced by Huawei. Lenovo was widely criticized as unpatriotic. When a second vote was conducted later that year, Lenovo supported Huawei, stating, "We all agree that Chinese companies should be united and cannot be played off one another by outsiders."[125] Zhao Houlin also publicly supported Huawei, stating, "Those preoccupations with Huawei's equipment, up to now there is no proof so far . . . if we don't have anything then to put them on the blacklist – I think this is not fair."[126]

As in the case of the Arctic, Beijing also places significant importance on expert committees. It floods expert committees with both Chinese proposals and participants. For example, in 2019, China offered 830 technical documents related to wired communications specifications in the ITU, more than the next three top submitters – South Korea, the United States, and Japan – combined.[127] In the area of surveillance technology, between 2016 and 2019, Chinese companies, including China Telecom, ZTE, Huawei, Hikvision, and Dahua, made every submission on technical standards to one section of the ITU, half of which were accepted. Most of the proposals were linked to "how footage from facial recognition cameras and recordings by audio surveillance devices are stored and analyzed."[128] In an interview with the *Financial Times*, the representative of the UK International Chamber of Commerce to the ITU, Nick Ashton-Hart, recalled a meeting in which the Chinese participants made 24 proposals one after the other related to the surveillance of people within cities. He noted, "They're very good at playing the numbers game. They use volume of contributions to have weight so that it's difficult for meetings not to reflect theirs as a dominant view."[129] And according to one participant, at the inaugural meeting of a standards subcommittee for AI under the auspices of the ISO and IEC, the Chinese and Russians brought such large delegations that it was difficult for others to push back on their initiatives.[130]

China's boldest move to enforce its internet governance vision on the rest of the world is its New IP initiative. Huawei, along with China's Ministry of Industry and Information Technology, China Unicom, and China Telecom, presented the proposal for New IP in the ITU in 2019. New IP contains within it the potential that the state, with its control over internet service providers, would have "control and oversight of every device connected to the network and be able to monitor and gate individual access."[131] It is the technical manifestation of China's political efforts to gain international acceptance for its vision of digital authoritarianism. It supports a "shut up command" in which a central point in the network can shut off communication to or from a particular address. This represents a significant shift from the current system, in which the network is an "agnostic postman that simply moves boxes around."[132] Huawei is also leading a group within the ITU that addresses future network technology, putting the company in an ideal position to advance its vision of New IP within the organization. As one UK ITU delegation member described the initiative, "You can now not only control access to certain types of content online, or track that content online, but you can actually control the access of a device to a network."[133] While most democracies have not responded favorably to the Chinese initiative, technology experts suggest that China could get traction simply by deploying its New IP framework and technology in countries where it already has a strong telecommunications presence[134] and political influence. It would be an important addition to its already comprehensive Digital Silk Road offerings.

Filling the Development Gap

Speaking before the second BARF in April 2019, UN Secretary General António Guterres lauded China's leadership in climate change, declaring that the BRI could play an important role in meeting the UN's 17 Sustainable Development Goals (SDGs), such as ending extreme poverty, and called for closely linking the SDGs with Belt and Road.[135] This was not the first time that Guterres had publicly supported the BRI. Just a few months earlier, he had affirmed the commitment of the UN itself to the BRI and enthused over its "immense potential."[136]

Guterres' remarks reflect the success Beijing has enjoyed in its multi-year effort to weave the BRI into the fabric of the United Nations. Xi Jinping himself made the case directly to the secretary general in 2016 that Belt and Road should be used to support the UN's 2030 Agenda for Sustainable Development.[137] And at the second BARF, Xi pledged an additional $1 billion in support of international organizations to implement projects that would benefit BRI countries.[138] By 2020, there were more than 25 studies, agreements, memorandums of understanding, and letters of intent signed between representatives of different agencies of the United Nations and Chinese officials affiliated with the BRI.[139] Some promised financial support, such as an agreement by the World Bank to commit more than $80 billion in advisory assistance to BRI efforts. Others appeared to offer little more than rhetorical support but were nonetheless noteworthy for their wholesale adoption of Chinese political language, such as a community of shared destiny for mankind.[140] As one observer noted, China is "UN-ising" Belt and Road.[141] For China, the United Nations provides a stamp of legitimacy for the initiative, an impressive organizational infrastructure through which to advance BRI projects, and a mechanism for amplifying the BRI message.

China's success in integrating the BRI mission and projects into a wide range of UN organizations and affairs is the result of years of stewardship of various UN organizations. Beijing has long played a leading role in UN DESA and UNIDO, organizations that Western countries have largely ignored.[142] A Chinese official has headed UN DESA since 2007; the current head, Liu Zhenmin, assumed the position of under-secretary general in 2017. As one European diplomat has commented, "DESA is a Chinese enterprise . . . everybody knows it and everybody accepts it."[143] In 2016, the Chinese government asked UN DESA to organize a study laying out how the BRI could be aligned with the UN's 2030 Agenda for Sustainable Development. One of UN DESA's Chinese nationals, Hong Pingfan, conducted the study and concluded that BRI could make a "great contribution" to the UN's 2030 agenda.[144] UN DESA has now initiated a China-funded program, "Jointly Building Belt and Road towards SDGs," the purpose of which is to support policies in BRI countries that "promote and harness the BRI for the acceleration of the SDGs."

UNIDO Director General Li Yong is also a former Chinese government official, who has served in his current position since 2013 and has used it to coordinate the organization's work closely with the BRI. At both BRI forums, UNIDO signed agreements with the Chinese government to strengthen cooperation, calling for UNIDO to "move towards coordinated strategies and policies, ensuring compatibility with BRI implementation in the participating countries and regions."[145] Cooperation between UNIDO and individual Chinese agencies also advances Chinese interests. For example, UNIDO signed an agreement with China's Ministry of Water Resources and the Standardization Administration of China to "work together to develop a series of guidelines in the area of small hydroelectric power plants."[146] Integrating Chinese technical standards into the development process advocated by the United Nations will provide Chinese firms with a permanent toehold in critical industries throughout the developing world.

Belt and Road arises in other aspects of China's UN-related development initiatives as well. In 2016, Beijing pledged $200 million over 10 years to establish a UN Peace and Development Trust Fund to support the 2030 Agenda for Sustainable Development and other initiatives in peace and security. Of the five-member steering committee, four officials are Chinese,[147] and projects explicitly linked to countries' participation in the BRI accounted for more than one-third of the $34 million distributed by 2019. Other political motivations may also play a role: a

$2 million grant was provided to enhance security against terrorism at major sporting events between 2019 and 2022, a period that included the Beijing Winter Olympics.[148]

Calling China Out

In recent years, China's quest to play a decisive role in international development institutions has encountered some resistance. In particular, its politicization of institutional processes has engendered criticism. In March 2020, I met with Kelley Currie, who served as the US representative to the UN Economic and Social Council during 2017–18. She suggested that China was known for trading votes and using other questionable methods to try to influence other countries' decisions. She is not alone in raising such concerns. In 2019, for example, Qu Dongyu was elected as the first Chinese director-general of the UN Food and Agriculture Organization (FAO). At the time, he was an outgoing Chinese vice minister of Agricultural and Rural Affairs who worked on the BRI's agricultural policy. In an editorial on the election, the scientific journal *Nature* criticized the politicization of the FAO election, noting that China was reportedly "unabashedly leveraging its influence and its investments in its massive Belt and Road Initiative to get votes for its candidate."[149] In particular, some observers noted that the candidate from Cameroon dropped out of the race when China canceled $78.4 million of debt owed by his government to Beijing.[150] The French newspaper *Le Monde* also reported that Beijing threatened "to block agricultural exports from Brazil and Uruguay" if the two countries did not vote for Qu.[151]

Cai Jinyong, who served as the CEO of the International Finance Corporation (IFC), the World Bank's private sector lending arm, also encountered criticism from shareholders for giving preference to Chinese companies in IFC lending. One of Cai's deals – a $300 million investment into the Postal Savings Bank of China – raised particular concerns, and countries representing more than 50 percent of the voting shares of the IFC, including the United States, Japan, the UK, Germany, and France, abstained from the vote. According to the critics, IFC funding is typically designated for important development projects that otherwise cannot get private backing; the Postal Savings Bank of China did not meet this criterion. It was, the *Financial Times* reported, a "dramatic rebuke" to Cai's leadership. The vote came after other controversial investments, such as a proposed $140 million investment in China's state-owned agriculture company, COFCO. In response to criticism of the investments, Cai said, "We have made so much money from our investments [in China]. We are so lucky. We thank the Chinese for giving us this opportunity." Cai's exit from his position was announced shortly after the vote.[152]

China's efforts to use the United Nations for its own narrow interests began to encounter significant pushback in 2019–20. In September 2019, the UN Security Council rejected Beijing's attempts, supported by Russia, to include a reference supporting China's BRI in the reauthorization bill for the UN Mission to Afghanistan. The reference had been included in previous authorizations in 2016, 2017, and 2018. In March 2019, however, the United States balked at its proposed inclusion. Acting US Ambassador to the United Nations Jonathan Cohen stated that China was holding UN negotiations hostage by "making it about Chinese national political priorities rather than the people of Afghanistan" and advancing inclusion of Belt and Road despite BRI's "tenuous ties to Afghanistan and known problems with corruption, debt distress, environmental damage and lack of transparency."[153] The Security Council agreed to a six-month extension and in September overcame the threat of a veto by China to pass the resolution.

While a significant part of China's engagement in international development organizations is targeted to advancing its own interests and standing, Beijing has also provided leadership in development finance by embracing existing norms.

I'm In with the In Crowd

Jin Liqun had an idea. The former World Bank and ADB official wanted to establish a joint infrastructure bank supported by CDB, the ADB, and Japan. The notion was not entirely new. Zheng Xinli, the executive vice chairman at the prominent think tank the China Center for International Economic Exchanges, had proposed a specialized infrastructure investment bank for Asian countries as early as 2009. Zheng pitched the bank as an alternative place for Chinese excess capital: rather than buying US treasury bonds that have exchange rate risks, Zheng argued, it would be better to invest the funds in Asia, where they would "definitely achieve higher profitability than American treasury bonds." His ambitions for the bank were great: "The Asian Infrastructure Investment Bank, in having a joint-stock system invested by Asian countries, will create conditions for Asia to attract foreign capital and achieve an economic take-off."[154]

Jin, however, pursued a different vision. He focused on a multilateral bank that would meet and even exceed the standards of his former employers. As planning for the bank began during 2009–10, China's Ministry of Finance, CBD, the Sumitomo Trust, and the Japan International Cooperation Agency were all enthusiastic. The ADB and the US investment fund Apollo also pledged to help capitalize the bank. Jin consulted with his friend and former ADB colleague Paul Speltz. Speltz, who had a long and distinguished career in business and government, culminating in a stint as US ambassador to, and executive director of, the ADB, recalled Jin talking about a bank headed by China, as well as the United States and Japan (and later India). In the end, the timing wasn't right for Japan. In the wake of the 2011 Tōhoku earthquake and tsunami, it could not justify investing in infrastructure in other countries when the need was so great at home. Yet Jin persisted. Speltz introduced Jin to top officials in the Obama administration, including members of the National Security Council, and found enthusiasm, but some caution, for the idea of the bank in a number of quarters. Nonetheless, the United States decided not to join and, additionally, placed pressure on several allies, including Japan, South Korea, Singapore, and Australia, to abstain as well. Washington saw two potential problems: corruption and Chinese dominance of the bank.[155] Ultimately, few countries found the United States' argument persuasive; and of the major economies originally invited to join, only Japan and the United States did not do so.

The AIIB is China's first attempt at creating a truly multilateral institution. By most accounts, it has been a success. Jin's mantra for the bank has been "clean, lean, and green." And observers agree that Jin is trying to keep the bank transparent and free of corruption. Established in 2016, the bank is small, but the transparency of the bank's lending terms, its complete list of projects, and its formal institutional mechanisms, such as the Complaints-Resolution, Evaluation, and Integrity Unit, help ensure that it operates at international standards. When the ADB and World Bank pulled out of a project for reasons of corruption, Jin refused to step in to fill the gap.[156] As pressure mounted on China to green the BRI, Jin pledged in 2020—one year before the rest of the Chinese government–not to build any new coal-fired power plants (and also to avoid building roads that lead to the plants). As one member of the AIIB's International Advisory Board explained to me, Jin is very clear that all loans must be compliant with AIIB standards, and many BRI projects are not. The bank also operates with a high degree of transparency. It has approved 118 projects as of the first quarter of 2021, and each has a webpage that offers progress updates and corresponding documents, although none has been completed in the five years since the first projects were approved in summer 2016. While initial projects were mostly all co-financed with other multilateral banks, the AIIB has more recently undertaken more independent projects, bringing the total of self-funded projects to 40 percent.

Observers nonetheless caution that Jin's verbal pledge around greening the AIIB must be matched by regulations written into the actual charter of the bank.[157] One former ADB official notes that the ADB had rejected a plan to expand a port in Sri Lanka, 30 minutes north of an airport, because it would have required a massive population shift as well as flooding of substantial areas. China, however, with help from the AIIB, had no such qualms. It moved forward with the port's development and has now secured a shipping and repair base. Some international observers suggest that the AIIB is not as attractive to the Chinese government because its transparency translates into a significant reduction in Beijing's negotiating leverage around Belt and Road projects,[158] which may account for its continued small role in BRI financing. American University professor Tamar Gutner also offers a more systemic critique of the AIIB in the context of China's development banks: "A clear or growing contradiction between China's actions outside the AIIB and the bank's policies and goals could still risk turning the AIIB into the Potemkin village of international organizations – a showcase of good intentions in a larger sea of hypocrisy."[159]

Still the AIIB stands as an important example of China's ability and interest in adapting its norms and values to those of the existing international system. Jin has ensured that, unlike CDB and the Export–Import Bank of China, the AIIB has a high degree of international participation in all of its business. When the bank launched its first global bond in

2019, several foreign banks, including Goldman Sachs, Barclays, TD securities, and Credit Agricole, were listed alongside the People's Bank of China; a European firm won the bid to design the AIIB's new headquarters; and even the United States has played an important role. Two Americans, Natalie Lichtenstein, the former general counsel of the World Bank, and Arthur Mitchell, a lawyer based in Japan, helped develop the AIIB's regulatory guidelines. In addition, AIIB lending is open to multinationals, whereas the vast majority of CDB and Export–Import Bank of China funding, as well as Silk Road funding (targeted at energy infrastructure projects), is tied to Chinese firms.

Conclusion

Xi Jinping's ambition for China to lead in reforming the global governance system is reflected across multiple policy arenas. By shaping the system of international institutions and arrangements that govern states' interactions, China ensures that it has the greatest opportunity to advance its domestic political, economic, and security interests, to protect itself from international criticism of its domestic policies around issues such as human rights, and to prevent Taiwan from expanding its independence and international space through membership in international organizations.

Its global governance playbook combines both deft diplomacy and brute force. Xi frequently delivers keynote addresses at major global governance gatherings that elevate China's image as a global leader. China also mobilizes significant resources to advance its interests. It places its officials in leadership positions within the UN system and other international governmental organizations and deploys large numbers of experts into the technical bodies of these organizations to advance Chinese standards and norms. The sheer number of Chinese participants and proposals they present shapes the debate in significant ways. China also uses its financial wherewithal to advance its interests: for example, by investing in scientific research and research stations in the Arctic or by providing support to organizations such as UN DESA. In addition, China has sought to gain support for its positions by trading votes and offering financial incentives to – or in some cases threatening economic consequences against – other countries.

China's participation and efforts to reform international institutions are also often designed to serve its narrower interests. Beijing requires that Chinese officials and other Chinese actors in international institutions support domestic priorities as opposed to fulfilling the mandates of the agencies they serve. Wu Hongbo, for example, prevented Uyghur World Congress President Dolkun Isa from testifying at the United Nations; Lenovo was pressured to support the standard put forward by Huawei in the ITU; and Cai Jinyong favored lending to Chinese companies that would not normally fall within the portfolio of IFC lending. China has also integrated the BRI into over two dozen international organizations. When the United States and other countries prevented the BRI from being written into the reauthorization bill for the UN Mission to Afghanistan, China threatened to veto the mission.

China has made significant strides toward enhancing its position in global institutions and in reforming norms and values in those institutions in ways that align them more closely with its own. Increasingly, however, it faces pushback in its efforts to enhance its economic stakes in the Arctic, to advance the BRI in the United Nations, and to place its officials in leadership positions. The greater China's success in using the global governance system to advance its own domestic policy preferences, the greater the resistance from other actors and the more difficult future progress becomes.

7

The China Reset

Speaking before the United Nations Climate Ambition Summit in December 2020, Xi Jinping announced yet another impressive pledge. He promised that China would lower its carbon intensity – the amount of CO_2 emissions per unit of GDP – by over 65 percent by 2030 and increase the share of non-fossil fuels in its energy consumption to around 25 percent. The new pronouncement came on the heels of an earlier commitment in September that China would achieve carbon neutrality by 2060. Once again, Xi appeared to have captured the rhetorical high ground and positioned himself and China for another round of international accolades. Yet this time the response from the international community was more muted. International experts and the media noted that China's current energy practices made it more climate sinner than savior. China contributes 28 percent of the world's emissions of the greenhouse gas CO_2, more than the next three emitters (the United States, India, and Russia) combined. And while it remains the largest investor in clean energy, additions to new wind and solar capacity have slowed,[1] while growth in coal-fired capacity has accelerated. Between January and June 2020, China provided permits for more new coal-fired capacity than in 2018 and 2019 combined;[2] and its 2020 coal consumption increased 3 percent over 2019, even with the decreased industrial and transportation emissions associated with COVID-19.[3] China was also on track to invest approximately $50 billion in 240 coal projects globally. Even the usually sympathetic UN Secretary General Guterres implicitly criticized Beijing, noting in a July 2020 speech, "There is no such thing as clean coal, and coal should have no place in any rational recovery plan. It is deeply concerning that new coal powerplants are still being planned and financed, even though renewables offer three times more jobs, and are now cheaper than coal in most countries."[4]

That same December, coal also emerged as the headline in a different China-related story. Over a dozen Chinese cities were suffering the worst power outages in a decade and were forced to impose restrictions on power usage just as winter hit. The answer was a stone's throw away. More than 60 ships with 5.7 million tons of Australian coal were waiting to unload their cargo at Chinese ports; some had been there for over a half-year. But Beijing refused to lift its wide-ranging ban on Australian exports, including coal. It preferred to let Chinese business pay the price and its own soft power take a hit. Unsurprisingly, the proportion of Australians who held an unfavorable view of China jumped from 57 percent in 2019 to 81 percent in 2020.[5]

China's claim to climate leadership and impressive investment in renewable energies, while at the same time contributing to a dramatic expansion of global coal consumption, appears inherently contradictory. Its decision to inflict economic pain on its domestic firms in order to punish Australia for a perceived political transgression also seems illogical. But as we have seen, China's foreign policy strategy reflects its own unique approach and priorities. It is willing, for example, to sacrifice the diplomatic soft power win of global leadership for narrower domestic political and economic gains. It also prioritizes sovereignty and social stability, as well as controlling the narrative around those core issues, above all else – even economic benefit. Understanding these Chinese leadership priorities, as well as how Beijing has deployed its domestic governance model in pursuit of its foreign policy objectives, is essential for the United States and its allies and partners in developing an effective China policy.

The Pursuit of Greatness

Chinese leaders offer a new vision of world order rooted in concepts such as "the great rejuvenation of the Chinese nation," a "community of shared destiny," a "new relationship among major powers," and a "China model." Once the rhetorical flourishes are stripped away, the vision translates into a radically transformed international system. The United States is no longer the global hegemon with a powerful network of alliances that reinforces much of the current rules-based order. Instead, a reunified and resurgent China is on a par with, or even more powerful than, the United States. China's technologies, trade and investment, and values flow through the BRI, define international institutions, and underpin a multipolar but still integrated international system. China is the preeminent power in Asia; and the United States operates there within the context of Chinese-led trade and security regimes. Responsibility for managing the global commons and providing global public goods is broadly shared among China and other responsible powers, as opposed to disproportionately borne by a single hegemon.

In pursuing their vision, China's leaders operate from their own distinctive playbook that reflects their domestic governance model: a highly centralized Party-state that possesses the ability to mobilize resources from the public and private sectors, to deploy those resources across multiple domains, to control the content and flow of information, to penetrate societies and economies globally, and to leverage the power of the country's vast market, as well as its military.

To date, Beijing has experienced mixed success in attaining its vision of a reordered international system. It has made progress in realizing its sovereignty claims through the imposition of the Hong Kong National Security Law and expanding military capabilities and presence in the South China Sea. It also has withstood international opprobrium and targeted economic sanctions for its violations of human rights in Xinjiang. Its trade initiative, the RCEP, has the potential to elevate its role within the Asia Pacific while diminishing that of the United States, which is not party to either the RCEP or the Japanese-led Comprehensive and Progressive Agreement for Trans-Pacific Partnership (CPTPP). Through the BRI, Beijing has laid the foundation for Chinese technology to provide much of the world's next-generation telecommunications, financial, and health infrastructure. Its dominance in UN technology standard setting bodies and capacity building on internet governance help reinforce acceptance of both Chinese technology and the more repressive norms and values it enables.

Yet China's vision remains unrealized in important respects. Its efforts to advance its sovereignty claims, human rights and internet governance norms, and its covert and/or coercive efforts to shape international actors' political and economic choices have produced a backlash that threatens its larger strategic objectives. Rather than undermining the United States' role in the Asia Pacific or the US-led alliance system, Chinese actions have resulted in calls to strengthen America's position. In the face of Chinese military aggression, India's prime minister, Narendra Modi, overcame deep-seated reluctance to support closer military ties with the United States. And the European Union has stepped up to enhance its political and security engagement in the Asia Pacific. Significant solidarity among advanced democracies emerged to protest Chinese policies in Xinjiang and Hong Kong, to call for an investigation into the origins of COVID-19, to ban or limit Huawei 5G technology, and to condemn China's support for Russia. And countries are increasingly scrutinizing and defending against Chinese behavior that attempts to subvert the democratic principles that underpin a range of international institutions.

For the United States, China's vision presents a set of important and difficult choices concerning the degree to which Washington is prepared to assert its own vision, accommodate Chinese preferences, seek compromise, or mount a vigorous defense. Neither the long-standing US policy of "engagement" nor the more recent competitive and containment-oriented approach of the Trump administration has yielded a positive and robust US–China relationship rooted in shared values and a common purpose. Each, however, has important lessons for US policy moving forward.

Lessons from History

Engaging with China has been a consistent theme of the US–China relationship dating back to before the establishment of diplomatic relations in 1979. In the 1950s, US secretary of state John Foster Dulles delivered a series of speeches in which he suggested that the United States should help Communist countries evolve peacefully to democracy by supporting opposition forces, cultural subversion, and information warfare.[6] After the opening of relations between the two countries, successive US presidents from Richard Nixon through to Barack Obama treasured the idea that the United States could influence China's political and economic trajectory, not through direct subversion, but through engaging China in the rules-based order. The notion was simple: the United States would encourage China's integration into the liberal international order; China would become a pillar of that order; and over time, along with the rise of the middle class, this integration process would accelerate economic and political liberalization within China.[7] In case US best hopes were not realized, Washington would also hedge its bets by retaining a strong military presence and system of alliances in the Asia Pacific region.

No US president expected that China would change overnight as a result of US policy. President Clinton, in discussing the importance of supporting China's entry into the World Trade Organization, had this to say:

> Of course the path that China takes to the future is a choice China will make. We cannot control that choice; we can only influence it. But we must recognize that we do have complete control over what we do. We can work to pull China in the right direction or we can turn our backs and almost certainly push it in the wrong direction. The WTO agreement will move China in the right direction. It will advance the goals America has worked for in China.[8]

Yet most administrations retained a belief that over time China would become a stakeholder in the international rules-based order and more closely approximate a market democracy at home. In his keynote address at the National Committee on US–China Relations' 2005 gala, the Bush administration's deputy secretary of state Robert Zoellick outlined a set of challenges posed by China's rise: a lack of transparency in supporting bad actors on the global stage; a failure to protect IP; a mounting US–China bilateral trade deficit; and China's desire for "predominance of power" in Asia. Solving these problems, Zoellick argued, would require China not only changing its behavior on the global stage but also transforming its domestic political system: "Our goal . . . is to help others find their own voice, attain their own freedom, and make their own way. . . . Closed politics cannot be a permanent feature of Chinese society. It is simply not sustainable. China needs a peaceful political transition to make its government responsible and accountable to its people."[9]

Engagement had both advocates and detractors within China, but in the aftermath of the 2008 global financial crisis, Chinese officials appeared less convinced by the US model. They advanced notions of a "new relationship among major powers." They also began to think more strategically about China's leadership on the global stage: Chinese economists set the stage for the BRI, scholars raised the prospect of China expanding its influence in the Arctic, and the PLA Navy moved from staking claims in the South China Sea to realizing them. The selection of

Xi Jinping as the country's leader in 2012–13 only reinforced this more ambitious and expansive global outlook.

The Obama administration's 2011 pivot or rebalance was in part a recognition of the changes underway in Chinese foreign policy. The United States strengthened the hedge element of its strategy: it bolstered its diplomatic and security outreach to Asian allies and partners; supported the decision of the Philippines to seek legal arbitration in its conflict with China in the South China Sea; promoted the negotiation of a regional trade deal, the Trans-Pacific Partnership, that excluded China; and redeployed forces from the Middle East to the Asia Pacific to enhance its military presence. Nonetheless, the Obama White House held on to the basic principles of engagement and remained committed to securing agreements on public health, cyber, and climate issues.

The election of Donald Trump as president of the United States in 2016, however, sounded the death knell for the notion of "engage but hedge." Campaigning under the banner of "America First," President Trump argued that the United States had sacrificed its own interests in support of others – that it had borne an unfair share of the burden of global security and fallen victim to unequal trade deals that disadvantaged the country.[10] He also dismissed the value of allies and multilateralism, viewing them as constraints on American interests and power.[11] In short order, he withdrew the United States from a half-dozen international institutions and arrangements, and he embraced a new priority on sovereignty in US foreign policy that suggested that the United States would no longer seek to influence the domestic political choices of others. In such a context, the two rationales for engagement – buttressing the current rules-based order and promoting political and economic reform – became irrelevant.

Senior members of the administration, along with a strong bipartisan consensus within the US Congress, instead drove a policy that challenged the fundamental understandings and underpinnings of engagement. The 2017 National Security Strategy asserted: "For decades, US policy was rooted in the belief that support for China's rise and for its integration into the post-war international order would liberalize China." Instead, as the report notes, "China seeks to displace the United States in the Indo-Pacific region, expand the reaches of its state-driven economic model, and reorder the region in its favor." The administration called for a "whole of government, whole of society" response to the threats posed by Chinese efforts to influence the American public.[12]

By the conclusion of its tenure in January 2021, the Trump administration had helped alert the world to the governance issues posed by the BRI and the security challenges presented by Huawei. It had stymied China's efforts to advance its interests in several UN forums, and cooperated with India, Australia, and Japan to reinvigorate the Quad and support the concept of a Free and Open Indo-Pacific (FOIP). The administration also undertook a sweeping campaign within the United States to address Chinese influence operations; to even the playing field for visas and access between Chinese and US scholars, journalists, and diplomats; to address Chinese IP theft; and to prevent US technology from being sold to Chinese firms that posed national security concerns or contributed to human rights violations.

Nonetheless, the administration's actions failed to improve the political situation in Xinjiang or Hong Kong or to stabilize the situation in the South China Sea or Taiwan. Its trade war with China inflicted greater costs on the US economy than on that of China. In addition, the bilateral diplomatic framework atrophied, contributing to a dramatic deterioration of the relationship. In the final months of the Trump administration, Chinese state councillor Wang Yi claimed that the US–China relationship was at risk of a "new Cold War," while scholars such as Niall Ferguson[13] and Timothy Garton Ash[14] claimed that the two countries had already arrived at such a state.

The Starting Point

The era of "engage but hedge" and the period of "compete, counter, and contain" reflect two sides of the same coin. "Engage but hedge" reflects a United States that is confident in its political and economic model, proactive in its support of the current rules-based order, understands allies as amplifying US influence, and is willing to sacrifice short-term interests for what it believes will be a longer-term gain in cooperating with China. "Compete, counter, and contain" reflects a United States that believes its model is under threat and seeks to prevent Chinese actors from accessing US human or financial capital to benefit the CCP. It pushes back against Chinese efforts to transform the international system but rarely leads in bolstering the current rules-based order. It also sees limited value in working to identify areas of cooperation with China. During the Trump administration, the US approach to allies was fragmented: the president characterized allies as free riders, while other administration officials sought cooperation.

The Biden administration, which took power in January 2021, retained many of the competitive and confrontational policies of the Trump administration but also embraced the traditional strengths of US foreign policy, such as allies and leadership in multilateral institutions. It also has reinforced the importance of the liberal international or rules-based order and the values that underpin that order in American foreign policy. This renewed focus on values provides a useful starting point for reconceptualizing the challenge China poses to the United States.

Reframing the Challenge

The United States and China both seek a future in which the world is prosperous, peaceful, and capable of addressing global challenges. They differ, however, in their conceptions of how power should be distributed and the norms and values that should underpin that future world.

Like China, the United States seeks an international order that reflects its values – both real and aspirational. This means reinforcing values such as a commitment to inclusion and equality, free trade and economic opportunity, innovation and sustainability, openness, human dignity, and the rule of law within the United States itself, and then developing institutions and arrangements that embody these values on the global stage. Many of these values are already embedded but not fully realized in the current rules-based order.

Such a frame makes clear that the central challenge China poses is a value- and norm-based one and not, as is often asserted, one defined by a rising power versus an established power. As noted previously, when competition is framed in a bilateral US–China context, China gains an important advantage. Every issue is elevated into a signal of relative power and influence; and as the rising power, any relative Chinese gain becomes a win. An increase in Chinese research funding relative to that of the United States is touted as an example of the inevitability of Chinese innovation leadership, despite the fact that the United States continues to lead the world in R&D. In addition, the bilateral competition frame, when applied to issues such as Huawei's 5G deployment or BRI governance practices, enables Beijing to claim that US actions are motivated by its desire to avoid losing primacy to China as opposed to normative concerns over data privacy or Chinese lending and investment practices.

A framework that embraces values and norms also is more likely to engage US allies and partners. Conflict in the South China Sea becomes a normative challenge by China to freedom of navigation and international law rather than a competition for military dominance between the United States and China in the Asia Pacific. It is a challenge that speaks not only to the United States but also to the 168 nations that are already party to UNCLOS.

Framing US policy toward China as "not about China" but rather about the broader context of the rules-based order advantages the United States. It provides a clear alternative to China's vision; forces Beijing to clarify where it is willing to uphold current norms and where it seeks to transform them; provides opportunities for prioritizing US policy initiatives; and engages with other countries to help bolster those same norms.

The US at Home is the US Abroad

For the United States to play a compelling role in shaping the future international system, it will need to ensure that its own governance system reflects its stated values and priorities. The polarized American polity and chaotic response of the US government to the pandemic in particular tarnished the United States' image and contributed to the impression of relative US decline.[15] The Biden administration established early on that a priority was to invest in the social, physical, and technological infrastructure of the United States. Before taking office, Biden administration National Security Council officials Kurt Campbell and Rush Doshi argued that the United States would need to rebuild and rethink the relationship between the state and the market in ways that addressed inequality, sustained growth, and ensured competitiveness with China. In part this would require rebuilding "the solidarity and civic identity that make democracy work."[16] President Biden, together with the U.S. Congress, has adopted legislation, including the CHIPS and Science Act, the Bipartisan Infrastructure law, and the Inflation Reduction Act, to bolster the foundations of U.S. competitiveness.

A renewed commitment to immigration is also important in affirming US values of openness and opportunity. Moreover, continuing to attract the best and the brightest to the United States for study and work is essential to US competitiveness. More than one million foreign students attend US colleges and universities annually. A 2020 Paulson Institute study of the top-flight researchers in AI revealed that the United States boasts 60 percent of the top AI researchers in the world, while China and Europe possess around 10 percent each. Two-thirds of the US research- ers, however, received undergraduate degrees from other countries.[17] The United States' ability to draw on the world's scientific talent is crucial to maintaining its technological competitiveness. The importance of welcoming foreign students, however, extends well beyond its ability to populate its technology firms. In 2020, 62 of the world's leaders had received education in the United States – more than anywhere else in the world.[18]

Reasserting US Leadership

The Trump administration's withdrawal from a number of international agreements and organizations limited its ability to shape international norms and values and left a vacuum in global leadership. Despite the expectations of many in the international community, China did not fill the vacuum. Although it stepped up to claim leadership on a number of global challenges, it hewed to a narrow opportunism that left it unable to forge a broader global consensus. Moreover, despite the lure of Chinese investment and the Chinese market, international surveys suggest a high degree of distrust in Xi Jinping and little interest in Chinese global leadership.

The Biden administration has made reestablishing US leadership in international institutions a priority. In a March 3, 2021 address, Secretary of State Antony Blinken described the US–China relation- ship as competitive, collaborative, and adversarial, noting: "The common denominator is the need to engage China from a position of strength." In defining strength, Blinken underscored the importance of US participa- tion in international organizations and partnership with allies.[19] The administration has moved quickly to reestablish the US commitment to global governance institutions. It rejoined the UNHRC, the Paris

Climate Agreement, and the WHO, and extended the New Strategic Arms Reduction Treaty. President Biden also convened a global climate summit in April 2021 to encourage more ambitious commitments from the world's largest emitters. Such steps are essential to the United States' ability to advance its notions of human rights, the rule of law, and sustainability, as well as to prevent Xi Jinping from achieving his objective of "leading in the reform of the global governance system." The United States should also build domestic support for acceding to UNCLOS. As Chinese military activities continue to ramp up in the Asia Pacific, US membership in UNCLOS offers an important platform for coordinating policies with ASEAN and other Asia Pacific countries.

US leadership will look different in the future, however. By 2030, or perhaps earlier, the size of China's economy will surpass that of the United States. China's population size already exceeds that of the United States by more than four times, providing it a distinct advantage in human capital, whether for advancing scientific and technological innovation or global political outreach. And within the Asia Pacific, China claims a clear military advantage simply by virtue of geography. The United States, as Blinken acknowledged, will increasingly need to rely on its allies and partners and act collectively to advance shared norms and interests. At the same time, it will need to mount a robust defense against China's foreign policy approach.

Building Coalitions: Allies, Partners, and More

The Biden administration has indicated that cooperating with allies and partners is central to its China strategy. One area where such cooperation is particularly important is technology. Technological competition with China has critical economic, national security, and value-based interests at stake. With China as a backdrop, the US Congress and Biden administration have committed to invest heavily in foundational technologies such as semiconductors, rethink critical supply chains, and constrain PRC access to technologies with national security applications. Determining where technological decoupling with China is necessary and where integration is beneficial, however, will be a challenging but essential part of the broader value and normative-based competition. The United States and other like-minded countries will need to decide among themselves which technologies should be protected, whether reshoring is more desirable than retaining a competitive free market approach within a like-minded group, and which Chinese technologies can be adapted for use in open societies. To this end, the United States and European Union have established the U.S.-EU Trade and Technology Council and the Quad critical and emerging technologies working group. These bodies coordinate on issues such as standards, supply chains, and export controls. Such bodies could also play an important role in assessing the implications of innovations such as China's digital currency/electronic payment system.

To address the multidimensional element of China's model, the United States and its allies should also establish a mechanism for coordinating policy in the United Nations and other international institutions to set standards, develop consensus candidates for leadership positions, and ensure strong representation by democracies in bodies such as the ITU. The Biden administration took an early step in this direction in April 2021 by proposing an American candidate to become the next head of the ITU.

One of the most challenging elements of Xi Jinping's playbook is his ability to leverage the Chinese market to shape others' political and strategic choices. There is a pressing need for countries to develop a coordinated response to Beijing's coercive economic diplomacy. In cases where China boycotts goods from countries on political grounds, as it has with Australia, the Philippines, and South Korea, among others, there should be a collective response in which economic alliances, akin to NATO or the Quad, would levy sanctions or even undertake boycotts in kind. Similarly, when China threatens retaliation against individual multinationals or even entire industries with loss of market access, countries should respond in kind by indicating that Chinese companies in those same sectors will face similar consequences. Reciprocity signals to China that other countries are prepared to respond with more than rhetorical condemnation and helps to level the playing field for future negotiation.

A Bigger Tent

In competing with China to define the values, norms, and institutions of the 21st century, cooperation with traditional allies will no longer suffice. The United States and other advanced market democracies need to expand the tent to include a broader range of partners and potential allies. China's BRI and efforts to transform norms and values in international institutions reflect a global challenge that necessitates a global response. The breadth and depth of China's engagement with the world's developing economies, particularly in Africa and the Middle East, provide it with fertile ground for its values, technologies, and policy preferences to take hold, and a strong and consistent base of support for policies in other areas, such as Xinjiang and Hong Kong. While China may claim reservoirs of elite support in some developing economies, however, polls suggest that the majority of citizens in many developing economies favor Japanese, EU, or US leadership over that of China.

Engagement with emerging economies should be rooted in new economic opportunities. The United States, in partnership with other large market democracies, such as Germany, France, the UK, Japan, and Australia, should consider a significant new initiative around urbanization, infrastructure, sustainable development, and innovation in 25 to 30 developing countries. The United States cannot and should not attempt to match the BRI. Instead, it should leverage its own strengths, and those of its democratic allies, around supporting growth that is rooted in the rule of law, transparency, and sustainability. The US Congress's 2021 Strategic Competition Act, which supports significantly increasing US funding for overseas infrastructure, political capacity building, and local media, among other areas, could serve as the basis for such an initiative.

Ongoing initiatives such as the US-led Clean Network or Quad-based efforts to establish resilient supply chains could also support such an effort. As multinationals diversify part of their supply chains away from China to develop regional manufacturing and distribution centers, these new investment opportunities should also become part of the larger initiative. In addition, the global economy should reflect greater integration of these economies into global innovation networks and technology supply chains in ways that both contribute to their economic development and bolster a commitment to norms of openness, the rule of law, and sustainability. Moreover, particularly where Huawei is not already deeply embedded, the Biden administration should continue the Trump administration policy of providing support for 5G and fiber optic cable alternatives to persuade countries of the benefits of adopting a technological future that prizes transparency and data security.

I'm Not Going Anywhere

Within the Asia Pacific, China is moving to assert sovereignty over contested territories and to create institutions and norms that cement its regional leadership. President Biden has moved decisively to support the Quad, which includes India, Australia, Japan, and the United States. Chinese officials have become increasingly concerned about the Quad's potential to harden into a more formal alliance-type arrangement: in October 2020, Chinese vice-foreign minister Luo Zhaohui referred to it as an "anti-China frontline" and a "mini-NATO."[20] While Chinese concerns may be misplaced, given India's long-standing com- mitment to non-alignment, as we have seen, China's military aggression on the Sino-Indian border triggered a new enthusiasm for the arrangement from Prime Minister Modi. With India's support, the Quad could serve an important role in helping to deter China from more aggressive military activity in the Indo-Pacific.

President Biden also stood-up negotiations around an Indo-Pacific Economic Framework (IPEF) in May 2022. IPEF, which includes 14 countries from the region, represents a high-standard agreement on supply chains, labor and tax, digital trade, and clean economy.

There is a significant opportunity to knit together a more formal partnership between the United States' Asian and European allies and partners. One hundred parliamentarians and members of Congress from 19 countries across Europe, North America, and Asia have already established the Interparliamentary Alliance on China to coordinate strategy toward China. NATO Secretary General Jens Stoltenberg has also called for NATO to play a larger role in the Asia Pacific region, coordinating with Australia, Japan, New Zealand, and South Korea to defend global rules and set norms and standards in space and cyberspace in the face of destabilizing Chinese behavior.[21] Germany, France, the Netherlands, and the UK have all deployed naval assets in the South China Sea in support of freedom of navigation. France and Germany have both published strategies for the Indo-Pacific, which were followed in April 2021 by the EU's own "Strategy of Cooperation" for the region. Echoing Stoltenberg's words, Germany's defence minister, Annegret Kramp-Karrenbauer, stated that Berlin wanted to increase its presence in the Indo-Pacific by teaming up with "like-minded allies" in the face of a China that was undermining the "rules-based world order."[22] While traditional security concerns might be the first priority for such a partnership, the Quad is already conducting conversations around supply chain resiliency, the pandemic, and disinformation campaigns. There is the potential to develop even more extensive cooperation between Asia, Europe, the UK, and the US on these issues.[23]

Deepening political and security engagement between these same actors could also play an important role in enhancing Taiwan's security. Xi's priority on sovereignty and reunification, as well as his success in advancing Beijing's claims in the South China Sea and subverting one country, two systems in Hong Kong, places Taiwan in an increasingly precarious position. Xi has asserted that unification with Taiwan should take place "sooner rather than later" and has refused to renounce the use of force. By integrating Taiwan more fully into the economic and security architecture of a Free and Open Indo Pacific, underpinned not only by Asian but also by European allies, the United States increases the probability of effective deterrence against Chinese military action. At the same time, the United States should resist unnecessarily provoking Beijing by adopting legislation, such as the Taiwan Travel Act, that draws attention to Taiwan as an independent actor but does not meaningfully enhance its security. The United States should focus on measured but consequential steps that help Taiwan enhance its ability to deter a Chinese attack, blockade, or quarantine and that more deeply embed the island in international institutions and arrangements.

While the United States maintains a strong position as the region's dominant guarantor of security, it should reestablish the economic pillar of its regional engagement, not only through IPEF, but ultimately by joining the CPTPP. The conclusion of the Chinese-led RCEP in 2020 has further emboldened Chinese thinkers and officials to argue that the United States is no longer a credible Asia Pacific power. Without a presence in either of the two dominant Asia Pacific trading regimes, the United States will not benefit from the economic dynamism of the world's fastest-growing region and its influence there will be diminished. Multinationals will reorient their supply chains in order to take advantage of the lower tariffs afforded to the agreement's member economies. The United States already operates at a deficit relative to China because much of the Asia Pacific region – and the world – believes that "the United States is essential for security, but China is indispensable for economic prosperity."

Tackling Tradeoffs

In April 2021, I received a request for advice from a US company that had signed on as a corporate sponsor for the 2022 Winter Olympics in Beijing. The human rights situation in Xinjiang had led governments in several countries, including the United States, to debate whether to push for a new venue for the games, carry out a full or selective boycott, or simply not send diplomatic representation. The company's China market was enormous, and while it didn't source goods from Xinjiang, it understood that its actions would be under a microscope in both Beijing and Washington.

I suggested that the firm reach out to other sponsors to develop a common platform that might include some combination of the following: a coordinated, behind-the-scenes push for China to begin releasing Uyghur Muslims from the labor and reeducation camps; an initiative to reform the International Olympic Committee's selection process for venues; and a public statement of concern about the situation in Xinjiang and boycott of any corporate representation at the games.

Issues in the US–China relationship frequently require balancing economic benefits against democratic values or national security interests. The CCP's penetration of democracies' educational and cultural institutions, business communities, and the media only adds to the challenge. There are heated debates, for example, over how to manage Chinese students and researchers working in labs with advanced technology:

what is the appropriate balance between national security and the value of American openness? How can the opportunities for the majority of Chinese students be protected in the face of malign actions by a few? Debates over CIs pit the opportunity for Chinese-language training that Beijing's financing enables against US universities' governance principles and the potential for CIs to influence students' views or universities' policies around issues such as inviting the Dalai Lama to speak on campus.

There are no simple answers to these issues, but lowering the temperature of these often inflamed debates is essential to ensuring the full consideration of all policy options. For example, many universities closed their CIs in the face of politically charged Congressional debates and tough actions. Without such a heated atmosphere, however, other options, such as allowing China to finance the CIs but not select the teachers or curriculum, could also have been explored. Over time, how these issues are resolved will shape the character of US policy toward China, and the US–China relationship, as much as, if not more than, the major US strategic initiatives pursued on the international stage.

A World Divided or United?

For most of the world, there is little appetite for the United States and China to allow tensions in the relationship to solidify into a new Cold War. Countries do not want to have to choose between the world's two largest economic and military powers. Moreover, prospects for addressing global challenges, such as climate change, pandemics, refugees, and financial crises, are all diminished in a world characterized by sharp divides and a zero-sum mentality.

For their part, Chinese scholars overwhelmingly see political conflict as inevitable. They identify structural reasons related to an existing and rising power, ideological differences, leadership and prestige, and economics and technology as the most important sources of contention.[24] They see little opportunity for US–China cooperation, and when they do, their ideas focus on narrow policy arenas within the construct of overall competition, such as developing international rules around infrastructure-related debt.[25] In December 2020, I reached out to several senior Chinese foreign policy scholars for their assessment of where the two countries might find common ground. The most frequently mentioned areas of potential cooperation were climate change, the Iran nuclear deal, and the pandemic. There were a few outlier ideas: Fudan University professor Wu Xinbo suggested that both countries could relax restrictions on media access, and PKU's Zha Daojiong raised the potential for civil society in each country to forge a more cooperative relationship; the governments, he lamented, were locked in a negative, deterministic, and threat-based framework.

The Chinese scholars' assessments are broadly shared by their American counterparts. Given the current political and economic realities, most Chinese and American experts concur that the scope for US–China cooperation remains limited. Engagement is likely to occur not at the level of grand bargain but at the level of technical cooperation around the big issues of global governance, such as climate change, public health, drug trafficking, and crisis management. The United States has made clear its interest in establishing guardrails for the bilateral relationship by working together with China in these areas. The United States and China are already co-chairing the G20's Sustainable Finance Study Group, and in February, 2022, signed a joint declaration to cooperate in areas such as the reduction of methane emissions. Opportunities also exist for the two countries to provide co-financing for clean energy projects in developing economies, and to establish a set of benchmarks that would lay out how they plan to achieve their emis- sion reduction targets. The two countries could also work together to strengthen and expand their carbon trading platforms.

Such cooperation would make a significant contribution to international security and help arrest the downward trajectory in the US–China relationship. It would not, however, alter fundamentally the contest underway between two distinct sets of values and world visions. On many of China's most important foreign policy priorities – such as reforming norms around human rights, realizing sovereignty over the South China Sea and Taiwan, promoting a state-centered internet governance regime, advancing the BRI, diminishing the US's role in Asia, enhancing China's role in the Arctic, and promoting Chinese technologies on the global stage – the United States understands China as subverting the norms of the current rules-based order. Moreover, it is concerned about the character and conduct of Chinese foreign policy: the coercive nature of

Chinese efforts to influence other actors' policy choices and decisions. Beijing, for its part, views the United States as a spoiler, attempting to block China's right to shape the rules governing states' behavior and trying to contain its rise through America's military alliance system and continued hold on fundamental technologies.

The emergence of two separate value-based technology – and perhaps even economic and military – ecosystems thus appears increasingly likely. The content and character of Chinese foreign policy suggest that the world according to China – one which celebrates Chinese centrality as a geographic, as well as political and economic, construct – is one that leaves little room for the United States, its allies, and the values and norms they support. The challenge for the United States and its allies and partners, therefore, is to develop and realize a more compelling vision of how the world is organized and the values and norms that inform it, such that a world according to China remains an ambition yet to be realized.

Notes

Chapter 1 Politics and the Plague

1 "Speech by President Xi Jinping at opening of 73rd World Health Assembly," *Global Times*, May 18, 2020.

2 "He talks: from disorder to a new world order," Video, China–US Focus, December 14, 2018.

3 William Zheng, "China's officials play up 'rise of the East, decline of the West'," *South China Morning Post*, March 9, 2021.

4 Kayla Wong, "China trumpets popular narrative that 'the East is rising & the West is declining'," Mothership, March 11, 2021.

5 Yan Xuetong, "The rise of China in Chinese eyes," *Journal of Contemporary China*, Vol. 10, No. 26 (2001), 33.

6 "中美经济对话格局生变 攻守更平衡 [A changing posture for Sino-US economic dialogue: toward a better offense–defense balance]," CCTV, June 19, 2008.

7 "Speech delivered by President Xi at the NPC closing meeting," *China Daily*, March 22, 2018.

8 Xi Jinping, *The Governance of China: Volume One* (Beijing: Foreign Languages Press, 2014), 261.

9 Ibid., 273.

10 Xi Jinping, *The Governance of China: Volume Three* (Beijing: Foreign Language Press, 2020), 540–7.

11 Ibid.

12 Xi, *The Governance of China: Volume One*, 390.

13 Wang Jisi, "A community with a shared future starts from the Asia Pacific," China–US Focus, December 15, 2019.

14 Wei Pan, "Western system versus Chinese system," China Policy Institute, July 2010.

15 Frank Ching, "China's economy not a model for emulation," *Japan Times*, August 31, 2011.

16 "关于坚持和发展中国特色社会主义的几个问题 [Several issues on upholding and developing socialism with Chinese characteristics]," *Qiushi*, April 1, 2019.

17 "Full text of Xi Jinping's report at 19th CPC National Congress," *China Daily*, October 18, 2017.

18 Yan Xuetong, "China model not for other countries," *Global Times,* July 23, 2019.

19 "Xi urges breaking new ground in major country diplomacy with Chinese characteristics," Xinhua, June 24, 2018.

20 "The Central Conference on Work Relating to Foreign Affairs was held in Beijing," Ministry of Foreign Affairs of the People's Republic of China, November 29, 2011.

21 Huang Jing, "The shield of multilateralism," China–US Focus, August 7, 2020.

22 Xi Jinping, *The Governance of China: Volume Two* (Beijing: Foreign Languages Press, 2017), 488.

23 Ying Fu, "Discussing changes in the international order," China–US Focus, July 31, 2018.

24 "Full text: Fu Ying's speech at Chatham House in London," *China Daily*, July, 8, 2016.

25 Liza Tobin, "Xi's vision for transforming global governance: a strategic challenge for Washington and its allies," *Texas National Security Review*, Vol. 2, No. 11 (November 2018).

26 Wang Jisi, "Wang Jisi: China–US ties today worse than Soviet–US relations during Cold War," Caixin, June 18, 2020.

27 Shen Dingli, "Why China is the new pillar of the world," *Global Times*, June 20, 2019.

28 Hillary Leung, "'An eternal hero.' Whistleblower doctor who sounded alarm on coronavirus dies in China," *Time*, February 7, 2020.

29 Laurie Chen, "Mourners pay tribute to Chinese doctor Li Wenliang who blew whistle on coronavirus that killed him," *South China Morning Post*, February 7, 2020.

30 Lily Kuo, "Coronavirus: Wuhan doctor speaks out against authorities," *The Guardian*, March 11, 2020.

31 Reese Oxner, "US and EU condemn jailing of lawyer who reported on coronavirus in Wuhan," NPR December 29, 2020.

32 Guo Rui, "Chinese citizen journalist detained after live-streaming on coronavirus from Wuhan," *South China Morning Post*, May 18, 2020.

33 Sheridan Prasso, "China's epic dash for PPE left the world short on masks," Bloomberg, September 17, 2020.

34 Michael R. Pompeo, "The United States announces assistance to combat the novel coronavirus," US Department of State, February 7, 2020.

35 Prasso, "China's epic dash for PPE."

36 Dian Septiari, "'Don't overreact': Chinese envoys responds to Indonesia's travel ban amid virus fears," *Jakarta Post*, February 4, 2020.

37 Alicia Chen and Vanessa Molter, "Mask diplomacy: Chinese narratives in the COVID era," Freeman Spogli Institute for International Studies, June 16, 2020.

38 Chad P. Brown, "China should export more medical gear to battle COVID-19," Peterson Institute for International Economics, May 5, 2020.

39 "China's response to COVID-19," filmed March 12, 2020, in Beijing, China.

40 Shu Chen et al., "Chinese medical teams in Africa: a flagship program facing formidable challenges," *Journal of Global Health*, Vol. 9, No. 1 (June 2019).

41 "Facing forwards along the Health Silk Road," *The Lancet Global Health*, Vol. 5, No. 10 (October 2017).

42 Kirk Lancaster, Michael Rubin, and Mira Rapp-Hooper, "Mapping China's Health Silk Road," Council on Foreign Relations, April 10, 2020.

43 Alberto Tagliapietra, "The European Union won't be fooled by China's Health Silk Road," German Marshall Fund of the United States, September 2, 2020.

44 Jacopo Barigazzi, "Italy's foreign minister hails Chinese coronavirus aid," *Politico*, March 13, 2020.

45 Tagliapietra, "The European Union won't be fooled by China's Health Silk Road."

46 "How Xi Jinping promoted traditional Chinese medicine to the world," *People's Daily*, October 12, 2020.

47 "Mao called it snake oil – how China uses the corona crisis to promote traditional medicine in Africa," MERICS, May 19, 2020.

48 David Cyranoski, "Why Chinese medicine is heading for clinics around the world," *Nature*, September 26, 2018.

49 "The World Health Organization's decision about traditional Chinese medicine could backfire," *Nature*, June 5, 2019.

50 Nectar Gan and Yong Xiong, "Beijing is promoting traditional medicine as a 'Chinese solution' to coronavirus. Not everyone is on board," CNN, March 16, 2020.

51 "Written statement submitted by World Federation of Acupuncture-Moxibustion Societies, a non-governmental organization in special consultative status," UN Human Rights Council, A/HRC/46/NGO/117, February 17, 2021.

52 Ben Westcott and Steven Jiang, "China is embracing a new brand of foreign policy. Here's what wolf warrior diplomacy means," CNN, May 29, 2020.

53 Stuart Lau, "Coronavirus: Germany's Angela Merkel plays down China's providing medical supplies to hard-hit European countries," *South China Morning Post*, March 18, 2020.

54 Jamie Smyth and Thomas Hale, "China targets Australian wine with anti-dumping investigation," *Financial Times*, August 17, 2020.

55 Daniel Hurst, "How much is China's trade war really costing Australia?" *The Guardian,* October 27, 2020.

56 Ben Westcott and Steven Jiang, "Chinese diplomat promotes conspiracy theory that US military brought coronavirus to Wuhan," CNN, March 13, 2020.

57 Anna Mulrine Grobe, "Wary Europe welcomes China's help – but not its disinformation," *Christian Science Monitor*, May 11, 2020.

58 "State Councilor and Foreign Minister Wang Yi meets the press," Ministry of Foreign Affairs of the People's Republic of China, May 24, 2020.

59 Alice Su, "Faulty masks. Flawed tests. China's quality control problem in leading global COVID-19 fight," *Los Angeles Times*, April 10, 2020.

60 Stephanie Nebehay, "WHO chief says widespread travel bans not needed to beat China virus," Reuters February 3, 2021.

61 "WHO, China leaders discuss next steps in battle against coronavirus outbreak," World Health Organization, January 28, 2020.

62 "WHO names disease caused by new coronavirus: COVID-19," Global Bio Defense, February 11, 2020.

63 Martin Enserik, "Update: 'A bit chaotic.' Christening of new coronavirus and its disease name create confusion," *Science*, February 12, 2020.

64 "What influence does China have over the WHO?" Deutsche Welle, April 17, 2020.

65 "Towards a Health Silk Road," World Health Organization, August 18, 2017.

66 Primrose Riordan and Sue-Lin Wong, "WHO expert says China too slow to report coronavirus cases," *Financial Times*, February 4, 2020.

67 "China delayed releasing coronavirus info, frustrating WHO," Associated Press, June 3, 2020.

68 Laura Silver, Kat Devlin, and Christine Huang, "Unfavorable views of China reach historic highs in many countries," Pew Research Center, October 6, 2020.

69 "中国加入'新冠肺炎疫苗实施计划' [China joins 'Novel Coronavirus Vaccine Implementation Plan']," Chinese Academy of Sciences, October 10, 2020.

70 Smriti Mallapaty, "China's COVID vaccines are going global – but questions remain," *Nature*, May 4, 2021.

71 "Chinese official says local vaccines 'don't have high protection rates'," BBC, April, 12, 2021.

72 Vincent Ni, "Shanghai's lockdown protests reveal tensions over zero-Covid," The Guardian, April 17, 2022.

73 Mark Moore, "Xi Jinping calls US 'biggest threat' to China's security," *New York Post*, March 3, 2021.

74 "How it happened: transcript of the US–China opening remarks in Alaska," Nikkei Asia March 19, 2021.

Chapter 2 Power, Power, Power

1 "Rockets' Tilman Fertitta distances team from Daryl Morey's tweet," ESPN, October 5, 2019.

2 Yaron Steinbuch, "Nets owner Joe Tsai weighs in on Rockets GM Daryl Morey's tweet backing Hong Kong protesters," *New York Post*, October 7, 2019.

3 Anthony Tao, "Everyone is jumping on Houston Rockets GM Daryl Morey's Hong Kong tweet," SupChina, October 7, 2019.

4 "Daryl Morey backtracks after Hong Kong tweet causes Chinese backlash," BBC, October 7, 2019.

5 Tania Ganguli and Alice Su, "Lakers arrive in Shanghai without much fanfare in wake of NBA–China dispute," *Los Angeles Times*, October 8, 2019.

6 Andrew Powel, "The Rockets lose $7 million in Chinese revenue, $20 million total," The Sports Geek, November 14, 2019.

7 Natsuko Fukue, "'We love China': NBA star James Harden apologizes for manager's tweet supporting Hong Kong protests," HKFP, October 7, 2019.

8 "NBA statement," NBA Communications, October 6, 2019, *https://pr.nba.com/nba-statement/*.

9 "Adam Silver's statement on the NBA and China," NBA Communications, October 8, 2019, *https://pr.nba.com/adam-silvers-statement-on-the-nba-and-china/*.

10 Sopan Deb, "NBA Commissioner: China asked us to fire Daryl Morey," *New York Times*, October 17, 2019.

11 Brian K. Patterson, "Houston Rockets: Silver's remarks further solidifies Daryl Morey's job," House of Houston, February 16, 2020.

12 Charles Clover and Michael Peel, "Philippines' Rodrigo Duterte announces 'separation' from US," *Financial Times*, October 20, 2016.

13 Anna Leah E. Gonzales, "China set to lift ban on PH banana exports," *Manila Standard*, October 6, 2016.

14 Andrew S. Erickson and Kevin Bond, "Archaeology and the South China Sea," The Diplomat, July 20, 2015.

15 Heekyong Yang and Hyunjoo Jin, "As missile row drags on, South Korea's Lotte still stymied in China," Reuters, June 16, 2017.

16 Andrew Salmon, "Korea still taking Chinese economic hits over US missile," *Asia Times*, October 6, 2019.

17 Jung Suk-yee, "Number of Chinese tourists visiting South Korea drops after China's travel ban," *BusinessKorea*, November 12, 2019.

18 Huileng Tan, "Descendants of the Sun smash hit prompts Beijing to warn on South Korean dramas," CNBC, March 16, 2016.

19 Jung H. Pak, "Trying to loosen the linchpin: China's approach to South Korea," Brookings Institution, July 2020.

20 Dean Takashi, "China is approving more foreign games, but not so many American ones," Venture Beat, February 18, 2020.

21 Chung Min Lee, "South Korea is caught between China and the United States," Carnegie Endowment for International Peace, October 21, 2020.

22 Laura Silver, Kat Delvin, and Christine Huang, "Unfavorable views of China reach historic highs in many countries," Pew Research Center, October 6, 2020.

23 Sui-Lee Wee, "Giving in to China, US airlines drop Taiwan (in name, at least)," *New York Times*, July 25, 2018.

24 Alexander Ma, "United Airlines made a tiny concession to recognize Taiwan and China is furious," *Business Insider*, August 30, 2018.

25 "NBA为何能恢复转播？中央广播电视总台发言人答记者问 [Why can the NBA return to broadcasting? CCTV answers reporters' questions]," CCTV, October 10, 2020.

26 "Rockets' Morey paid price for HK post, CCTV gloats," *Taipei Times*, October 17, 2020.

27 Stephen Wade and Tim Reynolds, "With China rift ongoing, NBA says free speech remains vital," AP News, October 8, 2019.

28 Christopher Walker and Jessica Ludwig, "The meaning of sharp power," *Foreign Affairs*, November 16, 2017.

29 Chris Fenton, *Feeding the Dragon: Inside the Trillion Dollar Dilemma Facing Hollywood, the NBA, & American Business* (New York: Simon & Schuster, 2020), 14–15.

30 "Strong revenue growth continues in China's cinema market," PricewaterhouseCooper, June 17, 2019.

31 "Aynne Kokas on Hollywood and China," National Committee on US–China Relations, February 27, 2017.

32 "Made in Hollywood, Censored in Beijing," PEN America, 2020.

33 "Christopher Robin: Winnie the Pooh film denied release in China," BBC, August 6, 2018.

34 Xi Jinping, *The Governance of China: Volume One* (Beijing: Foreign Languages Press, 2014), 64.

35 Mao Tse-Tung, *Selected Works of Mao Zedong: Volume II* (Beijing: Foreign Languages Press, 1967), 295.

36 Alex Joske, "The Party speaks for you: foreign interference and the Chinese Communist Party's United Front system," Australian Strategic Policy Institute, June 9, 2020.

37 Gerry Groot, "The expansion of the United Front under Xi Jinping" in Gloria Davies, Jeremy Goldkorn, and Luigi Tomba, eds., *China Story Yearbook 2015: Pollution* (Australia National University Press, 2016), 169.

38 Alexander Bowe, "China's overseas United Front work: background and implications for the United States," US–China Economic and Security Review Commission, August 24, 2018.

39 Anne-Marie Brady, "On the correct use of terms," Jamestown Foundation, May 9, 2019.

40 Stephanie Saul, "On campuses far from China, still under Beijing's watchful eye," *New York Times*, May 4, 2017.

41 Wang Dan, "Beijing hinders free speech in America," *New York Times*, November 26, 2017.

42 Rob Taylor, "China influence fears cost a rising political star his job," *Wall Street Journal*, December 12, 2017.

43 "ASIO identified political candidates with links to China," SBS News, September 12, 2017.

44 Tim Gosling, "As China eyes up Czech media, CME purchase renews concern," Rajawali Siber, November 26, 2020.

45 Kathrin Hille and James Shotter, "Czech university mired in Chinese influence scandal," *Financial Times*, November 10, 2019.

46 Ido Vock, "When Chinese influence fails," *New Statesman*, September 29, 2020.

47 Stuart Lau, "The Czech Republic's relationship with China? It's complicated," *South China Morning Post*, November 3, 2020.

48 Martin Hála, "United Front work by other means: China's 'economic diplomacy' in Central and Eastern Europe," *China Brief*, Vol. 19, No. 9 (May 9, 2019).

49 Martin Hála, "Making foreign companies serve China: outsourcing propaganda to local entities in the Czech Republic," *China Brief*, Vol. 20, No. 1 (January 17, 2020).

50 Alžběta Bajerová, "The Czech–Chinese centre of influence: how Chinese embassy in Prague secretly funded activities at the top Czech university," China Observers, November 7, 2019.

51 Daniela Lazarová, "Czech–Chinese centre at Charles University to be closed down," Czech Radio, November 13, 2019.

52 Keegan Elmer, "Czech prime minister Andrej Babiš hits back at Chinese diplomats' Huawei and ZTE claims," *South China Morning Post*, December 28, 2018.

53 Ibid.

54 Raphael Satter and Nick Carey, "China threatened to harm Czech companies over Taiwan visit: letter," Reuters, February 19, 2020.

55 "Czech prime minister says China's ambassador should be replaced," Reuters, March 9, 2020.

56 Security Information Service, "Annual Report of the Security Information Service for 2019," Publikovano, November 30, 2020.

57 "China hits out after Prague council cancels sister-city deal," *South China Morning Post*, October 9, 2019.

58 Gautam Chikermane, "Czech Republic's CETIN does what the government couldn't: reject Huawei," Observer Research Foundation, October 21, 2020.

59 Raymond Johnston, "Chinese state firm gets a majority stake in Czech media advertising agency," Expats CZ, April 22, 2020.

60 Sinophone Borderlands Project Palacky University Olomouc, "European public opinion on China in the age of COVID-19: differences and common ground across the continent," November 16, 2020.

61 "TikTok is No.1! Beats Facebook, Instagram to become most downloaded app in US," *Business Today*, February 27, 2020.

62 Taylor Nicole Rogers, "Meet Zhang Yiming, the secretive, 35-year-old Chinese billionaire behind TikTok who made over $12 billion in 2018," Business Insider, November 10, 2019.

63 Maria Abi-Habib, "India bans nearly 60 Chinese apps, including TikTok and WeChat," *New York Times*, June 29, 2020.

64 "Open apology from CEO of Toutiao following the ban of Neihan Duanzi," Pandaily, April 16, 2018.

65 Matthew Miller, "China's Xi strikes conciliatory note, broadens diplomatic focus," Reuters, November 30, 2014.

66 Joseph S. Nye, Jr., *Soft Power: The Means to Success in World Politics* (New York: PublicAffairs, 2004), 5, 11.

67 Lucy Handley, "The US is the world's top 'soft' power – but Trump has damaged its reputation, survey says," CNBC, February 25, 2020.

68 Xi Jinping, *The Governance of China: Volume One* (Beijing: Foreign Languages Press, 2014), 178–80.

69 "China is spending billions to make the world love it," *The Economist*, March 23, 2017.

70 Joseph S. Nye, Jr., "Squandering the US 'soft power' edge," *International Educator*, January/February 2007.

71 "Hu Jintao calls for enhancing 'soft power' of Chinese culture," *Beijing Review*, October 15, 2007.

72 Christopher Bodeen, "Communist Party will regulate China's media, film industry," Associated Press, March 22, 2018.

73 "The growing influence of Chinese media," *China Daily*, June 25, 2017.

74 Merriden Varrall, "Behind the news: inside China Global Television Network," Lowy Institute, January 16, 2020.

75 Lu Sun, "Developments and new approaches of internationalizing China's media: a case study of China Global Television Network (CGTN) in witness perspective," *Global Media Journal*, July 28, 2018.

76 "Live: Why Western media twist the reality of Xinjiang [新疆扶持就业政策, 却被西方媒体误读为强制劳动]," YouTube, January 2, 2020, *https://www. youtube.com/watch?v=LE9aZXqw1r4*.

77 "The Point with Liu Xin," YouTube, *https://www.youtube.com/playlist?list=PLt-M8o1W_GdSNhViAVk4Fq8IItW8PHBVf*.

78 Varrall, "Behind the news."

79 "The China story: reshaping the world's media," International Federation of Journalists, June 23, 2020.

80 Nathan Vanderklippe, "In Cambodia, independent media close as Chinese content moves in," *Globe and Mail*, December 29, 2017.

81 "The China story."

82 Ethan Epstein, "How China infiltrated US classrooms," *Politico*, January 16, 2018.

83 *China's Digital Authoritarianism: Surveillance, Influence, and Political Control Before the Permanent Select Committee on Intelligence*, 116th Cong. (2019) (testimony of Christopher Walker, Vice President, Studies and Analysis, National Endowment for Democracy).

84 Marshall Sahlins, "China U.," *The Nation*, October 30, 2013.

85 "On partnerships with foreign governments: the case of Confucius Institutes," American Association of University Professors, June 2014.

86 US Congress, House, *National Defense Authorization Act for Fiscal Year 2018*, HR 2810, 115th Congress, 1st sess., introduced in House, June 7, 2017.

87 Racqueal Legerwood, "As US universities close Confucius Institutes, what's next?" Human Rights Watch, January 27, 2020.

88 "How many Confucius Institutes are in the United States?" National Association of Scholars, September 8, 2020.

89 "Confucius Institutes around the world – 2020," Dig Mandarin, February 15, 2020.

90 Gary Sands, "Are Confucius Institutes in the US really necessary?" *The Diplomat*, February 20, 2021.

91 "About CIEF," Chinese International Education Foundation, *https://cief.org. cn/jj*.

92 Jack Farchy, "Kazakh language schools shift from English to Chinese," *Financial Times*, May 9, 2016.

93 Edem Selormey, "Africans' perceptions about China: a sneak peek from 18 countries," Afrobarometer, September 3, 2020.

94 Kathy Gilsinan, "How the US could lose a war with China," *The Atlantic*, July 25, 2019.

95 David Lague and Benjamin Kang Lim, "Special Report: How China is replacing America as Asia's military titan," Reuters, April 23, 2019.

96 "Providing for the Common Defense," Commission on the National Defense Strategy for the United States, November 13, 2018.

97 Damian Cave and Jamie Tarabay, "Suddenly, the Chinese threat to Australia seems very real," *New York Times*, November 28, 2019.

98 Diego Lopes da Silva, Nan Tian, and Alexandra Marksteiner, "Trends in world military expenditure, 2020," Stockholm International Peace Research Institute, April 2021.

99 "Secure a decisive victory in building a moderately prosperous society in all respects and strive for the great success of socialism with Chinese characteristics for a new era," *China Daily*, October 18, 2017.

100 Joel Wunthnow and Phillip C. Saunders, "Introduction: Chairman Xi remakes the PLA," in Phillip C. Saunders et al., eds., *Chairman Xi Remakes the PLA* (Washington, DC: National Defense University Press, 2019), 1.

101 Ibid., 1–42.

102 "Charting China's 'great purge' under Xi," BBC, October 23, 2017.

103 Minnie Chan, "China's military demotes over 70 senior officers 'for bribing Fang Fenghui,'" *South China Morning Post*, June 25, 2019.

104 "How are China's land-based conventional missile forces evolving?," China Power, September 21, 2020.

105 Ibid.

106 "Military and security developments involving the People's Republic of China 2020," US Department of Defense, September 1, 2020.

107 Michael R. Gordon and Nancy A. Youssef, "Pentagon says China could double nuclear weapons in Decade," *Wall Street Journal*, September 1, 2020.

108 "China's military strategy," The State Council of the People's Republic of China, May 27, 2015.

109 Derek Grossman and Logan Ma, "A short history of China's fishing militia and what it may tell us," RAND Corporation, April 6, 2020.

110 "China's 1st nuclear-powered icebreaker in the pipeline," *China Daily*, June 25, 2018.

111 Angela Poh and Weichong Ong, "PLA reform, a new normative contest, and the challenge for ASEAN," *Asia Policy*, Vol. 14, No. 4 (October 2019).

112 Christopher A. Ford, "Technology and power in China's geopolitical ambitions," US–China Economic and Security Review Commission, June 20, 2019.

113 Poh and Ong, "PLA Reform."

114 "Joint training and exercises," Ministry of National Defense of the People's Republic of China, *http://eng.mod.gov.cn/news/node_48741.htm*.

115 "Press communiqué issued after SCO Qingdao Summit," *Xinhua,* June 10, 2018.

116 Zhou Bo, "Unlike Nato, the SCO needs no enemy to justify its existence," *South China Morning Post*, June 21, 2017.

117 Nurlan Aliyev, "Military cooperation between Russia and China: the military alliance without an agreement," International Centre for Defence and Security, July 1, 2020.

118 Transcript of the "Meeting of the Valdai Discussion Club," October 22, 2020, *http://en.kremlin.ru/events/president/news/64261*.

119 Aliyev, "Military cooperation between Russia and China."

120 Zhang Xiaoming, "Locus of Chinese regional diplomacy: the Shanghai Co-operation Organization," *Global Asia*, Vol. 13, No. 4 (December 2018).

121 Sutirtho Patranobis, "India refused to endorses Chinas Belt and Road Initiative in SCO summit statement," *Hindustan Times*, June 10, 2018.

122 Sam LaGrone, "China sent uninvited spy ship to Russian Vostok 2018 exercise alongside troops, tanks," USNI News, September 17, 2018.

123 James M. Dorsey, "Now Russia accuses China of technology theft," The Globalist, January 2, 2020.

124 Grace Shao, "China, the world's second largest defense spender, becomes a major arms exporter," CNBC, September 26, 2019.

125 Paul Stronski and Nicole Ng, "Cooperation and competition: Russia and China in Central Asia, the Russian Far East, and the Arctic," Carnegie Endowment for International Peace, February 28, 2018.

126 Shen Dingli, "Don't shun the idea of setting up overseas military bases," China.org.cn, January 28, 2010.

127 "Secure a decisive victory."

128 "Full text: China's national defense in the new era," Xinhua, July 24, 2019.

129 Andrew S. Erickson, "China's blueprint for sea power," *China Brief*, Vol. 16, No. 11 (July 6, 2016).

130 "中华人民共和国国民经济和社会发展第十三个五年规划纲要 [Outline of the 13th Five-Year Plan for the Economic and Social Development of the People's Republic of China]," Central People's Government of the People's Republic of China, March 17, 2016.

131 "Yemen Crisis: China evacuates citizens and foreigners from Aden," BBC, April 3, 2015.

132 Matthieu Duchâtel, "China trends #2 – Naval bases: from Djibouti to a global network?" Institut Montaigne, June 26, 2019.

133 Wang Tianze, Qi Wenzhe, and Hai Jun, "海外军事基地运输投送保障探讨" [An exploration into logistical support of transportation and projection for military bases abroad], Defense Transportation Engineering and Techniques, No. 1, 2018, 32–6.

134 Ralph Jennings, "Experts: China renewing effort to squelch US influence in Southeast Asia," Voice of America News, September 16, 2020.

135 Dialogue, senior Chinese official, Beijing, January 2019.

136 Fu Mengzi, "大变局下的中国周边外交 [China's peripheral diplomacy under changing conditions]," Wuhan University Institute of Boundary and Ocean Studies, 2019.

137 "China's ambitious bid for Southeast Asia hegemony," Deutsche Welle, December 24, 2019.

138 Emil Avdaliani, "China's effect: a global NATO," Begin–Sadat Center for Strategic Studies, August 10, 2020.

139 "NATO's Jens Stoltenberg sounds warning on China's rise," Deutsche Welle, June 13, 2020.

140 "Remarks by NATO Secretary General Jens Stoltenberg on launching #NATO2030 – strengthening the Alliance in an increasingly competitive world," NATO, June 8, 2020.

141 "Annual Report to Congress: Military and security developments involving the People's Republic of China 2019," Office of the Secretary of Defense, May 2, 2019.

142 Jonathan McClory, "The Soft Power 30," Portland Communications, October 2019.

143 Silver et al., "Unfavorable views of China."

144 Pippa Morgan, "Can China's economic statecraft win soft power in Africa? Unpacking trade, investment and aid," *Journal of Chinese Political Science*, Vol. 22, No. 3 (2019).

145 Richard Q. Turcsányi et al., "European public opinion on China in the age of COVID-19," Central European Institute for Asian Studies, 2020.

146 Laura Silver, Kat Devlin, and Christine Huang, "Attitudes toward China," Pew Research Center, December 5, 2019.

147 Tang Siew Mun et al., "The state of Southeast Asia: 2020 Survey Report," ASEAN Studies Centre at ISEAS–Yusof Ishak Institute, January 16, 2020.

148 Richard Wike, Janell Fetterolf, and Christine Huang, "British, French and German publics give Biden high after US election," Pew Research Center, January 19, 2021.

149 Charissa Yong, "Singaporeans should be aware of China's 'influence operations' to manipulate them, says retired diplomat Bilahari," *Straits Times*, June 27, 2018.

150 Qi Wang, "Over 70% respondents believe China's global image has improved, wolf warrior diplomacy a necessary gesture: GT poll," *Global Times*, December 25, 2020.

151 Stephen McDonnell, "Xi Jinping calls for more 'loveable' image for China in bid to make new friends," BBC, June 2, 2021.

Chapter 3 Reunifying the Motherland

1 Under the proposed bill, Hong Kong would be able to detain people and extradite them to countries without a formal extradition treaty. This includes Taiwan and mainland China. See Mike Ives, "What is Hong Kong's extradition bill?" *New York Times*, June 10, 2019.

2 Michael Forsythe, "Billionaire is reported seized from Hong Kong hotel and taken into China," *New York Times*, January 31, 2017.

3 Alex W. Palmer, "The Case of Hong Kong's missing booksellers," *New York Times*, April 3, 2018.

4 Tsui-kai Wong, "Hong Kong protests: What are the 'five demands'? What do protestors want?" *South China Morning Post*, August 20, 2019.

5 "Full text of the Constitution and the Basic Law," Basic Law Promotion Steering Committee, last modified July 17, 2020.

6 "The practice of the 'one country, two systems' policy in the Hong Kong Special Administrative Region," State Council Information Office of the People's Republic of China, June 2014.

7 "China says Sino-British Joint Declaration on Hong Kong no longer has meaning," Reuters, June 30, 2017.

8 "Full text of Xi Jinping's speech on 'one country, two systems' and how China rules Hong Kong," *South China Morning Post*, July 1, 2017.

9 Megan K. Stack, "Joshua Wong's long campaign for the future of Hong Kong," *New Yorker*, October 23, 2019.

10 Alexander Chipman Koty, "The US position on Hong Kong's special status," China Briefing, June 10, 2020.

11 John Ruwitch, "What to know about Hong Kong's special status and what happens if the US removes it," NPR, May 28, 2020.

12 Jessie Pang and Twinnie Siu, "Landslide democratic win puts pressure on leader of Chinese-ruled Hong Kong," Reuters, November 24, 2019.

13 Ibid.

14 Robert Delaney and Owen Churchill, "Donald Trump signs Hong Kong Human Rights and Democracy Act into law, brushing off China's warnings," *South China Morning Post*, November 28, 2019.

15 "Chinese media blames 'foreign forces' for interfering in Hong Kong; brushes aside pro-democracy wins," *South China Morning Post*, November 25, 2019.

16 Anna Fifield, "China's ominous warning to Hong Kong: less tolerance, more patriotic education," *Washington Post*, November 1, 2019.

17 Jiangtao Shi, "Xia Baolong – from toppling church crosses to overseeing Hong Kong affairs," *South China Morning Post*, February 13, 2020.

18 "HK needs new national security laws: liaison chief," RTHK, April 15, 2020.

19 Elaine Yu and Austin Ramzy, "Amid pandemic, Hong Kong arrests major pro-democracy figures," *New York Times*, April 18, 2020.

20 "Protest violence in Hong Kong is a 'political virus,' says Beijing," Hong Kong Free Press, May 6, 2020.

21 Ibid.

22 Javier C. Hernandéz, "Harsh penalties, vaguely defined crimes: Hong Kong's security law explained," *New York Times*, June 30, 2020.

23 "Lam says national security law will not undermine HK autonomy," Reuters, June 30, 2020.

24 Dan Strumpf, "Hong Kong libraries pull books for review under China's Security Law," *Wall Street Journal*, July 5, 2020.

25 Scott Neuman, "Hong Kong activist Nathan Law says he has fled abroad amid Beijing-backed crackdown," NPR, July 2, 2020.

26 "The end of one country, two systems? Implications of Beijing's National

Security Law in Hong Kong," US House of Representatives Committee on Foreign Affairs, July 1, 2020.

27 Helen Davidson, "Concern as Hong Kong postpones elections for a year, citing Covid-19," *The Guardian*, July 31, 2020.

28 "Foreign Ministry spokesperson Hua Chunying's Regular Press Conference on June 12, 2020," Foreign Ministry of the People's Republic of China.

29 "Joshua Wong and fellow activists plead guilty in Hong Kong protests trial," BBC, November 23, 2020.

30 "Joint Statement on the Human Rights Situation in Xinjiang and the Recent Developments in Hong Kong, delivered by Germany on behalf of 39 countries," United States Mission to the United Nations, October 6, 2020.

31 Anwar Iqbal, "Pakistan leads 55-nation group supporting China on Hong Kong," *Dawn*, October 8, 2020.

32 "Joint Statement on Xinjiang at Third Committee made by Belarus on behalf of 54 Countries," Permanent Mission of the People's Republic of China to the UN, October 29, 2019.

33 "Xi Focus: China celebrates 40th anniversary of Shenzhen SEZ, embarking on new journey toward socialist modernization," Xinhua, October 14, 2019.

34 Ken Chu, "Hong Kong still has a place in Beijing's grand reforms after Shenzhen," *South China Morning Post*, October 17, 2020.

35 Xi Jinping, "Secure a decisive victory in building a moderately prosperous society in all respects and strive for the great success of socialism with Chinese characteristics for a new era," *China Daily*, October 18, 2017.

36 Ibid.

37 Xi Jinping, "Vice President Xi Jinping policy speech, February 15, 2012," filmed at the National Committee on US–China Relations, New York.

38 Robert G. Sutter and Chin-Hao Haung, "China's growing resolve in the South China Sea," *Comparative Connections*, Vol. 15, No. 1 (January–April 2013).

39 "Actions and tricks to split China doomed to fail: Xi," Xinhua, March 20, 2018.

40 "China's Xi says political solution for Taiwan can't wait forever," Reuters, November 6, 2013.

41 "Highlights of Xi's speech at Taiwan message anniversary event," State Council Information Office of the People's Republic of China, January 2, 2019.

42 "Xinhua Headlines: Xi says 'China must be, will be reunified' as key anniversary marked," Xinhua, January 2, 2019.

43 "It's not just India, China has border disputes with 18 countries," India TV, June 26, 2020.

44 Jesse Johnson, "China's 100-day push near Senkaku Islands comes at unsettling time for Sino-Japanese ties," *Japan Times*, July 27, 2020.

45 Dai Lun, "北京学者：习近平传承毛泽东 国安立法终结香港'无政府'状态 [Beijing scholar: Xi Jinping inherits Mao Zedong's national security legislation and ends Hong Kong's 'anarchist' state]," Deutsche Welle, July 9, 2020.

46 Nick Aspinwall, "Taiwan is exporting its coronavirus successes to the world," *Foreign Policy*, April 9, 2020.

47 "Full text of Xi Jinping's report at the 19th CPC National Congress," *China Daily*, November 4, 2017.

48 Yuwen Deng, "Why China will wait until 2030 to take back Taiwan – unless the island forces Xi Jinping's hand," *South China Morning Post*, November 26, 2018.

49 "Struggle to restore China's lawful seat in the United Nations," Ministry of Foreign Affairs of the People's Republic of China.

50 "A policy of 'one country, two systems' on Taiwan," Ministry of Foreign Affairs of the People's Republic of China.

51 Zhao Xinying, "More Taiwan students studying in mainland universities," *China Daily*, November 6, 2015.

52 Sindy Leng and Liu Zhen, "'We are brothers': Xi hails closer ties with Taiwan as closed-door talks with Ma wrap up at historic Singapore summit," *South China Morning Post*, November 7, 2015.

53 Xi Jinping, *The Governance of China: Volume One* (Beijing: Foreign Language Press, 2014), 254.

54 Ibid., 258.

55 "What was the CSSTA?" Daybreak, July 20, 2017.

56 "What was the movement attempting to address?" Daybreak, July 22, 2017.

57 "President Ma Ying-jeou's National Day Address," Taipei Economic and Cultural Office in Thailand, October 17, 2014.

58 Javier C. Hernández and Vanessa Piao, "Tsai Ing-wen, Taiwan's first female leader, is assailed in China for being 'emotional'," *New York Times*, May 25, 2016.

59 Ching-chi Ko, "Taiwan's 2016 presidential election," Carnegie Endowment for International Peace, September 9, 2015.

60 Aurelio Insisa, "Taiwan 2012–2016: from consolidation to the collapse of cross-strait rapprochement," *Asia Maior*, Vol. 27 (2016).

61 Lawrence Chung, "Beijing cuts Ma-era cross-strait communication channel with Taiwan," *South China Morning Post*, June 26, 2016.

62 Chun-hung Lee et al., "Evaluating international tourists' perceptions on cultural distance and recreation demand," *Sustainability*, Vol. 10, No. 12 (2018).

63 Lawrence Chung, "Beijing cuts number of students allowed in Taiwan," *South China Morning Post*, May 30, 2017.

64 Joyce Lau, "Post-pandemic, will China use its students as bargaining chips?" *Inside Higher Ed*, June 26, 2020.

65 Cheng Jiawen, "林中斌：中共對台政策是'窮台' [Lin Chong-pin: China's policy toward Taiwan is to 'impoverish Taiwan']," *United Daily News*, July 22, 2016.

66 "MUJI 無印良品," MUJI, *https://www.muji.com/tw/*.

67 Elliot Waldman, "Chinese interference casts a dark cloud over local elections in Taiwan," *World Politics Review*, November 29, 2018.

68 Tom O'Connor, "Which countries still recognize Taiwan? Two more nations switch to China in less than a week," *Newsweek*, September 20, 2019.

69 John Dotson, "Military activity and political signaling in the Taiwan Strait in early 2020," Jamestown Foundation, April 1, 2020.

70 "China says Taiwan military drills are over after Pelosi visit," BBC, August 10, 2022.

71 Minnie Chan, "China tries to calm 'nationalist fever' as calls for invasion of Taiwan grow," *South China Morning Post*, May 10, 2020.

72 H.I. Sutton, "If China invades Taiwan, this is what the fleet could look like," *Forbes*, June 7, 2020.

73 Chan, "China tries to calm 'nationalist fever'."

74 Minnie Chan, "'Too costly': Chinese military strategist warns now is not the time to take back Taiwan by force," *South China Morning Post*, May 4, 2020.

75 "Taiwan Relations Act," American Institute in Taiwan, *https://www.ait.org.tw/our-relationship/policy-history/key-u-s-foreign-policy-documents-region/taiwan-relations-act/*.

76 "H.R.535 – Taiwan Travel Act," Congress.gov, last updated March 16, 2018, *https://www.congress.gov/bill/115th-congress/house-bill/535*.

77 "S.1678 – Taiwan Allies International Protection and Enhancement Initiative," Congress.gov, last updated March 26, 2020, *https://www.congress.gov/bill/116th-congress/senate-bill/1678/text*.

78 John Ruwitch, Biden, again, says "U.S. would help Taiwan if China attacks," NPR, September 19, 2022.

79 "Taiwanese foreign trade in figures," Santander, September 2020, *https://santandertrade.com/en/portal/analyse-markets/taiwan/foreign-trade-in-figures*.

80 Isabella Steger, "China tried to threaten Taiwan by weaponizing tourism, but it didn't work," Quartz, January 7, 2020.

81 Charlotte Gifford, "Going it alone – what the New Southbound Policy means for Taiwanese independence," World Finance, May 1, 2020.

82 "Taiwanese companies returning to the island because of growing aggressiveness from Beijing," MercoPress, September 16, 2020.

83 John Sudworth, "China needs to show Taiwan respect, says president," BBC, January 14, 2020.

84 "Joint multidimensional landing drill conducted in sea areas of East and South China Seas," YouTube, October 11, 2020, *https://www.youtube.com/watch?v=DPp_Guk3GEc&feature=youtu.be*.

85 "China threatens to take over Taiwan by conducting live-fire military drill of 'soldiers seizing an island' as political tensions spike to new high," *Daily Mail*, October 12, 2020.

86 David Alexander, Michael Martina, and Dean Yates, "China's land reclamation in South China Sea grows: Pentagon report," Reuters, August 21, 2015.

87 Ankit Panda, "It's official: Xi Jinping breaks his non-militarization pledge in the Spratlys," The Diplomat, December 16, 2016.

88 Rachael Bale, "One of the world's biggest fisheries is on the verge of collapse," *National Geographic*, August 29, 2016.

89 Quoted in Robert Kaplan, *Asia's Cauldron: The South China Sea and the End of a Stable Pacific* (New York: Random House, 2014), 41.

90 "Declaration on the Conduct of Parties in the South China Sea," Association of Southeast Asian Nations, November 4, 2002.

91 South China Sea Expert Working Group, "A blueprint for a South China Sea Code of Conduct," Asia Maritime Transparency Initiative, October 11, 2018.

92 Mingjiang Li, "Reconciling assertiveness and cooperation? China's changing approach to the South China Sea dispute," *Security Challenges* Vol. 6, No. 2 (Winter 2010).

93 "Historical evidence to support China's sovereignty over Nansha Islands," Ministry of Foreign Affairs of the People's Republic of China, November 17, 2000.

94 Natalie Thomas and Michael Martina, "China tightens rules on maps amid territorial disputes," Reuters, December 16, 2015.

95 Andrew S. Erickson and Kevin Bond, "Archaeology and the South China Sea," *The Diplomat*, July 20, 2015.

96 Mike Ives, "A defiant map-hunter stakes Vietnam's claims in the South China Sea," *New York Times*, November 25, 2017.

97 "Maps question China's claims over Vietnamese islands," *Tuoi Tre News*, May 30, 2016.

98 Raul Pedrozo, "China versus Vietnam: an analysis of competing claims in the South China Sea," CNA, August 2014.

99 Andrew Chubb, "Xi Jinping and China's maritime policy," Brookings Institution, January 22, 2019.

100 "Annual Report to Congress: Military and security developments involving the People's Republic of China 2018," Office of the Secretary of Defense, May 16, 2018.

101 Lynn Kuok, "Countering China's actions in the South China Sea," *LawFare*, August 1, 2018.

102 Ibid.

103 AMTI Leadership, "Arbitration Support Tracker," Center for Strategic and International Studies, June 16, 2016.

104 Douglas Guilfoyle, "A new twist in the South China Sea Arbitration: the Chinese Society of International Law's critical study," *EJIL:Talk! Blog of the European Journal of International Law*, May 25, 2018.

105 Kristin Huang, "'Prepare for war', Xi Jinping tells military region that monitors South China Sea, Taiwan," *South China Morning Post*, October 26, 2018.

106 Shinji Yamaguchi, "Strategies of China's maritime actors in the South China Sea: a coordinated plan under the leadership of Xi Jinping," *China Perspectives* 3 (September 2016).

107 Megha Rajagopalan, "China trains 'fishing militia' to sail into disputed waters," Reuters, April 30, 2016.

108 China Power Team, "Are maritime law enforcement forces destabilizing Asia?" China Power, August 18, 2016, updated August 26, 2020.

109 Ralph Jennings, "After show of military might, China offers to restart S. China Sea talks," Voice of America, July 8, 2020.

110 Kristin Huang, "Beijing marks out claims in South China Sea by naming geographical features," *South China Morning Post*, April 20, 2020.

111 Alan Robles, "'Any suggestion?' Philippine president Duterte asks after Xi Jinping reaffirms South China Sea claims," *South China Morning Post*, September 5, 2019.

112 Laura Zhou, "Asean members up the ante on South China Sea amid code of conduct talks," *South China Morning Post*, December 29, 2019.

113 Brad Lendon, "Philippines says it won't end US military access agreement amid South China Sea Tensions," CNN, June 3, 2020.

114 Jim Gomez, "Philippines calls for Beijing to follow ruling on South China Sea dispute," *Global News*, July 12, 2020.

115 Phuong Nguyen and Neil Jerome Morales, "Vietnam, Philippines denounce China military drills in disputed waters," *US News*, July 2, 2020.

116 Felix K. Chang, "Uncertain prospects: South China Sea Code of Conduct negotiations," Foreign Policy Research Institute, October 6, 2020.

117 "Bilahari Kausikan's speech on ASEAN & US–China Competition in Southeast Asia," *Today*, March 31, 2016.

118 Laura Zhou, "Asean members up the ante on South China Sea."

119 Dzirhan Mahadzir, "China pushes back against US statement on South China Sea claim, ASEAN stays silent," USNI News, July 14, 2019.

120 Jason Loh, "South China Sea: time to display firm resolve," *The ASEAN Post*, July 25, 2020.

121 Tony Walker, "Naval exercises in South China Sea add to growing fractiousness between US and China," *The Conversation*, July 8, 2020.

122 Michael R. Pompeo, "US position on maritime claims in the South China Sea," US Department of State, July 13, 2020.

123 Philip Davidson and Nicholas Burns, "Military competition with China: maintaining America's edge," filmed July 18, 2019, at Aspen Strategy Group, Aspen, CO, video, 21:19.

124 Ibid., 21:42.

125 "China condemns US for South China Sea freedom of navigation operation," Reuters, October 1, 2018.

126 Ben Werner, "Maritime standoff between China and Malaysia winding down," USNI News, May 13, 2020.

127 Pompeo, "US position on maritime claims in the South China Sea."

128 "Foreign Ministry spokesperson Zhao Lijian's Regular Press Conference on July 14, 2020," Ministry of Foreign Affairs of the People's Republic of China, July 14, 2020.

129 Chunhao Lou, "为何美日澳总是搅局南海问题? [Why do the United States, Japan, and Australia always disrupt the South China Sea Issue?]" opinion. china.com.cn, 2017.

Chapter 4 The Dragon's Bite

1 "Port of Piraeus," World Port Source, *http://www.worldportsource.com/ports/review/GRC_Port_of_Piraeus_1041.php*.

2 "China's Cosco makes Piraeus 2nd largest port in Mediterranean," *The National Herald*, October 21, 2019.

3 Angeliki Koutantou, "COSCO sees Greece's Piraeus among world's top 30 ports by 2018," Reuters, September 22, 2016.

4 Yanis Varoufakis, *Adults in the Room* (New York: Farrar, Straus, and Giroux, 2017), 315.

5 Ibid., 316.

6 Ibid., 138.

7 Ibid., 321.

8 "Cosco (Hong Kong) Group Limited 51% shareholder of PPA," Hellenic Republic Asset Development Fund, August 10, 2016.

9 "China is making substantial investment in ports and pipelines worldwide," *The Economist*, February 6, 2020.

10 Theresa Fallon, "The EU, the South China Sea, and China's successful wedge strategy," Asia Maritime Transparency Initiative, October 13, 2016.

11 Robin Emmott and Angeliki Koutantou, "Greece blocks EU statement on China human rights at the UN," Reuters, June 18, 2017.

12 Ibid.

13 Angus Berwick and Renee Maltezou, "EU suspects tax fraud at China's new gateway to Europe," Reuters, April 20, 2018.

14 Stuart Lau, "Greece's ancient civilisation was once a lure for China's leaders. Now it could prove their nemesis," *South China Morning Post*, April 7, 2019.

15 "Meeting Asia's infrastructure needs," Asian Development Bank, February 2017.

16 Shai Oster, "China: new dam builder for the world," *Wall Street Journal*, December 28, 2007.

17 Jin Ling, "The 'New Silk Road' Initiative: China's Marshall Plan?" China Institute of International Studies, June 11, 2015.

18 Zhou Jiayi, He Kaile, and Han Weiyi, "一带一路'恐带来的风险 [The risks posed by the Belt and Road Initiative]," 中外对话 [China Dialogue], July 7, 2015.

19 Min Ye, "Domestic politics of China's Belt and Road Initiative," The Asan Forum, June 17, 2019.

20 Feng Pan, "中国与21世纪亚洲基础设施互联互通进程 [China's infrastructure interconnection process towards Asia in the 21st century]," 国际研究参考 [International Research Reference], No. 8 (2015).

21 Liu Yazhou, "大国策 [Great power policy]," Aisixiang, April 15, 2004.

22 Jiang Zhida, "一带一路:以'空间'换'时间'的发展战略 [One Belt One Road: a development strategy trades 'space' with 'time']," 和平与发展 [Peace and Development], No. 4 (2015).

23 Zheng Yongnian and Hang Chi, "一带一路与中国大外交 [One Belt, One Road and China's big diplomacy]," 当代世界 [Contemporary World], February 2016.

24 Andrea Ghiselli, "The domestic drive behind China's Belt and Road Initiative," The Asia Dialogue, June 7, 2017.

25 Wang Jisi, "China's search for a grand strategy," *Foreign Affairs*, March/April 2011.

26 Xinyi Wang and David A. Parker, "Buckling down: how Beijing is implementing its 'One Belt, One Road' vision," CogitAsia, May 7, 2015.

27 Ghiselli, "The domestic drive behind China's Belt and Road Initiative."

28 Ye, "Domestic politics of China's Belt and Road Initiative."

29 François Godement et al., "'One Belt, One Road': China's Great Leap Forward," European Council on Foreign Relations, June 2015, 10.

30 Jinghan Zeng, "Narrating China's Belt and Road Initiative," *Global Policy*, Vol. 10, No. 4 (March 2019), 2.

31 Ye, "Domestic politics of China's Belt and Road Initiative."

32 Li Xiaojun and Zeng Ka, "To join or not to join? State ownership, commercial interests, and China's Belt and Road Initiative," *Pacific Affairs*, Vol. 92, No. 1 (2019).

33 World Bank Group, *Belt and Road Economics: Opportunities and Risks of Transport Corridors* (Washington, DC: World Bank Publications, 2019).

34 "BRI Connect: an initiative in numbers," Refinitv, *https://www.refinitiv. com/content/dam/marketing/en_us/documents/reports/belt-and-road-initiative-in-numbers-issue-2.pdf.*

35 "BRI Projects," Belt and Road Initiative, *https://www.beltroad-initiative.com/ projects/.*

36 Leonie Kijewski, "Sihanoukville, Cambodian magnet for Chinese casinos, loses its pull, leaving thousands owed money and unable to move on," *South China Morning Post*, February 20, 2020.

37 "BRI Projects."

38 China Power Team, "How will the Belt and Road Initiative advance China's interests?" China Power, updated October 18, 2019.

39 James Kynge and Sun Yu, "China faces wave of calls for debt relief on 'Belt and Road' projects," *Financial Times,* April 30, 2020.

40 "China's investment in Belt & Road Initiative countries averaging US$12.76 billion a month," Silk Road Briefing, January 14, 2020.

41 "China's investment in Belt and Road Initiative cools," Radio Free Asia, January 17, 2020.

42 China Power Team, "Does China dominate global investment?" China Power, updated January 27, 2020.

43 Adva Saldinger, "China's Belt & Road Initiative out-lends MDBs, sees itself as a 'global public good'," Devex, October 23, 2019.

44 Jamie P. Horsley, "Working Paper: Challenging China to make good project governance a centerpiece of the Belt and Road Initiative," Paul Tsai China Center, Yale Law School, December 2018.

45 Tom Mitchell and Alice Woodhouse, "Malaysia renegotiated China-backed rail project to avoid $5bn fee," *Financial Times*, April 15, 2019.

46 Stephen Chin, "Is the BRI a corruption magnet?" *The Asean Post*, October 10, 2018.

47 Dipanjan Roy Chaudhury, "Tanzania president terms China's BRI port project exploitative," *The Economic Times*, July 6, 2019.

48 Jonathan E. Hillman, "China's Belt and Road Initiative: five years later," Center for Strategic and International Studies, January 25, 2018.

49 "Success of China's Belt & Road Initiative depends on deep policy reforms, study finds," World Bank, June 18, 2019.

50 "The road less travelled: European involvement in China's Belt and Road Initiative," European Chamber of Commerce in China, January 16, 2020.

51 Sebastian Horn, Carmen M. Reinhart, and Christopher Trebesch, "How much money does the world owe China?" *Harvard Business Review*, February 26, 2020.

52 Sebastian Horn, Carmen Reinhart, and Christoph Trebesch, "China's overseas lending," Kiel Institute for the World Economy, June 2019.

53 Tan Weizhen, "About half of China's loans to developing countries are 'hidden,' study finds," CNBC, July 12, 2019.

54 Horn et al., "How much money does the world owe China?"

55 World Bank Group, *Belt and Road Economics*.

56 Kliman, et al., "Grading China's Belt and Road," Center for a New American Security, April 8, 2019.

57 World Bank Group, *Belt and Road Economics*.

58 Ben Bartenstein, "Ecuador eyes new financing after world's first virtual debt deal," Bloomberg, August 5, 2020.

59 Elliot Smith, "Zambia's spiraling debt offers glimpse into future of Chinese loan financing in Africa," CNBC, January 14, 2020.

60 Joseph Cotterill, Jonathan Wheatley, and Tommy Stubbington, "Zambia resists Chinese pressure on arrears," *Financial Times*, October 12, 2020.

61 Sebastian Horn, Carmen M. Reinhart, and Christoph Tresbesch, "China's overseas lending: a response to our critics," Center for Global Development, May 7, 2020.

62 Agatha Kratz, Matthew Mingey, and Dew D'Alelio, "Seeking relief: China's overseas debt after COVID-19," Rhodium Group, October 8, 2020.

63 "Interactive database of Chinese loan commitments to African governments (2000–2018)," Johns Hopkins School of Advanced International Studies, China Africa Research Initiative.

64 Discussion with Brazilian experts and officials via Zoom, November 4–5, 2020.

65 "2017 Report on the Sustainable Development of Chinese Enterprises Overseas," United Nations Development Program, May 2017.

66 Global Policy Development Center, "China's global energy finance," Boston University, 2020.

67 Hans Nicholas Jong, "Survey: Less coal, more solar, say citizens of Belt & Road countries," Mongabay, April 25, 2019.

68 George Obulutsa, "Power from Kenya's planned Lamu plant could cost 10 times more than estimated: study," Reuters, June 11, 2019.

69 "Kenya halts Lamu coal power project at World Heritage Site," BBC, June 26, 2019.

70 Obulutsa, "Power from Kenya's planned Lamu plant could cost 10 times more than estimated: study."

71 James Ellsmoor, "US ambassador pushes coal plant on African World Heritage Site, Kenya fights back," *Forbes*, June 27, 2019.

72 Lewis Nyaundi, "Lamu coal plant: China ready to leave," *The Star*, June 29, 2019.

73 Christian Shepherd, "China pours money into green Belt and Road projects," *Financial Times*, January 26, 2021.

74 Han Chen and Wei Shen, "China's no new coal power overseas pledge, one year on" China Dialogue, September 22, 2022.

75 Zafar Bhutta, "Chinese offer to finance whole $2B LNG project," *The Express Tribune*, May 13, 2016.

76 Vishnu Prakash, "Pakistan's 'China Dilemma': is the CPEC a Boon or a burden?" *The Quint,* August 20, 2020.

77 Tom Hussain, "Where does Imran Khan's government stand on China's Belt and Road?" *South China Morning Post*, August 12, 2018.

78 Nadia Naviwala, "Pakistan's $100B deal with China: what does it amount to?" Devex, August 24, 2017.

79 David Lipton, "IMF Executive Board approves US$6 billion 39-Month EFF arrangements for Pakistan," International Monetary Fund, July 3, 2019.

80 Adnan Amir, "Why is Pakistan cutting funding from Belt and Road projects?" China–US Focus, July 15, 2019.

81 Stephanie Findlay and Farhan Bokhari, "Pakistan revives Belt-and-Road projects under Chinese pressure," *Financial Times*, December 10, 2019.

82 Adnan Amir, "Pakistan and CPEC are drawn into the US–China rivalry," *China Brief,* Vol. 20, No. 1 (January 17, 2020).

83 Masayuki Masuda, "China as regional actor," in *China Goes to Eurasia*, National Institute for Defense Studies, Japan, November 2019, 19.

84 Kaswar Klasra, "China's Huawei protests after Pakistan authorities tear down security barriers at its Islamabad office," *South China Morning Post*, May 17, 2019.

85 "Rising attacks by Baloch separatists increase risks, costs of BRI projects in Pakistan: Report," *The Economic Times*, July 20, 2020.

86 Adnan Aamir, "China moves for more control over Belt and Road in Pakistan," Nikkei Asia, February 16, 2021.

87 "Pakistan's Gwadar port leased to Chinese company for 40 years," *Economic Times*, April 20, 2017.

88 "Commentary: China's Djibouti base not for military expansion," Xinhua, July 13, 2017.

89 Masuda, "China as regional actor," 19.

90 Liu Zhen, "Pakistan port on China's radar for naval base, Pentagon report says," *South China Morning Post*, June 7, 2017.

91 James Kynge et al. "How China rules the waves," *Financial Times*, January 12, 2017.

92 Mohan Malik, "Countering China's maritime ambitions," Indo-Pacific Defense Forum, March 23, 2020.

93 Mohan Malik, "Dimensions, detours, fissures, and fault lines," The American Interest, February 19, 2018.

94 Guifang (Julia) Xue, "The potential dual use of support facilities in the Belt and Road Initiative," in Nadège Rolland, ed., *Securing the Belt and Road Initiative*, NBR Special Report #80 (September 2019), 53.

95 Qingsi Li and Chunyu Chen, "试析中国的海外港链基地战略 [Analysis of Chinese overseas port bases strategy]," *CNKI 知网空间* [*CNKI Online Knowledge Space*], No. 2 (2019).

96 Tianze Wang, Wenzhe Qi, and Jun Hai, "海外军事基地运输投送保障探讨 [Discussion of transportation and delivery guarantees for military bases]," 国防交通工程与技术 [*National Defense Transportation, Engineering, and Technology*], No. 1 (2018).

97 Mathieu Duchâtel, "China Trends #2 – Naval bases: from Djibouti to a global network?" Institut Montaigne, June 26, 2019.

98 Cassandra Garrison, "China's military-run space station in Argentina is a 'black box'," Reuters, January 31, 2019.

99 Jeremy Page, Gordon Lubold, and Rob Taylor, "Deal for naval outpost in Cambodia furthers China's quest for military network," *Wall Street Journal*, July 22, 2019.

100 Shaun Turton and Bopha Phorn, "US questions Cambodia over possible Chinese military presence," *Nikkei Asian Review*, July 1, 2019.

101 "The latest: China refutes report of Cambodia naval base," AP News, July 24, 2019.

102 Prak Chan Thul, "Cambodia says to increase arms purchases from China," Reuters, July 29, 2019.

103 Ankit Panda, "Cambodia's Hun Sen denies Chinese naval base again – but what's really happening?" The Diplomat, June 2, 2020.

104 Guifang Xue and Hao Zheng, "中国21世纪海外基地建设的现实需求与风险应对 [The realistic demand and risk response of China's overseas base construction in the 21st century]," 国际展望 [International Outlook], No. 4 (2017).

105 "Xi urges major risk prevention to ensure healthy economy, social stability," Xinhua, January 22, 2019.

106 Bradley Jardine and Edward Lemon, "Tajikistan's security ties with China a Faustian bargain," Eurasia.net, March 2, 2020.

107 Charles Clover, "Chinese private security companies go global," *Financial Times*, February 26, 2017.

108 "Xi's statements on the Belt and Road Initiative," *China Daily*, April 15, 2017.

109 Clayton Cheney, "China's Digital Silk Road could decide the US–China competition," The Diplomat, July 17, 2019.

110 Shen Hong, "Beijing takes stakes in private firms to keep them afloat," *Wall Street Journal*, September 30, 2019.

111 Simon Denyer, "Command and control: China's Communist Party extends reach into foreign companies," *Washington Post*, January 28, 2018.

112 Zhang Lin, "The three dangers of China's mixed-ownership reform," *South China Morning Post*, August 7, 2018.

113 Kieran Green, "Securing the Digital Silk Road," Center for Advanced China Research, February 11, 2019.

114 Johannes Ledel and Sam Kingsley, "Can Nokia, Ericsson compete with Huawei?" *Asia Times*, February 3, 2020.

115 "China Safe Cities Technologies and Market Report 2020: rising impressive business opportunities analysis forecast by 2022," MarketWatch, August 19, 2020.

116 "Huawei announces safe city compact solution to protect citizens in small and medium cities," Huawei, October 15, 2018.

117 Jonathan E. Hillman and Maesea McCalpin, "Watching Huawei's 'safe cities'," Center for Strategic and International Studies, November 4, 2019.

118 Klasra, "China's Huawei protests after Pakistan authorities tear down security barriers at its Islamabad office."

119 Daniel Newman, "Opinion: These 7 tech companies are today's 5G winners," MarketWatch, March 9, 2019.

120 Jonathan Kaiman, "'China has conquered Kenya': Inside Beijing's new strategy to win African hearts and minds," *Los Angeles Times*, August 7, 2013.

121 Ibid.

122 "Chinese TV series gaining popularity in Africa," Balancing Act, April 4, 2013.

123 Fu Ying, "Telling China's story," China–US Focus, April 19, 2020.

124 "Chinese TV series gaining popularity in Africa."

125 Jenni Marsh, "How China is slowly expanding its power in Africa, one TV set at a time," CNN Business, July 24, 2019.

126 Edem Selormey, "Africans' perceptions about China: a sneak peek from 18 countries," Afrobarometer, September 3, 2020.

127 Marsh, "How China is slowly expanding its power in Africa."

128 Asterius Banzi, "Tanzania seeks Chinese help in social media," *The East African*, August 1, 2017.

129 Shayera Dark, "Strict new internet laws in Tanzania are driving bloggers and content creators offline," The Verge, July 6, 2018.

130 Samuel Woodhams, "Huawei, Africa and the global reach of surveillance technology," Deutsche Welle, December 9, 2019.

131 "Uganda's Bobi Wine: pop star MP charged with treason," BBC, August 23, 2018.

132 Joe Parkinson, Nicholas Bariyo, and Josh Chin, "Huawei technicians helped African governments spy on political opponent," *Wall Street Journal*, August 15, 2019.

133 Dark, "Strict new internet laws in Tanzania."

134 "Freedom of the Net 2019: Uganda," Freedom House, 2019, *https://freedom house.org/country/uganda/freedom-net/2019*.

135 Parkinson et al., "Huawei technicians helped African governments spy on political opponent."

136 "Latvia: trade statistics," Global Edge, *https://globaledge.msu.edu/countries/latvia/tradestats*.

137 "2019 Annual Report," Constitution Protection Bureau of the Republic of Latvia, April 24, 2019.

138 Siew Mun Tang et al., "The state of Southeast Asia: 2020," ISEAS–Yusof Ishak Institute, January 16, 2020.

139 "Thousands protest against Myanmar mega-dam," *The Asean Post*, April 23, 2019.

140 "Experts warn of 'debt-trap' for Vietnam in Belt and Road Initiative as China bids for projects," Radio Free Asia, May 22, 2019.

141 Catherine Putz, "Kyrgyz–Chinese joint venture scrapped after protests," The Diplomat, February 20, 2020.

142 Laura Zhou, "Thailand nixed China's Mekong River blasting project. Will others push back?" *South China Morning Post*, February 22, 2020.

143 Thitinan Pongsudhirak, "China's Belt & Road needs to listen more," *Bangkok Post*, November 30, 2018.

144 Wenguang Sun, "孙文广：致习总之8：出访不要大撒币 [Sun Wenguang: To Xi in brief: don't throw away money when visiting abroad]," Canyuwang, July 20, 2018.

145 "Chinese police remove professor during broadcast of VOA program," Voice of America News, August 1, 2018.

146 Zhangrun Xu, "我們當下的恐懼與期待 [Our current fears and expectations]," Initium, July 24, 2018.

147 Chris Buckley, "A Chinese law professor criticized Xi. Now he's been suspended," *New York Times*, March 26, 2019.

148 Yongniang Zheng, "贸易战与特朗普的国际新秩序 [The trade war and Trump's new international order]," Cfisnet, July 6, 2018.

149 Ankur Shah and Vivek Pisharody, "BRI draws skepticism in China's northeast," Reconnecting Asia, November 8, 2019.

150 World Bank Group, *Belt and Road Economics*.

151 Edward Wong, "Competing against Chinese loans, US companies face long odds in Africa," *New York Times*, January 13, 2019.

152 "President Donald J. Trump signs H.R. 302 into Law," White House Press Office, October 5, 2018.

153 Asia Reassurance Initiative Act of 2018, Pub. L. No. 114-409, 132 Stat. 5387 (2018).

154 "EU steps up its strategy for connecting Europe and Asia," European Commission, September 19, 2018.

155 "Text adopted by Parliament, single reading," European Parliament, December 9, 2018.

156 Michelle Jamrisko, "China no match for Japan in Southeast Asia infrastructure race," Bloomberg, June 22, 2019.

157 Peter McCawley, "Connecting the dots on the Blue Dot Network," The Interpreter, November 12, 2019.

158 "'一带一路'：和平发展的经济纽带 ['The Belt and Road': the economic link for peaceful development]," Development Research Center of the State Council, January 28, 2015.

159 "Xi's statements on the Belt and Road Initiative," *China Daily*, April 15, 2017.

160 Wentao Zhou, "'一带一路':报道中这些雷区千万不要碰 ['The Belt and Road': don't touch the minefields in this report]," Tea Party Media, April 17, 2017.

161 Jizhong Zhang et al., "The Belt and Road Initiative 2020 Survey – a more sustainable road to growth?" Central Banking, April 16, 2020.

162 Mark Plant and Scott Morris, "China's new debt sustainability framework is largely borrowed from the World Bank and IMF. Here's why that could be a problem," Center for Global Development, July 19, 2019.

163 Adva Saldinger, "China's Belt & Road Initiative out-lends MDBs, sees itself as a 'global public good'," Devex, October 23, 2019.

164 Shahar Hameiri and Lee Jones, "The misunderstood AIIB," Lowy Institute, May 17, 2018.

165 "China's coal projects outside its borders," Belt & Road News, July 5, 2020.

166 Tan Hui Yee, "Many not sold on Beijing's new stance on Belt and Road Initiative: survey," *Straits Times*, January 16, 2020.

167 Ivana Karásková et al., "Empty shell no more: China's growing footprint in Central and Eastern Europe," CHOICE, April 7, 2020.

168 John Psaropoulos, "Greece and China hail Strategic Partnership, as US and EU look on" Al Jazeera, November 11, 2019.

169 Ibid.

170 Elias Bellos, "Τα ανοικτά μέτωπα του Δημοσίου με την Cosco [The open fronts between the state and Cosco]," *Kathimerini*, January 2, 2021.

171 Louis Charbonneau, "Countries blast China at UN over Xinjiang abuses," Human Rights Watch, October 31, 2019.

172 Bojan Stojkovski, "As US, China fight trade war, Greece opens up to Huawei's 5G ambitions," ZD Net, August 19, 2019.

173 "Cosmote picks Sweden's Ericsson for Greece's 5G Network," *The National Herald*, March 30, 2020.

174 Benjamin Weinthal, "Iran threatens retaliation against Greece for US use of military bases," *The Jerusalem Post*, January 15, 2020.

175 Stuart Lau, "US pushes Greece to stop acting as China's 'dragon's head' into Europe," *South China Morning Post*, November 3, 2020.

176 Michael R. Pompeo, "Announcing expansion of the Clean Network to safeguard America's assets," US Department of State, August 5, 2020.

177 Lau, "US pushes Greece to stop acting as China's 'dragon's head' into Europe."

Chapter 5 From Bricks to Bits

1 "China has new US$1.4 trillion plan to seize the world's tech crown from the US," *South China Morning Post*, May 21, 2020.

2 Campbell Kwan, "WeChat Pay follows Alipay in allowing foreign visitors to make payments in China," ZDNet, November 8, 2019.

3 Yaqiu Wang, "WeChat is a trap for China's diaspora," Human Rights Watch, August 14, 2020.

4 Miles Kenyon "WeChat surveillance explained," Citizen Lab, May 7, 2020.

5 P.W. Singer and Taylor A. Lee, "China's version of GPS is almost complete. Here's what that means," *Popular Science*, March 31, 2020.

6 Rajesh Uppal, "China's Beidou navigation satellite system (BDS) to provide global coverage with millimeter level accuracy," *International Defence, Security & Technology*, November 9, 2020.

7 Scott Tong, "China charges forward into 5G wireless future, despite pandemic, weak economy," Market Place, October 8, 2020.

8 John Hendel and Michael Farrel, "Questions for Robert Blair, Trump's point man on 5G," Politico, February 25, 2020.

9 Jeremy Page, Kate O'Keefe, and Rob Taylor, "America's undersea battle with China for control of the global internet grid," *Wall Street Journal*, March 12, 2019.

10 Palan Balakrishnan, "China's digital route to dominance," *Hindu Business Line*, October 15, 2019.

11 "White Paper on China International Optical Cable Interconnection (2018)," China Academy of Informational and Communications Technology, August 2018.

12 Page et al., "America's undersea battle with China for control of the global internet grid."

13 World Bank Group and Development Research of the State Council, "Innovative China: new drivers of growth," World Bank Group, 2019.

14 "A coffee with Ren III: digital sovereignty, from words to action," Huawei, November 6, 2019.

15 Arjun Kharpal, "Huawei's growth slowed dramatically in 2020 as US sanctions take their toll," CNBC, March 31, 2021.

16 Chua Kong Ho, "Huawei founder Ren Zhengfei on why he joined China's Communist Party and the People's Liberation Army," *South China Morning Post*, January 16, 2019.

17 Li Yuan, "Huawei's communist culture limits its global ambitions," *New York Times*, May 1, 2019.

18 "Ren Zhengfei's interview with UK documentary producer," Huawei, *https://www.huawei.com/en/facts/voices-of-huawei/ren-zhengfeis-interview-with-uk-documentary-producer*.

19 Jeffrey Melnik, "China's 'national champions': Alibaba, Tencent, and Huawei," Association for Asian Studies, Fall 2019.

20 "Ren Zhengfei's interview with UK documentary producer."

21 "Ren Zhengfei's Interview with *South China Morning Post*," Huawei, March 24, 2020.

22 "Transcript: Huawei founder Ren Zhengfei's responses to media questions at a round table this week," *South China Morning Post*, January 16, 2019.

23 Keith Johnson and Elias Groll, "The improbable rise of Huawei," *Foreign Policy*, April 3, 2019.

24 Bruce Gilley, "Huawei's fixed line to Beijing," *Far Eastern Economic Review*, December 2000–January 2001.

25 Melnik, "China's 'national champions'."

26 Alberto F. De Toni, *International Operations Management: Lessons in Global Business* (New York: Routledge, 2016).

27 Matthew Dalton, "EU finds China gives aid to Huawei, ZTE," *Wall Street Journal*, February 3, 2011.

28 Chuin-Wei Yap, "State support helped fuel Huawei's global rise," *Wall Street Journal*, December 25, 2019.

29 Reilly Gregson, "Huawei aims to become a global force: vendor makes mobile-industry push," RCR Wireless, March 1, 2001.

30 "Ren Zhengfei's interview with UK documentary producer."

31 Alan Carlton, "How polar codes work," Computer World, September 28, 2017.

32 Steven Levy, "Huawei, 5G, and the man who conquered noise," *Wired*, November 16, 2020.

33 Christopher Rhoads, "Motorola claims Huawei plot," *Wall Street Journal*, July 22, 2010.

34 Chuin-Wei Yap et al., "Huawei's yearslong rise is littered with accusations of theft and dubious ethics," *Wall Street Journal*, May 25, 2019.

35 Erik Shatzker, "Huawei sting offers rare glimpse of the US targeting a Chinese giant," *Bloomberg Businessweek*, February 4, 2019.

36 Qasim Khan, "Ren Zhengfei: Huawei didn't, and will never steal intellectual property," Equal Ocean, June 18, 2020.

37 "Commerce addresses Huawei's efforts to undermine Entity List, restricts products designed and produced with US technologies," US Department of Commerce, May 15, 2020.

38 Alex Capri, "Semiconductors at the heart of the US–China tech war: how a new era of techno-nationalism is shaking up semiconductor value chains," Hinrich Foundation, January 2020.

39 "Ren Zhengfei says he will never hate US, desire for survival makes Huawei work harder," CN Tech Post, August 20, 2020.

40 Xi Jinping, *The Governance of China: Volume One* (Beijing: Foreign Language Press, 2014), 124–35.

41 See ibid., 48–65 and 124–35; "Keynote speech by Chinese President Xi Jinping at the APEC CEO Summit," *Global Times*, November 19, 2016; "习近平：在科学家座谈会上的讲话 [Xi Jinping: Speech at Scientists' Symposium]," Xinhua, September 11, 2020.

42 "[Xi Jinping: Speech at Scientists' Symposium]."

43 "习近平：在企业家座谈会上的讲话 [Xi Jinping: Speech at Forum for Entrepreneurs]," Xinhua, July 21, 2020.

44 "[Xi Jinping: Speech at Scientists' Symposium]."

45 CGTN, "Jack Ma does Michael Jackson dance for Alibaba's 18th birthday," September 14, 2017, video, *https://www.youtube.com/watch?v=Vja8nIqVUw0*.

46 Gong Shou Dao, "Gong Shou Dao – official film," February 13, 2018, video, 22:10, *https://www.youtube.com/watch?v=wfS9Uf5SKu8*.

47 Baidu Inc., "Robin Li's book recommendations," May 21, 2020, video, 2:25, *https://www.youtube.com/watch?v=XWxP9HVbrDs*.

48 "Meet Pony Ma, the billionaire tech CEO who is neck-and-neck with Jack Ma to be China's richest man," Business Insider India, July 14, 2019.

49 "Global 500," *Fortune*, 2020, *https://fortune.com/global500/2020/search/*.

50 Antonio Graceffo, "China's national champions: state support makes Chinese companies dominant," *Foreign Policy Journal*, May 15, 2017.

51 Sarah Dai, "China adds Huawei, Hikvision to expanded 'national team' spearheading country's AI efforts," *South China Morning Post*, August 30, 2019.

52 Samm Sacks, "Data security and US–China tech entanglement," Lawfare, April 2, 2020.

53 Laura He, "China is sending government officials into companies like Alibaba and Geely," CNN Business, September 24, 2019.

54 Joseph Horwitz, "China's Communist Party is all in on the power of technology," Quartz, October 25, 2017.

55 Jiayang Fan, "Why China cracked down on the social-media giant ByteDance," *The New Yorker*, April 19, 2018.

56 Louise Lucas, "Tencent's losing game with Chinese regulators," *Financial Times*, June 18, 2019.

57 Pei Li and Brenda Goh, "'Homeland Dream': Chinese gaming giants unveil titles that play up patriotic values," Reuters, August 5, 2019.

58 Raymond Zhong and Paul Mozur, "Tech giants feel the squeeze as Xi Jinping tightens his grip," *New York Times*, May 2, 2018.

59 Yoko Kubota, "Alibaba's Jack Ma says government should stick to governing," *Wall Street Journal*, September 17, 2018.

60 Kevin Xu, "Bonus: Jack Ma's Bund Finance Summit speech," Interconnected, November 9, 2020.

61 Jacky Wong, "Chinese Fintech is hot. Regulators could still cool it down," *Wall Street Journal*, October 16, 2020.

62 Faith Brar, "TikTok is reportedly removing videos of people with 'abnormal body shapes'," Shape, March 19, 2020.

63 Sarah Perez, "TikTok explains its ban on political advertising," TechCrunch, October 3, 2019.

64 Lily Kuo, "TikTok sorry for blocking teenager who disguised Xinjiang video as make-up tutorial," *The Guardian*, November 28, 2019.

65 Yuan Yang and Xinning Liu, "Tencent denies storing WeChat conversations," *Financial Times*, January 2, 2018.

66 Jialing Xie, "'Don't download this app!' – a top 10 of harmful Chinese apps," What's on Weibo, September 18, 2019.

67 Michael Martina, "China's President Xi pledges more support for technology firms," Reuters, May 20, 2016.

68 Marco Di Capua, "Technology innovation in China," *The Bridge*, Vol. 28, No. 2 (Summer 1998).

69 Micah Springut, Stephen Schlaikjer, and David Chen, "China's Program for Science and Technology Modernization: implications for American competitiveness," CENTRA Technology, January 2011.

70 "Testimony of Robert D. Atkinson, President, Information Technology and Innovation Foundation," Information Technology and Innovation Foundation, July 11, 2018.

71 Miyu Ono and Hannah Cabot, "The disappearance of Chinese capital in US biotechnology," Back Bay Life Science Advisors, September 5, 2019.

72 Ezekiel Emanuel, Amy Gadsden, and Scott Moore, "How the US surrendered to China on scientific research," *Wall Street Journal*, April 9, 2019; Dennis Normile, "Surging R&D spending in China narrows gap with United States," *Science*, October 10, 2018.

73 Meng Jing, "Tianjin city in China eyes US$16 billion fund for AI work, dwarfing EU's plan to spend US$1.78 billion," *South China Morning Post*, May 16, 2018.

74 Sintia Radu, "US looks to boost non-defense AI research," *US News*, September 26, 2019.

75 Thomas J. Colvin, "A brief examination of Chinese government expenditures

on artificial intelligence R&D," Science and Technology Policy Institute, February 2020.

76 Christo Petrov, "Top R&D spenders: the biggest investors of 2020," Spend Me Not, August 3, 2020.

77 James A. Lewis, "Learning the superior techniques of the barbarians: China's pursuit of semiconductor independence," Center for Strategic & International Studies, January 2019.

78 C. Textor, "Share of GDP expenditure on research and development (R&D) in China from 2010 to 2017," Statista, November 29, 2019.

79 Kathleen McLaughlin, "Science is a major plank in China's new spending plan," *Science*, March 7, 2016; "China R&D spending rises 10% to record $38 billion in 2020," Bloomberg News, March 1, 2021.

80 Stephen Chen, "Two Sessions 2020: China cuts science budget by 9 per cent but national R&D still tipped to grow," *South China Morning Post*, May 22, 2020.

81 Jost Wübbeke et al., "Made in China 2025: the making of a high-tech super-power and consequences for industrial countries," Mercator Institute for China Studies, December 2016.

82 Karen M. Sutter, "'Made in China 2025' industrial policies: issues for Congress," Congressional Research Service, August 11, 2020.

83 "US–China Economic and Security Review Commission: Economics and Trade Bulletin," US–China Economic and Security Review Commission, January 11, 2019.

84 Max J. Zenglein and Anna Holzmann, "Evolving Made in China 2025: China's industrial policy in the quest for global tech leadership," Mercator Institute for China Studies, July 2019.

85 Maximilian Nadicksbernd, "Made in China 2025 – a halftime analysis," China Tech Blog, March 3, 2020.

86 Zenglein and Holzmann, "Evolving Made in China 2025."

87 "Market access challenges in China," The American Chamber of Commerce in Shanghai, 2017.

88 Zenglein and Holzmann, "Evolving Made in China 2025."

89 "China has a new US$1.4 trillion plan to seize the world's tech crown from the US," *South China Morning Post*, May 21, 2020.

90 Tom Hancock, "Multinationals lose ground in China's medical devices," *Financial Times*, May 27, 2018.

91 Ibid.

92 Michael Collins, "Protected at home, China's medical device industry looks abroad," Asia Unbound, December 3, 2019.

93 "Unpacking Made in China 2025 for US healthcare cos," American Chamber of Commerce in China, January 15, 2016.

94 Frank Tang, "Chinese officials bemoan 'significant catch-up' needed with US on chipmaking, as industrial decoupling looms," *South China Morning Post*, July 10, 2020.

95 Issaku Harada, "China ousts reformist official who called Made in China 2025 'waste'," *Nikkei Asian Review*, April 5, 2019.

96 Arati Shroff, "'Made in China 2025' disappears in name only," Indo-Pacific Defense Forum, March 23, 2020.

97 Cao Cong, "China's approaches to attract and nurture young biomedical researchers," National Academies, 6–7.

98 "Hundreds Talents Program," School of Engineering Science, University of Science and Technology of China, 2011.

99 Ellen Barry and Gina Kolata, "China's lavish funds lured US scientists. What did it get in return?" *New York Times*, February 7, 2020.

100 Remco Zwetsloot, "China's approach to tech talent competition: policies, results, and the developing global response," Brookings, April 2020.

101 Ibid.

102 Cong Cao et al., "Returning scientists and the emergence of China's science system," *Science and Public Policy*, Vol. 47, No. 2 (April 2020).

103 Launched on May 4, 1919, the May 4th movement ushered in an era of revolutionary political and social action across China and was a central part of the country's New Culture Movement.

104 Jiayun Feng, "'Modern Chinese intellectuals are spineless': Peking University vice dean reportedly resigns after provocative essay," SupChina, March 27, 2018.

105 "Chinese national who worked at Monsanto indicted on economic espionage charge," US Department of Justice, November 21, 2019.

106 Rebecca Trager, "Theft of universities' secrets fuels US crackdown on Chinese talent programs," Chemistry World, January 27, 2020.

107 Andrew Silver, "Scientists in China say US government crackdown is harming collaborations," *Nature*, July 8, 2020.

108 Christopher Burgess, "China's 1000 Talents Program continues to harvest US knowledge," Clearance Jobs, May 13, 2020.

109 "Harvard University professor indicted on false statement charges," US Department of Justice, June 9, 2020.

110 Ryan Lucas, "The Justice Department is ending its controversial China Initiative," NPR, February 23, 2022.

111 Anil Wadhwa, "Make in China 2025 – is it on track?" Institute of Chinese Studies Delhi, March 2019.

112 Alex Lykken, "China-driven M&A in North America is nearly MIA this year," Pitchbook, November 1, 2019.

113 Huang Yongfu, "Foreign firms eyeing Chinese market prove forced technology transfer claims don't hold up," *Global Times*, October 8, 2019.

114 Daniel Shane, "How China gets what it wants from American companies," CNN Business, April 5, 2018.

115 "2018 China Business Report," American Chamber of Commerce in Shanghai, July 12, 2018.

116 Julie Wernau, "Forced tech transfers are on the rise in China, European firms say," *Wall Street Journal*, May 20, 2019.

117 Dan Prud'homme, "Reform of China's 'forced' technology transfer policies," Oxford Business Law Blog, July 22, 2019.

118 Lee G. Brantetter, "China's forced technology transfer problem – and what to do about it," Peterson Institute for International Economics, June 2018.

119 Rob Barry and Dustin Volz, "Ghosts in the clouds: inside China's major corporate hack," *Wall Street Journal*, December 30, 2019; Christopher Bing, Jack Stubbs, and Joseph Menn, "Exclusive: China hacked HPE, IBM and then attacked clients," Reuters, December 20, 2018.

120 "Update to the IP Commission Report," The National Bureau of Asian Research, 2017.

121 John C. Demers, "Statement of John C. Demers, Assistant Attorney General, National Security Division, US Department of Justice, before the Committee on the Judiciary United States Senate," US Department of Justice, December 12, 2018.

122 Ellen Nakashima and Paul Sonne, "China hacked a Navy contractor and secured a trove of highly sensitive data on submarine warfare," *Washington Post*, June 8, 2018.

123 White House Office of the Press Secretary, "Fact Sheet: President Xi Jinping's State Visit to the United States," September 25, 2015.

124 "2016 Report to Congress of the US–China Economic and Security Review Commission," US–China Economic and Security Review Commission, November 2016.

125 Alexander Chipman Koty, "What is the China Standards 2035 Plan and how will it impact emerging industries?" China Briefing, July 2, 2020.

126 Christopher Ashley Ford, "Huawei and its siblings, the Chinese tech giants:

national security and foreign policy implications," US Department of State, September 11, 2019.

127 Christopher Balding and Donald C. Clarke, "Who Owns Huawei?" Social Science Research Network, April 17, 2019.

128 Li Tao, "Who controls Huawei? Chinese telecom's leader's ownership structure explained in more detail," *South China Morning Post*, April 29, 2019.

129 Ford, "Huawei and its siblings, the Chinese tech giants."

130 Wesley Rahn, "Huawei boss Liang Hua: 'Our top priority is to ensure survival'," Deutsche Welle, December 18, 2019.

131 "Declaration of Jihong Chen and Jianwei Fang," The China Collection, May 27, 2018.

132 Paul Sandle, "Huawei willing to sign 'no-spy' pacts with governments: chairman," Reuters, May 14, 2019.

133 Rob Davies, "The giant that no one trusts: why Huawei's history haunts it," *The Guardian*, December 8, 2018.

134 Guy Fulconbridge and Martin Quinn Pollard, "China warns UK: 'dumping' Huawei will cost you," Reuters, July 15, 2020.

135 Margaret McCuaig-Johnston, "China's threats on behalf of Huawei are becoming desperate," *The Globe and Mail*, July 4, 2019.

136 Joe Panettieri, "Huawei: banned and permitted in which countries? List and FAQ," Channel e2e, December 15, 2020.

137 David Lawder, "US Commerce chief warns against China semiconductor investment binge," Reuters, December 3, 2016.

138 Christopher Thomas, "A new world under construction: China and semiconductors," McKinsey & Company, November 1, 2015.

139 "US semiconductor manufacturing: industry trends, global competition, federal policy," Congressional Research Service, June 27, 2016.

140 Cheng Ting-Fang, "China's semiconductor 'Big Fund' to focus on advanced chips," *Nikkei Asian Review*, March 16, 2018.

141 Capri, "Semiconductors at the heart of the US–China tech war."

142 John VerWey, "Chinese semiconductor industrial policy: past and present," *United States International Trade Commission Journal of International Commerce and Economics*, July 2019.

143 Ibid.

144 "Global semiconductor sales increase 6.5% to $439 billion in 2020," Semiconductor Industry Association, February 1, 2021.

145 Capri, "Semiconductors at the heart of the US–China tech war."

146 "2019 Factbook," Semiconductor Industry Association, 2019.

147 Danny Manners, "China's IC efforts could be a waste of money," *Electronics Weekly*, August 27, 2019.

148 Frank Tang, "Chinese officials bemoan 'significant catch-up' needed with US on chipmaking, as industrial decoupling looms," *South China Morning Post*, July 10, 2020.

149 Executive Office of the President and the President's Advisors on Science and Technology, "Report to the President: Ensuring Long-Term US Leadership in Semiconductors," Obama White House, January 2017.

150 Sophia Yang, "Tycoon recalls Chinese chipmaker Tsinghua Unigroup's bid for Taiwan TSMC5 years ago," Taiwan News, November 16, 2020.

151 Keith Bradsher and Paul Mozur, "Political backlash grows in Washington to Chinese takeovers," *New York Times*, February 16, 2016.

152 Graham Webster et al., "Full translation: China's 'new generation artificial intelligence development plan' (2017)," Center for a New American Security, August 1, 2017.

153 Meng Jing, "Are China's investments in semiconductors all for naught? US expert says China is at a crossroads," *South China Morning Post*, August 26, 2019.

154 "Findings of the Investigation into China's Acts, Policies, and Practices Related to Technology Transfer, Intellectual Property, and Innovation under Section 301 of the Trade Act of 1974," Office of the United States Trade Representative, March 22, 2018, 23.

155 David Barboza, "How this US tech giant is backing China's tech ambitions," *New York Times*, August 4, 2017.

156 Cyrus Lee, "Thousands of Taiwanese chip experts moved to China for better pay," ZDNet, December 5, 2019.

157 "PRC state-owned company, Taiwan company, and three individuals charged with economic espionage," US Department of Justice, November 1, 2018.

158 Alexander Gillis, "DRAM (dynamic random access memory)," Search Storage, *https://searchstorage.techtarget.com/definition/DRAM*.

159 Sarah Dai, "Chinese memory chip maker Fujian Jinhua says there's been 'no stealing of technology' amid US export ban," *South China Morning Post*, November 5, 2018.

160 Anton Shilov, "US government indicts Chinese DRAM maker JHICC on industrial espionage; bans exports to firm," AnandTech, November 1, 2018.

161 Billy Huang, "Chinese chip maker Fujian Jinhua is accused of stealing US technology. This time, China is fully prepared to fight back," *South China Morning Post*, November 21, 2018.

162 Arjun Kharpal, "'Bleak but salvageable': Huawei has limited options as US sanctions cut off supply to smartphone chips," CNBC, August 11, 2020.

163 Michael Herh, "Engineers of Huawei's HiSilicon move to Tsinghua Unigroup's subsidiary," *Business Korea*, June 17, 2020.

164 Douglas Fuller, "Trump's sanctions won't put Huawei out of business," *Asia Nikkei*, June 12, 2020; Cheng-Ting Fang and Lauly Li, "China aims to shake US grip on chip design tools," Caixin, November 26, 2020.

165 Danny Vincent, "How China plans to lead the computer chip industry," BBC, November 19, 2019.

166 He Shujing and Mo Yelin, "In depth: China chip sector has the money, now it just needs the workers," Caixin, September 15, 2020.

167 Kathrin Hille and Sun Yu, "Chinese groups go from fish to chips in new 'Great Leap Forward'," *Financial Times*, October 12, 2020.

168 China Money AI, "How a con man with primary education defrauded billions out of a Wuhan chip project," China Money Network, January 9, 2021.

169 He and Mo, "In depth: China chip sector has the money."

170 Sidney Leng and Orange Wang, "China's semiconductor drive stalls in Wuhan, exposing gap in hi-tech production capabilities," *South China Morning Post*, August 28, 2020.

171 "China's pursuit of semiconductor independence," filmed February 28, 2019, at CSIS, Washington, DC, video, *https://www.youtube.com/watch?v=ZHN2l-7dkoM*.

172 Shuhei Yamada, "China's chip self-sufficiency drive in need of factory investment", *Nikkei Asia*, January 25, 2023.

173 "Tsinghua Unigroup fighting to become a top chipmaker," Global SMT & Packaging, *https://globalsmtseasia.com/technology_news/tsinghua-unigroup-fighting-to-become-a-top-chipmaker/*.

174 Sherisse Pham, "Taiwan could become the next flashpoint in the global tech war," CNN Business, July 31, 2020.

175 Stephen Nellis and Alexandra Alper, "US chipmakers quietly lobby to ease Huawei ban," Reuters, June 16, 2019.

176 Scott Kennedy, "Washington's China policy has lost its Wei," Center for Strategic and International Studies, July 27, 2020.

177 Shaun Nichols, "How the US–China trade war is felt stateside: Xilinx trims workforce after lucrative Huawei sales pipe blocked," The A Register, February 16, 2020.

Chapter 6 *Rewriting the Rules of the Game*

1 Choi Chi-yuk, "China's removal of Meng Hongwei completes reshaping of public security ministry," *South China Morning Post*, October 14, 2018.

2 William Zheng, "Former Chinese Interpol president Meng Hongwei facing prosecution on bribery charge," *South China Morning Post*, April 24, 2019.

3 "Meng Hongwei: China sentences ex-Interpol chief to 13 years in jail," BBC, January 21, 2020.

4 Hu Yiwei, "In numbers: China's anti-graft campaign after achieving 'sweeping victory'," CGTN, January 16, 2020.

5 China Power Team, "Is China contributing to the United Nations' mission?" China Power Project, March 7, 2016, updated August 26, 2020.

6 "Full text of Xi Jinping keynote at the World Economic Forum," CGTN, January 17, 2017.

7 Yen Nee Lee, "China says it has no intention of 'becoming another United States'," CNBC, August 5, 2020.

8 Yong Wang, "China's new concept of global governance and action plan for international cooperation," Centre for International Governance Innovation, November 13, 2019.

9 Ibid.

10 Ibid.

11 Joseph Foundy, "How China's Xi Jinping is filling the 'global leadership vacuum' left by Trump," CNBC, April 12, 2018.

12 Beth Mole, "China joins global vaccine alliance, filling 'leadership vacuum' left by Trump," ArsTechnica, October 9, 2020.

13 Chloé Farand and Megan Darby, "Xi Jinping: China will aim for carbon neutrality by 2060," Climate Home News, September 22, 2020.

14 Matt Ferchen, "How China is reshaping international development," Carnegie Endowment for International Peace, January 8, 2020.

15 Ting Shi and David Tweed, "Xi Jinping outlines 'big country diplomacy' for China," *Sydney Morning Herald*, December 2, 2014.

16 Alice Ekman, "China and the 'definition gap': shaping global governance in words," Asan Forum, November 4, 2017.

17 Ibid.

18 Sam Boone, "CSR 2019: China's influence on Interpol – progress and pushback," *The SAIS China Studies Review*, October 30, 2019.

19 Yi Zhang, "Training begins in Beijing for UN police missions," *China Daily*, August 9, 2016.

20 "Interpol to help promote security along Belt & Road," Xinhua, May 14, 2019.

21 "Interpol: address China's 'Red Notice' abuses," Human Rights Watch, September 25, 2017.

22 Boone, "CSR 2019: China's Influence on Interpol."

23 Nicolas LePan, "The final frontier: how Arctic ice melting is opening up trade opportunities," World Economic Forum, February 13, 2020.

24 "About," The Arctic Council, *https://arctic-council.org/en/about/*.

25 Linda Jakobson, "China prepares for an ice-free Arctic," Stockholm International Peace Research Institute, March 2010.

26 Sissel Finstad, "The Svalbard Treaty," Svalbard Museum, *https://svalbard museum.no/en/kultur-og-historie/svalbardtraktaten*.

27 "The evolution of CNARC: 2013–2018," China–Nordic Arctic Research Center, December 2018.

28 "China," Arctic Institute, *https://www.thearcticinstitute.org/countries/china/*.

29 Laura Zhou, "China's new icebreaker Snow Dragon II ready for Antarctica voyage later this year," *South China Morning Post*, July 12, 2019.

30 "Past ASSWs," International Arctic Science Committee, *https://iasc.info/assw/past*.

31 "Observers," The Arctic Council, *https://arctic-council.org/en/about/observers/*.

32 Steven Lee Myers, "Arctic Council adds 6 nations as observer states, including China," *New York Times*, May 15, 2013.

33 Brandi Buchman, "US ratifies 'Arctic 5' deal to preserve and fish warming waters," Courthouse News Service, August 27, 2019.

34 Linda Jakobson and Jingchao Peng, "China's Arctic aspirations," Stockholm International Peace Research Institute, 2012.

35 Peiqing Guo, "New cold wars over Arctic wealth," *Global Times*, July 27, 2009.

36 Sanna Kopra, "China's Arctic interests," *Arctic Yearbook*, September 2013.

37 Liu Huirong,"中国可以在北极做什么 [What can China do in the Arctic?]," 经济参考报 [Economic Information], December 27, 2011.

38 David Curtis Wright, "The dragon eyes the top of the world," Naval War College China Maritime Institute, August 2011.

39 David Curtis Wright, "China's growing Interest in the Arctic," *Journal of Military and Strategic Studies*, Vol. 15, No. 2 (2013), 57.

40 Kopra, "China's Arctic interests."

41 "而论深入学习贯彻习近平主席重要讲话精神 [Study and implement the important speech of Chairman Xi Jinping]," 中国海洋日报 [*China Ocean Daily*], November 20, 2014.

42 "China unveils vision for 'Polar Silk Road' across Arctic," Reuters, January 26, 2018.

43 Michael R. Pompeo, "Looking north: sharpening America's Arctic focus," US Department of State, May 6, 2019.

44 David Auerswald, "China's multifaceted Arctic strategy," War on the Rocks, May 24, 2019.

45 Malte Humpert, "China acquires 20 percent stake in Novatek's latest Arctic LNG project," *High North News*, April 29, 2019.

46 Auerswald, "China's multifaceted Arctic strategy."

47 "Sweden designates China's, Russia's actions as main security threats – report," *Sputnik News*, March 14, 2019.

48 Simon Johnson, "Sweden to tighten foreign takeover rules amid security worries," Reuters, May 8, 2020.

49 Sveinn K. Einarsson, Ingjanur Hannibalsson, and Alyson Bailes, "Chinese investment and Icelandic National Security," University of Iceland, October 2014.

50 Yves Eudes, "Iceland: money from China," Pulitzer Center, August 7, 2013.

51 Auerswald, "China's multifaceted Arctic strategy."

52 "China denies threatening to pull plug on Faroe Islands' salmon trade deal over Huawei 5G contract," Salmon Business, December 11, 2019.

53 Danish Defence Intelligence Service, *Intelligence Risk Assessment 2020*, December 2020, 21.

54 Ibid., 16.

55 Timo Koivurova et al., "China in the Arctic; and the opportunities and challenges for Chinese–Finnish Arctic co-operation," Valtioneuvoston Selvitys – Ja Tutkimustoiminta (Government Investigation and Research), December 2, 2019.

56 Linda Jakobson, "Preparing for an ice-free Arctic," China Dialogue, April 22, 2010.

57 Stephen Chen, "China launches its first fully owned overseas satellite ground station near North Pole," *South China Morning Post*, December 16, 2016.

58 Keegan Elmer, "Swedish defense agency warns satellite station could be serving Chinese military," *South China Morning Post,* January 14, 2019.

59 Aspen Institute, "Great powers clash in the Arctic: the struggle for the Northern Frontier," YouTube video, 59:41, July 18, 2019, *https://www.youtube.com/watch?v=bxlj7-76Su8.*

60 Frank Jüris, "Handing over infrastructure for China's strategic objectives 'Arctic Connect' and the Digital Silk Road in the Arctic," Sinopsis, July 3, 2020.

61 Karen Marie Oseland, "The Arctic this week Take Five: week of September 28, 2020," Arctic Institute, October 2, 2020.

62 David Brennan, "Battle for the Arctic: US warns Russia 'is way ahead of us' in race to control new frontier," *Newsweek*, July 19, 2019.

63 "China's Arctic policy," State Council Information Office of the People's Republic of China, January 26, 2018.

64 Pompeo, "Looking north."

65 "China's Arctic Policy."

66 Nong Hong, *China's Interests in the Arctic: Opportunities and Challenges*, Institute for China-America Studies, March 2018, 3.

67 Trym Aleksandr Eiterjord, "China's busy year in the Arctic," The Diplomat, January 30, 2019.

68 Amy H. Liu and Kevin Peters, "The Hanification of Xinjiang, China: the economic effects of the Great Leap West," *Studies of Ethnicity and Nationalism*, Vol. 17, No. 2 (2017).

69 Murray Scot Tanner and James Bellacqua, "China's response to terrorism," CNA, June 2016.

70 Rachel Harris, "Securitization and mass detentions in Xinjiang: how Uyghurs became quarantined from the outside world," Quartz, September 4, 2018.

71 "China: free Xinjiang 'political education' detainees," Human Rights Watch, September 10, 2017.

72 Austin Ramzy and Chris Buckley, "'Absolutely no mercy': leaked files expose how China organized mass detentions of Muslims," *New York Times*, November 16, 2019.

73 Emma Graham Harrison, "China has built 380 internment camps in Xinjiang, study finds," *The Guardian*, September 23, 2020.

74 Adrian Zenz, "'Wash brains, cleanse hearts': evidence from Chinese government documents about the nature and extent of Xinjiang's extrajudicial internment campaign," *Journal of Political Risk*, Vol. 7, No. 11 (November 2019).

75 Blaine Kaltman, *Under the Heel of the Dragon: Islam, Racism, Crime, and the Uighur in China* (Athens: Ohio University Press, 2007).

76 Yuan Yang, "Xinjiang security crackdown sparks Han Chinese exodus," *Financial Times*, December 21, 2019.

77 Ramzy and Buckley, "'Absolutely No Mercy'."

78 Mimi Lau, "Wanted: Chinese cadres to hold Beijing's line in Xinjiang as Han Chinese head for exits," *South China Morning Post*, December 4, 2019.

79 "Joint Statement, delivered by UK Rep to UN, on Xinjiang at the Third Committee Dialogue of the Committee for the Elimination of Racial Discrimination," United States Mission to the UN, October 29, 2019.

80 Hong Xiao, "Statement at UN supports China on Xinjiang," *China Daily*, October 20, 2019.

81 "Joint Statement on the human rights situation in Xinjiang and the recent developments in Hong Kong, delivered by Germany on behalf of 39 countries," United States Mission to the UN, October 6, 2020.

82 "Nearly 70 countries voice support for China human rights issues," CGTN, October 8, 2020.

83 Amr Essam, "The Like Minded Group: speaking truth to power," Universal Rights Group, May 10, 2016.

84 Nithin Coca, "Are Indonesia and Malaysia ready to stand up for China's Muslims?" The Diplomat, January 28, 2019.

85 Tamara Qiblawi, "Muslim nations are defending China as it cracks down on Muslims, shattering any myths of Islamic solidarity," CNN, July 17, 2019.

86 "UN: China responds to rights review with threats," Human Rights Watch, April 1, 2019.

87 "Dolkun Isa participates in UN Indigenous Forum despite growing Chinese influence," European Interest, May 12, 2019.

88 Ibid.

89 World Uyghur Congress, "CCTV interview with Wu Hongbo," Facebook, April 25, 2019.

90 Louis Charbonneau, "China again in UN hotseat over Xinjiang abuses," Human Rights Watch, March 6, 2019.

91 "China's top diplomat Wang Yi dismisses European rights concerns over Xinjiang," Associated Press, August 31, 2020.

92 "Convention on the Prevention and Punishment of the Crime of Genocide," United Nations, December 9, 1948.

93 Helen Davidson, "Beijing 2022: 180 human rights groups call for Winter Olympics boycott," *The Guardian*, February 4, 2021.

94 "UN treaty bodies and China," Human Rights in China, 2014, *https://www.hrichina.org/en/un-treaty-bodies-and-china*.

95 Danny Mok, "Canto-pop singer Denise Ho calls on UN Human Rights Council to remove China over 'abuses' in Hong Kong," *South China Morning Post*, July 9, 2019.

96 *The Cost of International Advocacy: China's Interference in United Nations Human Rights Mechanisms*, Human Rights Watch, September 5, 2017.

97 Ibid., 87–90.

98 Ted Piccone, "China's long game on human rights at the United Nations," Brookings Institution, September 2018.

99 Ibid., 7.

100 Hillel C. Neuer, "Why China picked Amnesty International's ex-chief as UN free speech monitor – opinion," *Newsweek*, July 17, 2019.

101 "Contribution of development to the enjoyment of all human rights," UN Human Rights Council, *https://www.ohchr.org/EN/HRBodies/HRC/AdvisoryCommittee/Pages/DevelopmentEnjoymentAllHR.aspx*.

102 Kata Insenring-Szabó, "China's views on the UNHRC," European Council on Foreign Relations, April 12, 2018.

103 Julian Borger, "China and Russia accused of waging 'war on human rights' at the UN," *The Guardian*, March 27, 2018.

104 Piccone, "China's Long Game on Human Rights."

105 "习近平：自主创新推进网络强国建设 [Xi Jinping: independent innovation to promote the construction of network power]," Xinhua, April 21, 2018.

106 Sarah McKune and Shazeda Ahmed, "The contestation and shaping of cyber norms through China's internet sovereignty agenda," *International Journal of Communication*, Vol. 12 (2018).

107 Samm Sacks, "Beijing wants to rewrite the rules of the internet," *The Atlantic*, June 18, 2018.

108 Sarah Cook, "China's long, hot summer of censorship," Freedom House, June 25, 2019.

109 Shastri Ramachandaran, "WIC in Wuzhen: cyber security is the challenge," China.org.cn, November 16, 2016.

110 "Full text: white paper on the internet in China," *China Daily*, June 8, 2010.

111 James T. Areddy, "Anti-Wikipedian translation at China's internet conference," *Wall Street Journal*, December 17, 2015.

112 Lorand Laksai and Adam Segal, "The encryption debate in China," Carnegie Endowment for International Peace, May 30, 2019.

113 Mary Hui, "Hong Kong's protest movement keeps getting stymied by Apple," Quartz, July 14, 2020.

114 McKune and Ahmed, "The contestation and shaping of cyber norms."

115 "Countering the use of information and communications technologies for criminal purposes," 74th Session of the UN General Assembly, November 25, 2019.

116 "Countering the use of information and communications technologies for criminal purposes," 73rd Session of the UN General Assembly, November 2, 2018.

117 Kubo Mačák, "This is cyber: 1 + 3 challenges for the application of interna-

tional humanitarian law in cyberspace," Exeter Center for International Law, February 2019.

118 Julian Ku, "Forcing China to accept that international law restricts cyber warfare may not actually benefit the US," Lawfare, August 25, 2017.

119 "国家标准委：正制定'中国标准2035'[National Standards Committee: Preparing 'China 2035 Standards']", Xinhua, January 5, 2018.

120 Jeffrey Ding, Paul Triolo, and Samm Sacks, "Chinese interests take a big seat at the AI governance table," New America, June 20, 2018.

121 Emily de La Bruyère and Nathan Picarsic, "China's next plan to dominate international tech standards," TechCrunch, April 11, 2020.

122 "China in international standards setting," US–China Business Council, February 2020.

123 Kong Wenzheng, "ITU vows to join hands with China," *China Daily*, April 24, 2019.

124 "China in international standards setting."

125 Lindsay Gorman, "The US needs to get in the standards game – with like-minded democracies," Lawfare, April 2, 2020.

126 Tom Miles, "Huawei evidence driven by politics not evidence: UN telecoms chief," Reuters, April 5, 2019.

127 Hideaki Ryugen and Hiroyuki Akiyama, "China leads the way on global standards for 5G and beyond," *Financial Time*s, August 4, 2020.

128 Anna Gross and Madhumita Murgia, "China shows its dominance in surveillance technology," *Financial Times*, December 26, 2019.

129 Ibid.

130 Peter Cihon, "AI & global governance: using international standards as an agile tool for governance," UN University Centre for Policy Research, July 8, 2019.

131 Madhumita Murgia and Anna Gross, "Inside China's controversial mission to reinvent the internet," *Financial Times*, March 27, 2020.

132 Anna Gross and Madhumita Murgia, "China and Huawei propose reinvention of the internet," *Financial Times*, March 27, 2020.

133 Murgia and Gross, "Inside China's controversial mission to reinvent the internet."

134 Stephen Shankland, "China has big ideas for the internet. Too bad no one else likes them," Cnet, July 17, 2020.

135 "At China's Belt and Road Forum, Guterres calls for 'inclusive, sustainable and durable development'," UN News, April 26, 2019.

136 "Guterres affirms UN role in China-proposed Belt and Road Initiative," Xinhua, January 19, 2019.

137 Pingfan Hong, "Strengthening national policy capacity for jointly building the Belt and Road towards the Sustainable Development Goals," UN Department of Economic and Social Affairs, May 2017.

138 "Focus on agriculture is key to ensure that Belt and Road Initiative promotes sustainable development," UN Food and Agriculture Organization, May 15, 2017.

139 "UN agencies Belt and Road Initiative involvement," UN Environmental Programme, October 1, 2018.

140 William Lacy Swing, "Statement, Belt and Road Forum for International Cooperation," UN Migration, May 15, 2017.

141 Maaike Okano-Heijmans, Frans-Paul van der Putten, and Louise van Schaik, "Welcoming and resisting China's growing role in the UN," Clingendael, February 8, 2019.

142 Ibid.

143 Colum Lynch, "China enlists UN to promote its Belt and Road project," *Foreign Policy*, May 10, 2018.

144 Hong, "Strengthening national policy capacity."

145 "UNIDO further engages with the Belt and Road Initiative," UN Industrial Development Organization, April 25, 2019.

146 Ibid.

147 "Steering Committee," UN Peace and Development Trust Fund.

148 "2030 Agenda for Sustainable Development Sub-Fund," UN Peace and Development Trust Fund, *https://www.un.org/en/unpdf/2030asd.shtml*.

149 "Pick a leader with a vision for the Food and Agriculture Organization," *Nature*, June 19, 2019.

150 Hilary Clarke, "Why does new Chinese head of UN food agency feed suspicion?" *South China Morning Post*, July 8, 2019.

151 Gerardo Fortuna, "China's Qu Dongyu beats EU candidate for FAO leadership," Euractiv, June 24, 2019.

152 Shawn Donnan, "World Bank exit highlights China's fears," *Financial Times*, December 30, 2015.

153 "US at UN takes aim at China's Belt and Road Initiative," *Strait Times*, March 16, 2019.

154 "'会员通讯' 2009 第2期 ['Member Newsletter' 2009 Issue Two]," China Center for International Economic Exchanges, June 23, 2009.

155 Geoff Dyer and George Parker, "US attacks UK's 'constant accommodation' with China," *Financial Times*, March 12, 2015.

156 "Jin Liqun emphasizes 'cooperation and coordination' between AIIB and World Bank," Asia Society Policy Institute, April 13, 2016.

157 Petra Kjell, "Why is the world's newest development bank investing in coal despite its green promise?" Climate Home News, June 21, 2018.

158 James Lo, "Why isn't China's Belt and Road Initiative acting through the Asian Infrastructure Bank?" Medium, January 12, 2020.

159 Tamar Gutner, "AIIB: is the Chinese-led development bank a role model?" *The Internationalist*, June 25, 2018.

Chapter 7 The China Reset

1 Anders Hove, "Trends and contradictions in China's energy patterns," Columbia Center on Global Energy Policy, August 28, 2020.

2 Center for Research on Energy and Clean Air, "A new coal boom in China," Global Energy Monitor, June 2020.

3 Cissy Zhou and Wang Zixu, "China suffers worst power blackouts in a decade, on post-coronavirus export boom, coal supply shortage," *South China Morning Post*, December 23, 2020.

4 Chloé Farrand, "Guterres confronts China over coal boom, urging a green recovery," Climate Home News, July 23, 2010.

5 Laura Silver, Kat Delvin, and Christine Huang, "Unfavorable views of China reach historic highs in many countries," Pew Research Center, October 6, 2020.

6 Russell Ong, *China's Security Interests in the Post-Cold War Era* (Richmond, Surrey: Curzon Press, 2002).

7 Leah Bitounis and Jonathon Price, eds., *The Struggle for Power: US–China Relations in the 21st Century* (Washington, DC: Aspen Institute, 2020).

8 "Full text of Clinton's speech on China Trade Bill," Institute for Agriculture & Trade Policy, March 9, 2000.

9 "Whither China? From membership to responsibility," National Committee on US–China Relations, September 21, 2005.

10 Ryan Teague Beckwith, "Read Donald Trump's 'America First' foreign policy speech," *Time*, April 2016.

11 Steven Erlanger and Jane Perlez, "America's allies fear that traditional ties no longer matter under Trump," *New York Times*, December 21, 2018.

12 "Bureaucracy and counterstrategy: meeting the China challenge," US Department of State, September 11, 2019.

13 Niall Ferguson, "Cold War II has America at a disadvantage as China courts Russia," *Boston Globe*, January 20, 2020.

14 Timothy Garton Ash, "The US and China are entering a new cold war. Where does that leave the rest of us?" *The Guardian*, June 20, 2020.

15 Richard Wike, "The Trump era has seen a decline in America's global reputation," Pew Research Center, November 19, 2020.

16 Kurt Campbell and Rush Doshi, "The China challenge can help America avert decline," *Foreign Affairs*, December 3, 2020.

17 "The global AI talent tracker," MacroPolo, The Paulson Institute, June 2020.

18 Nick Hillman, "HEPI's Annual Soft-Power Ranking, 2020: The UK slips further behind the US," Higher Education Policy Institute, August 27, 2020.

19 Antony J. Blinken, "A foreign policy for the American people," Speech at US Department of State, March 3, 2021.

20 Daniel Hurst, "Australia to discuss critical supply chains with Japan, India and US as China relationship frays," *The Guardian*, October 2, 2020.

21 Sebastian Sprenger, "NATO chief seeks to forge deeper ties in China's neighborhood," *Defense News*, June 8, 2020.

22 Laura Tingle, "Germany looks to join Australian military in Indo-Pacific as it faces 'major challenge' in China," Australian Broadcast Corporation, November 6, 2020.

23 Garima Mohan, "Europe in the Indo-Pacific: a case for more coordination with Quad countries," German Marshall Fund of the United States, January 14, 2020.

24 Minghao Zhao, "Is a new Cold War inevitable? Chinese perspectives on US–China strategic competition," *The Chinese Journal of International Politics*, Vol. 12, No. 3 (Autumn 2019).

25 Yiwei Wang, "中美就一带一路开展合作是否可能? [Is China–US cooperation under the BRI possible?]" 学术前沿 [*Academic Frontiers*], No. 4 (2017).

Index

275

Printed in the USA
CPSIA information can be obtained
at www.ICGtesting.com
JSHW011043280524
63677JS00004B/29

9 781509 537495